Strategies for
Culturally
and
Linguistically
Responsive Teaching
and Learning

Author
Sharroky Hollie, Ph.D.

Foreword by
Felicia Homberger, M.Ed.

Publishing Credits

Corinne Burton, M.A.Ed., *President* and *Publisher*
Aubrie Nielsen, M.S.Ed., *EVP of Content Development*
Kyra Ostendorf, M.Ed., *Publisher, professional books*
Véronique Bos, *Vice President of Creative*
Cathy Hernandez, *Senior Content Manager*
Jill Malcolm, *Cover Designer*

Library of Congress Cataloging-in-Publication Data

Names: Hollie, Sharroky, 1967- author. | Hollie, Sharroky, 1967- Culturally and linguistically responsive teaching and learning.
Title: Strategies for Culturally and linguistically responsive teaching and learning / by Sharroky Hollie ; foreword by Felicia Homberger.
Description: Second edition. | Huntington Beach, CA : Shell Educational Publishing, Inc., 2025. | Includes bibliographical references.
Identifiers: LCCN 2024033368 (print) | LCCN 2024033369 (ebook) | ISBN 9798765965559 (paperback) | ISBN 9798765965566 (ebook)
Subjects: LCSH: English language--Study and teaching.
Classification: LCC LB1576 .H6263 2025 (print) | LCC LB1576 (ebook) | DDC 428.0071--dc23/eng/20241002
LC record available at https://lccn.loc.gov/2024033368
LC ebook record available at https://lccn.loc.gov/2024033369

Image Credits: all images from iStock and/or Shutterstock

5482 Argosy Avenue
Huntington Beach, CA 92649
www.tcmpub.com/shell-education
ISBN 979-8-7659-6555-9
© 2025 Shell Educational Publishing, Inc.
Printed by: 51497
Printed in: China

TABLE OF CONTENTS

Let me begin with a flashback to 2013…

> Dr. Hollie: "Why did you do a Silent Appointment?"
>
> Felicia: "I have no idea. Because it was in your book."

This is direct from the conversation I had with Dr. Hollie the first time he observed me attempting CLR—cultural and linguistic responsiveness—in my classroom. Such began our relationship, and as two people who subscribe to the cultural behavior of realness, you can only imagine the conversations we have had since. Back then, I was referring to the first edition of *Culturally and Linguistically Responsive Teaching* (the orange book). All I had was the handful of strategies explained in the appendix and a gut feeling that CLR would be a game changer for me and my students.

Dr. Hollie wrote the first edition of the blue *Strategies for Culturally and Linguistically Responsive Teaching* binder when he was working as a consultant at my high school in Minnesota because he recognized the need for more detailed explanations of the CLR activities and the rationale behind them. The practical nature of this binder has been a godsend for many teachers.

But a few things have happened since that binder was first published, including, of course, a global pandemic. With Dr. Hollie no longer flying to a different city every day during the shutdown, he had some time to reflect and fine-tune his work, most noticeably in his articulation of the sixteen most common cultural behaviors of the underserved. His work has progressed significantly since the release of the first binder, which is why he now offers this second edition.

I have had the privilege of working with Dr. Hollie as a program specialist and lead CLR practitioner since 2013. In that capacity, I have worked with hundreds of teachers around the country. But I also keep one foot in the classroom, using CLR each and every day with my students. CLR kept me afloat during the pandemic. CLR was a lifesaver when we returned post-pandemic and found that things weren't going to just go back to normal. As my colleague and partner in crime at my high school, Beth Ocar, said, "There is nothing that has been thrown at me as an educator that CLR hasn't made better." True dat.

For those of you who are picking up this book, thank you for being willing to stretch yourself in service to your students. I was nineteen years into my career when I started my CLR journey, and I was highly regarded in my school. But nothing, and I mean nothing, has been more impactful for me as a professional and for my students than CLR.

If you choose to join us on the journey to responsiveness, please know, it isn't easy. I once told Dr. Hollie that every time he gave me feedback, I had to work my feelings out on my elliptical machine that night. He laughed, and said, "Elliptical machines are so white." But seriously, working with teachers, I have seen the frustration they feel when they first start their CLR journey. While I empathize, I also want you all to know, I started with that orange book and no clue of what I was doing, and look how far I have come. You can do it too! Really, you can. In fact, you will be modeling for your students all the things you ask of them when they are learning something new and challenging.

We now have many more resources to offer the educators who work with us, from videos, to a members portal, to exemplar lessons, to this new and improved strategies book. You have what you need to develop your CLR skill set. If I can offer any advice as someone who has stumbled, fallen, gotten up, soared, and stumbled again: be patient with yourself, be willing to fail and feel uncomfortable. It is worth it—for you and, more importantly, for your students.

I am so excited about this second edition, because it encompasses the changes we have made in our approach to the work. One thing I found so inspiring when I first met Dr. Hollie (besides his jokes) was that, unlike other trainers we had worked with, he not only pushed our thinking (mindset) but he also offered concrete ideas of what to do in the classroom (skill set). While the CLR activities are critical, and so important to teachers who crave pragmatic solutions to responding to the underserved, they are nothing if not rooted in the mindset.

This edition of the book puts the cultural behaviors at the center, where they belong. It helps teachers focus on their students culturally before choosing activities so that true validation and affirmation of students' authentic selves guides the pedagogy. It also focuses on how to make CLR part of the culture of a school, as this work is best done in community.

This book is for teachers in that it will help them develop their CLR practice, but ultimately it is for the students. Developing a CLR practice takes time, which is in short supply for teachers. But if you invest that time, there is no telling the difference you can make. One of my former students who was living in North Minneapolis during the unrest that followed the murder of George Floyd told me that the culturally authentic book we read and the discussions we had saved him during that difficult time. That is the power of CLR.

CLR isn't a magic bullet—it won't fix everything in your classroom—but it is magical. Dr. Hollie offers us this book to give us the technical support we need to make that magic happen. So, with this book in your backpack and outrageous love in your heart, you have what it takes to be VABBulous! Carry on!

—Felicia Homberger, Teacher and Professional Development Coordinator
Hopkins Public Schools, Minnesota

PREFACE

A Lot Has Changed

What I am about to say will not come as a surprise to you. A lot has changed in our world since 2015, when the first edition of this book was published. When I say *our world*, I am not necessarily talking about the world in which we live. You know those changes all too well because they have impacted our lives in ways that we would have never imagined—in 2016, a historic presidential election; in 2020, a historic pandemic, the historic civil rights protests and so-called racial reckoning sparked by the murder of George Floyd, and another historic presidential election; in 2021, a historic attack on the US Capitol; in 2022, the Ukrainian-Russian War; in 2022, the increasing momentum of the book banning movement; in 2023, the War in the Middle East; and in 2024, yet another historic presidential election.

When I say a lot has changed in our world, I am talking about our culturally and linguistically responsive world, affectionately known as our CLR world. Since 2015, our CLR world has evolved profoundly, especially when you consider the happenings that occurred in our other world. The lockdown during the pandemic brought CLR to the virtual world, growing its reach to people and in places that my team and I would not otherwise have encountered. The sociopolitical turmoil created an even greater need for CLR. More than ever, educators needed a safe space where they could advocate for underserved students while at the same time staying focused on teaching and learning, on community and collaboration, and on students' cultural and linguistic assets. Fortunately, we were able to meet that need; the changes on the outside caused us to change CLR on the inside. The second edition of this book is the evidence of those changes. We are validating and affirming, building and bridging a lot differently than we did in 2015. However, the need for cultural and linguistic responsiveness has not changed over time. In fact, what has been most compelling is that CLR has survived the times, so to speak, despite everything that has happened. Our charge now is to move forward in a different way that impactfully represents not only the CLR work described here but also any work rooted in the equitable treatment of underserved students.

What's New in This Book

When I wrote the second edition of *Culturally and Linguistically Responsive Teaching and Learning: Classroom Practices for Student Success* (Hollie 2018), I learned that most readers or potential book buyers of the second edition had one question: What is the difference between the first edition and the second edition? After being asked the question dozens of times, I formulated a simple answer—about 100 pages. That was the only way I could briefly capture the many changes. With the second edition of *this* book, I want to be more linear in my response. There are several changes in this new edition.

The first and most significant change is a focus and emphasis on the sixteen cultural behaviors that are most likely not validated and affirmed in the milieu of school. In the first edition, the cultural behaviors were presented as almost an afterthought, which led to an overemphasis on the CLR activities, and, more importantly, a discounting of the cultural and linguistic behaviors that each student brings to school. Indeed, the focus on cultural behaviors did not appear in the first edition until chapter 12, defeating the purpose of CLR, which is to validate and affirm our students' cultural and linguistic behaviors. The emphasis on the cultural behaviors is the center of CLR in this book and is a recurring theme in every chapter. This emphasis includes a deeper understanding of each of the behaviors and more clarity around how they align with the CLR activities.

A second change reflects an acknowledgment that CLR is meant to be done in community and collaboration. This second edition encourages readers by providing starter activities for doing the CLR work in collaboration within grade-level teams, subject-area departments, PLCs, and so forth. An exciting development that followed publication of the first edition was the organic growth of educators meeting for CLR binder studies. My immediate takeaway was that CLR is better together, and aspects of the CLR binder study have now become part of this edition with the hope that they will support your CLR community and collaboration.

There are other additions and modifications. A new BeYou section is included with each chapter. BeYou stands for "Be Engaged Your Own Unique Way," and it speaks to giving students opportunities to be their cultural and linguistic selves at school without fear that their behavior will be seen as a problem. A significant misconception with CLR is that we only validate and affirm so that students can then build and bridge to school culture. The truth is that there are times when we must validate and affirm cultural and linguistic behaviors simply because it is the right thing to do, meaning that it does not have to always be in the context or for the purpose of building and bridging. Students should be allowed to BE themselves at school. Putting the focus on the cultural behaviors is a major shift from the first edition that will lead to more impactful validation and affirmation. Briefly, here are a few other things that changed:

- More than twenty new protocols or strategies have been added throughout the book. In addition, fifty new attention signals have been added to chapter 3.
- In several chapters, the directions for the protocols or strategies have been updated to make them more user friendly.
- The end-of-chapter exercises have been revised and updated.
- The new edition is no longer a binder. It is a bound book. Kudos to the publisher for following the recommendations of dozens of teachers.
- Our online CLR community of educators continues to grow. For resources and more, join us at: culturallyresponsive.org, vabbacademy.thinkific.com (our professional learning portal), and facebook.com/culturallyresponsive/.

Lastly, those familiar with the first edition know that each chapter has a "reflective process" section, which takes the reader through a series of reflective questions, thought-provokers for moving forward, and potential thought-blockers that can keep one stagnant in one's mindset. These reflective questions are instructive as well, because they allow the educator to gauge where they are in relation to what we call their CLR-ness. To strengthen the reflective process, a year-long CLR journal has been provided in the digital resources for this edition. This journal is a reflective guide for your journey in cultural and linguistic responsiveness. There are more than forty reflection prompts, essentially one for each week of the school year, and there are four types of prompts: shifting your mindset, building your skill set, loving yourself, and loving your community.

Let's Go Swimming: Dive into the Pool of Cultural Responsiveness

The primary purpose of this book is to make clear the process for diving into the pool of cultural responsiveness, using the teaching skills necessary to be culturally and linguistically responsive (CLR). I use the metaphor of a pool because I liken the process of becoming culturally responsive to learning how to swim. (I was inspired by the swim lessons of my twin daughters, Biko and Zora.) At their swim school, there are five swim levels, with a set of discrete skills for each level. The pre-beginner level is an Emerger, which means standing on the side of the pool, daring oneself to get in. The top level is a Freestyler, which means you are ready for Olympic competition. (Keep in mind that this is all being interpreted by a non-swimmer, me.) These swimming levels are a perfect way to look at the infusion or implementation of the culturally and linguistically responsive pedagogy into instruction. Thus, I borrowed the labels from the swim school and created five infusion levels for becoming CLR.

Continuum of Infusion Levels

	Emerger ➜	Splasher/ High Splasher ➜	Floater/High Floater ➜	Kicker ➜	Freestyler
Number of CLR Instructional Areas (1–4)	*One Area:* Management Vocabulary Literacy + Language	*One Area:* Management Vocabulary Literacy + Language	*Two Areas:* Management Vocabulary Literacy + Language	*Three Areas:* Management Vocabulary Literacy + Language	*Four Areas:* Management Vocabulary Literacy + Language
Quantity	1–2 CLR activities	3–5 CLR activities	6–7 CLR activities	8–9 CLR activities	10–12 CLR activities
Quality	Minimal fidelity + accuracy	Some fidelity + accuracy	Fidelity + accuracy	Strong fidelity + accuracy	Strong fidelity + accuracy
Strategy	Does not VA/BB with intent and purpose	Attempts to VA/BB with intent and purpose	VA/BBs with clear intent and purpose	VA/BBs with intent, purpose, and juxtaposition	VA/BBs with intent, purpose, and juxtaposition

The quantity of CLR activities implemented for each level is based on observing teachers in hundreds of classrooms. Floaters and above move beyond using only management or engagement activities (Section 1). Each infusion level increases your instructional activity in cultural responsiveness. Most times, teachers enter the pool splashing and then move toward kicking. Some teachers are emerging. Regardless of where you begin, it is where you end that counts.

The end goal of this book is for you to become a culturally responsive Kicker or Freestyler in your CLR pool—your classroom. A Kicker is a teacher who validates, affirms/builds, and bridges cultural behaviors with explicit intent and purpose and does so with fidelity and accuracy. Teachers at the Kicker level are typically using eight to nine CLR activities in an instructional block. If you make it to Freestyle, you are working on all eight cylinders, so to speak. It means that you have the ultimate mix of quantity, quality, and strategy.

The secondary purpose of this book is to challenge your pedagogy. Becoming culturally responsive means that your instruction changes for the better. I call this change in instruction *transformative instructional practices*, or TIPs. CLR can renovate or overhaul your instruction. CLR is rooted in seeing and feeling the change for yourself, no different than getting a new hairstyle or buying a new outfit. In other words, you can see the difference without any external endorsement or research because you know that it feels right. This, however, is not to say that there is not ample research support for the effectiveness of these practices. In fact, the number of researchers providing supportive evidence is overwhelming (Zeichner 2003; Goodwin 2011; Tate 2025; Johnson and Johnson 1987; Slavin 2010; Dolan et al. 1993). Regardless, the most important evidence is when your students become more engaged and invested in their learning.

The question is, are you willing to be transformed? It can be a difficult question to answer. After more than twenty years of training thousands of teachers, I have realized that most educators are not necessarily opposed to CLR and its principles. However, some are simply unwilling to change their instructional practices. I assume, though, that if you are reading this text, you are ready for change. The objectives of this book are twofold—to give practicing teachers the what to do (the quantity) and to coach teachers on the how (the quality). Each of the CLR categories presented in this book is intentionally connected to a general area of instruction that impacts your daily teaching.

Being culturally responsive is not so much about doing one activity instead of another activity, but about how your overall teaching dynamic is influenced, nudged, tweaked, or changed with the use of CLR. For example, academic vocabulary. The CLR pedagogy teaches you how to validate and affirm your students' vocabulary for the purpose of building and bridging them to use academic vocabulary more proficiently in their speaking and writing. In doing this, your vocabulary teaching is enhanced. As you work your way through this text, keep telling yourself that the change in your instruction is not only about the cultural responsiveness. It is about transforming all of your teaching and how you approach instruction overall.

Anyone who has read *Culturally and Linguistically Responsive Teaching and Learning: Classroom Practices for Student Success, Second Edition* (Hollie 2018) knows that the journey to cultural responsiveness happens in two ways: a change in mindset and a change in skill set. As the initial step to changing the instructional dynamic in the classroom and the overall school climate, educators have to see their students' cultural and linguistic behaviors differently. This change in mindset is rooted in four areas: speaking a common language, listening to your deficit monitor, knowing your race-ethno cultural identity, and identifying the students who are most in need of cultural responsiveness.

The second way the journey to responsiveness happens is in the change in skill set: a culturally responsive use of a set of strategies and activities that validates, affirms, builds, and bridges. Validating and affirming refer to explicit acknowledgment of the legitimate and positive cultural and linguistic behaviors of all students through proactive, strategic instructional planning and through reactive teachable moments. *Proactive* means that you are planning specific activities with intention and purpose to culturally appeal to students. *Reactive* means using unplanned moments—teachable moments—to validate and affirm students. For example, a student may utter something in their home language during class. At that moment, you can let the student know that you appreciate the use of home language or how the student expressed the idea, rather than "correcting" it. Building and bridging is acknowledging those behaviors and using them to teach the academic, social, and cultural skills your students need for success in mainstream culture and academia. Building and bridging moves students toward being situationally appropriate. Situational appropriateness is determining which cultural or linguistic behaviors are most appropriate for a situation.

> **Note:** For an in-depth exploration of the change in mindset needed for successful responsive teaching, see *Culturally and Linguistically Responsive Teaching and Learning: Classroom Practices for Student Success, Second Edition* (Hollie 2018).

A change in skill set is rooted in four aspects: knowing the gatekeepers of success, using traditional to culturally responsive instruction, jumping into the pool of responsive activities, and reimaging the learning environment. With these aspects of the skill set in mind, we examine how the change in mindset is associated with the skill set.

Change in Mindset Leads to Change in Skill Set

We start with the change in mindset. The first step to changing the classroom dynamic and school climate is seeing students' cultural and linguistic behaviors differently. As mentioned above, a change in mindset is rooted in four areas:

1. Speaking a common language
2. Listening to your deficit monitor
3. Knowing your cultural identity
4. Identifying the students who are most in need of cultural responsiveness

Let's look at each of the four aspects of mindset to gain an understanding of how they are linked to the strategies and activities in this book.

Speaking a Common Language

Being culturally and linguistically responsive begins with understanding what it means and having consensus about how to name it. My term, *culturally and linguistically responsive teaching and learning (CLR)*, speaks to comprehensiveness and complexity. There is an in-depth focus on culture and language. This focus is a benefit to both teachers and learners. The use of the word *responsive* is strategic and purposeful because it forces a thought process beyond such common monikers as *relevance*, *proficiency*, or *competency*. To be responsive, educators must be willing to validate and affirm students through instruction, which leads to the skill set and the pool of activities described in this book. In short, educators must be responsive to who their students are culturally and linguistically. Use of the strategies and activities begins with the use of common terminology.

Listening to Your Deficit Monitor

Your *deficit monitor* is the internal signal that warns you when you are looking at a student's behavior solely as negative, as lacking, or as a liability, without consideration that it might be culturally or linguistically based and, therefore, an asset. Those who practice responsiveness as a way of being constantly ask reflectively, *What will prevent me from validating and affirming a student culturally and linguistically?* This reflection keeps us honest about our potential for bias, prejudice, misinformation, and ignorance. We have to be omni-aware of our implicit biased thinking, so we can combat it with the cultural lens of validation and affirmation. If we stay stuck in the deficit lens, then we are unlikely to validate and affirm. This can affect our instructional practices, along with the school climate and organizational issues related to equity and institutional racism. Being attuned to your deficit thinking is the key to cultural responsiveness in the classroom. It highlights the path to teaching in a way that validates and affirms.

> *Responsiveness* means the validation and affirmation of indigenous (home) culture and language for the purpose of building and bridging the student to success in the culture of academia and in mainstream society.

Knowing Your Cultural Identity

The research is clear. To the extent that you know who you are racially, ethnically, and nationally, the more likely you are to validate and affirm others (Villegas and Lucas 2004; Villicana, Rivera, and Dasgupta 2011). The concept is simple. When you know who you are culturally and linguistically, and love yourself, you are likely to love others. The worrisome part of this concept is its opposite. If you do not love who you are culturally, then you are unlikely to be validating and affirming or to change your instruction to fit your student population. Similar to listening to your deficit monitor, knowing your identity is a prerequisite to changing your skill set or instruction in the classroom and impacting the school climate. Discovering yourself culturally is a liberating experience because it increases empathy. Empathy opens up your teaching and allows you to be more validating and affirming. In other words, when you are able to consider your cultural background with confidence, whether it is ethnically or socioeconomically, then you are able to walk in the shoes of your students.

Identifying the Beneficiaries of Responsiveness

Without a doubt, changing your mindset and changing your skill set benefits all students, regardless of their culture. Validation and affirmation are for everyone. There are some students, however, who will benefit more from this than others. Identifying who these students are focuses your advocacy and instruction. Since the beginning of state-mandated standardized testing, there are four groups (Mexican American, African American, Hawaiian American, and Native American) that have been traditionally underserved—failing academically or behaviorally because schools are not culturally responsive (Hollie 2018; New America Foundation 2008). CLR teaching and learning calls for specific discussions around certain students and particular issues that directly affect them. Educators identify the most underserved—any student who is not successful academically, socially, and/or behaviorally because of the school's unresponsiveness to the student's needs.

Keep in mind that these four aspects work together to allow for the transition from a change in mindset to a change in skill set—the focus on instructional strategies emphasized in this book. Read on for summaries of the four aspects of the skill set (gatekeepers of success, methods of instruction continuum, pool of responsive activities, and reimaging the learning environment).

Changes in Skill Set

The four gatekeepers of success are classroom management, academic vocabulary, academic literacy, and academic language (Orange and Hollie 2014, 68). They are considered "gatekeepers" because they are essential for student success in school. As educators, we must ensure that our classroom management supports students' success and that our instruction leads to their proficiency or mastery of academic vocabulary, academic literacy, and academic language. This book is divided into four sections based on these gatekeepers with a brief review of what research says about their importance.

Methods of Instruction Continuum

Most instructional methodology used in the classroom falls into one of three broad categories—traditional methodology, responsive methodology, and culturally responsive methodology. Traditional instruction is teacher centered with a higher affective filter and reliance on one-way interaction. Responsive instruction is student centered with a lowered affective filter and reliance on two-way interaction. Culturally responsive instruction adds cultural (anthropological) elements, such as language, rhythm (music), movement, social interactions, and other aspects of culture. The objective is to have a balance of activities across the continuum. If this can be accomplished, then culturally responsive instruction is achieved: validating and affirming activities (responsive and culturally responsive) as well as building and bridging activities (traditional) are utilized. By implementing activities across the continuum, you are meeting the needs of all students. This book will fill your toolbox with responsive and culturally responsive activities.

Pool of Culturally and Linguistically Responsive Activities

The pool of responsive activities is organized by categories. These activities provide the what and the how of the pedagogy of cultural responsiveness, which includes traditional instruction as well. The challenge for most teachers is utilizing these activities strategically and intentionally. There is one goal: to validate and affirm or build and bridge students' cultural and linguistic behaviors. Doing the activities just for the sake of doing them completely misses the point of CLR. There should never be random acts of teaching. The CLR formula for success is Quantity + Quality + Strategy. All three of these equal CLR, resulting in increased student engagement and better student outcomes. The pool of activities is listed on page 7 and becomes the content of the subsequent sections for this book.

CLR Formula for Success

Quantity	+	Quality	+	Strategy	=	CLR
using many different activities with frequency		using the activities with fidelity and technical precision		knowing when to use a particular activity and for what purpose		Cultural and Linguistic Responsiveness

Reimaging the Learning Environment

A culturally responsive learning environment is one that conveys respect for every student, notably respect for the knowledge, experiences, and language students bring to the classroom. The last skill set is to critically examine your classroom environment for opportunities to make it more culturally responsive. Putting on your cultural lens, you'll want to consider three revisions to your learning environment:

1. De-Blumenbach your classroom. Johann Friedrich Blumenbach was a German anthropologist who developed a system of racial classification that divided humans into five races based on skin color and perceived beauty. To de-Blumenbach your classroom, you make deliberate decisions about the images you display and seek materials that represent your students' cultures, rather than accepting Caucasian representations as the standard.

2. De-commercialize your classroom. The best way to ensure that your classroom environment is representative of your student population is to display students' work, rather than commercial products. The most authentic piece that can be put on the walls is student work.

3. De-superficialize your classroom. Go beyond superficial images of cultural diversity and strive for authentic and genuine historical and visual representations of your students' cultures.

The last chapter of this book provides tips and suggestions for a responsive learning environment.

In summary, successful infusion of these four areas into your instruction constitutes a change in skill set and leads you on the path to becoming a Kicker. The chapters that follow delve into the CLR categories and provide a host of activities. Each chapter begins with the rationale for the general pedagogy of each category and then explores its specific connection to CLR. Steps to success follow, with detailed explanations. When applicable, tips, suggestions, sample lessons, and opportunities for reflection and assessment are provided for each chapter.

Are you ready to dive into the pool? You say, "Yes, I am!"

CLR Pool of Instructional Activity Categories

CULTURALLY AND LINGUISTICALLY RESPONSIVE MANAGEMENT

- Use of attention signals
- Use of protocols for responding
- Use of protocols for discussing
- Use of movement
- Use of extended collaboration activities

CULTURALLY AND LINGUISTICALLY RESPONSIVE ACADEMIC VOCABULARY

- Use of leveled vocabulary words
- Use of Personal Thesaurus or Personal Dictionary tools
- Use of vocabulary acquisition strategies
- Use of reinforcement activities/assessments

CULTURALLY AND LINGUISTICALLY RESPONSIVE ACADEMIC LITERACY

- Use of CLR text
- Use of engaging read-alouds
- Use of effective literacy activities

CULTURALLY AND LINGUISTICALLY RESPONSIVE ACADEMIC LANGUAGE

- Use of sentence lifting
- Use of role-playing
- Use of retellings
- Use of revising

CULTURALLY AND LINGUISTICALLY RESPONSIVE LEARNING ENVIRONMENT

- Use of de-Blumenbach
- Use of de-commercialize
- Use of de-superficialize

How to Use This Book

Strategies for Culturally and Linguistically Responsive Teaching and Learning, Second Edition is designed to maximize student learning by arming teachers with the skills they need to validate and affirm students' home lives and languages to build and bridge them to their academic lives. This book provides the philosophy and models the strategies to support culturally and linguistically diverse students through responsive management, vocabulary, literacy, and environment.

Most chapters begin and end with a **self-assessment chapter survey** and have **reflective thoughts** throughout to encourage contemplation and drive adjustments in practice.

After an overview of the chapter and an examination of the research, a **reflection checklist** is provided.

Following the reflection checklist, **each item from the checklist is thoroughly explained** and examined. **Thought-provokers and thought-blockers** follow, providing insight into the mindset that either promotes or prevents forward progress.

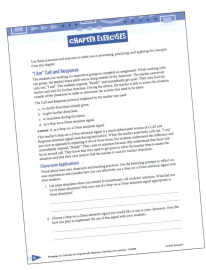

Chapter exercises provide **classroom applications and sample lessons** to visualize implementation of the protocols, strategies, or activities in an instructional setting.

How to Use This Book (cont.)

A **"Student Voice: BeYou"** section explores how students might express the importance of being validated and affirmed when demonstrating cultural behaviors and reminds teachers to adjust instruction and classroom practices, ensuring students can be themselves at school.

A **"Be Community and Collaborate"** section provides starter activities for doing the CLR work in collaboration within grade-level teams, subject-area departments, and PLCs.

The **Appendices** provide the **student pages** and **teacher forms** mentioned in the book.

The **Digital Resources** include a **Year of Reflections Journal** with more than forty reflection prompts, essentially one for each week of the school year. You'll also find digital versions of the **student pages** and **teacher forms** in this book.

Is That Cultural or Not? Focusing on Cultural Behaviors

Understanding the Context

The essence of cultural responsiveness is the validation and affirmation of cultural behaviors. With our CLR lens, we must ask ourselves, "Is this behavior cultural or not?" If teachers don't ask this question, they might unintentionally mistake behaviors that are recognized as cultural or linguistic for *bad* or *wrong* behaviors, which leads to unwarranted punishment, negative consequences, or microaggressions. Those in turn then affect the quality of the relationship between the student and the teacher. On the flipside, validating and affirming cultural behaviors builds and strengthens relationships.

Before delving into the CLR pedagogy—the four instructional areas and the accompanying CLR activities—educators **must know these cultural behaviors and recognize their biases toward them** in order to validate, affirm, build, and bridge. Knowing the behaviors means understanding their meaning, recognizing individual biases as well as institutional biases, and then learning how and when to validate and affirm accordingly. This knowledge reduces the likelihood of cultural misunderstandings, or worse, outright bias.

Focusing on cultural behaviors goes hand in hand with the proactive approach of utilizing engagement activities that culturally appeal to students. These engagement activities validate and affirm students' sociocentrism, kinesthetic learning, communalism, and verbal expression. When students are more engaged, they are less likely to go off task and cause classroom management problems. The activities for engagement are provided in Section 1, Culturally and Linguistically Responsive Management.

> Being *proactive* in your responsiveness begins when you plan your instruction.
>
> Being *reactive* in your responsiveness includes using teachable moments to help students learn to be linguistically or culturally appropriate based on the situation.

This section focuses on cultural behaviors in the context of situational appropriateness and zeroes in on those times when you will have to react in the moment, in teachable moments, by making a split-second decision about whether the behavior is cultural or not.

Each of us expresses our cultural behaviors differently, depending on our home cultures or ethnic identities and in relation to the other Rings of Culture (religious or non-religious affiliations, age, gender, socioeconomic status, orientation, and so on). Expressions of cultural behaviors are not race-dependent.

Cultural behaviors can be conceptualized in two ways:

1. They are meant to stand alone, have value on their own, and be representations of who students are culturally and linguistically for the purpose of validation and affirmation. They are meant to be examined independently of the behaviors of school culture, which, historically speaking, has been rooted in "WASness" or White Anglo-Saxon culture. To only see cultural behaviors in comparison to school culture, then, misses the purpose of validation and affirmation and treads on deficit thinking about who our students are culturally and linguistically.

2. In the context of school culture (or any cultural context), expressions of cultural behaviors can be seen as skills. Different expressions (or skills) are appropriate depending on the context. For example, in the context of school culture, the cultural norm of maintaining eye contact with teachers is a sign of respect or attentiveness. In many other cultures, however, students are taught that looking adults directly in the eye communicates disrespect. Eye contact is a cultural behavior that is expressed differently at school than in some homes and communities. Neither expression or norm of eye contact is wrong; rather, it is about the appropriate use given the context.

Considering the Research

Research supports the importance of identifying cultural behaviors and teaching situational appropriateness with regard to these behaviors. The following works support the significant role of cultural behaviors in a culturally responsive classroom:

- In the extremely well-researched *Culturally Responsive Teaching: Theory, Research, and Practice, Third Edition* (2018), Geneva Gay makes a strong argument for recognizing the relationship between culture, language, and education.

- In *Culture in School Learning: Revealing the Deep Meaning, Third Edition* (2015), Etta R. Hollins strongly argues that understanding and utilizing knowledge of students' culture is essential to the process of education.

- *Culturally and Linguistically Responsive Teaching and Learning: Strategies for Student Success, Second Edition* lays out complementary research and arguments to those presented in this book (Hollie 2018).

- Barbara J. Shade, Cynthia Kelly, and Mary Oberg wrote a comprehensive analysis of the impact of culture on learning and how to spot and address cultural differences in the classroom. Their work, *Creating Culturally Responsive Classrooms* (1997), includes information about specific ethnographic groups and incorporates theory into an "action guide" that can be used by classroom teachers. This book is foundational to the CLR approach.

- Wade W. Nobles' landmark article "Psychometrics and African American Reality: A Question of Cultural Antimony" (1987) argues that traditional mental functioning assessments are biased and reinforce ideas of Eurocentric superiority when used to assess Afrocentric psychology and behavior.

Before continuing, reflect on how you currently focus on cultural behaviors. As you rate yourself on figure P.1, think about how frequently you focus on cultural behaviors as positive versus negative. If you are not focusing on cultural behaviors, think about the ways that you can start by the end of the chapter.

Figure P.1 Focusing on Cultural Behaviors Survey: Before Infusing the CLR Principles

0: *Never Emerging* 1: *Rarely Splashing* 2: *Sometimes Floating* 3: *Mostly Kicking* 4: *Always Freestyling*					
I recognize the cultural behaviors of my students.	0	1	2	3	4
I reactively use teachable moments to help my students be linguistically or culturally appropriate depending on the situation.	0	1	2	3	4
I verbally validate and affirm my students' cultural and linguistic behaviors daily.	0	1	2	3	4

Beginning the Reflective Process

Though practicing cultural responsiveness with fidelity requires the broad skill set that is described in the chapters to come, the heart and soul of CLR lies in the split-second decision of determining whether a student's behavior is cultural or not. It is here, in the blink of an eye, that your mindset, disposition, and attitude toward your students' Rings of Culture (figure P.2) and possibly their race are put to the test. It is here, in a matter of seconds, that you need to reflect on your filter:

◆ Where have you received your information to make this decision? You must question your belief system.

◆ How does all that you believe, rightly or wrongly, factor into your decision? You need to listen to your deficit monitor.

◆ Do you trust the voice or the feeling that says you are thinking with bias?

There is no expectation that you get it right every time. However, as a culturally and linguistically responsive educator, you are mandated to ask the question: Is it cultural or not? Doing so requires courage, conviction, and consistency, and over time you will answer the question with accuracy more often than not. Teachers often ask me, "How can I learn about all of the cultures in my classroom to make the right decision?" You cannot. Your students are your best teachers, so long as you put on your cultural lens and see your students as unique individuals with their own cultural behaviors, you will be on the right track. So, are you ready to focus on cultural behaviors?

> Though practicing cultural responsiveness with fidelity requires the broad skill set that is described in the chapters to come, the heart and soul of CLR lies in the split-second decision of determining whether a student's behavior is cultural or not.

Figure P.2 Rings of Culture

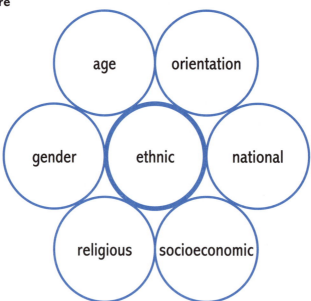

Use the following checklist to gauge your readiness and ability to effectively integrate situational appropriateness and cultural behaviors into your teaching. Each item represents an important aspect of understanding and using cultural behaviors in a culturally responsive classroom. After completing the checklist, read the information about each item and reflect on how you plan to help your students learn about the situational appropriateness of cultural behaviors.

☑ Cultural Responsiveness Reflection Checklist		
Item P.1	Do I recognize the cultural behaviors of my students?	◯ Yes ◯ No
Item P.2	Do I reactively use teachable moments to have my students be linguistically or culturally appropriate depending on the situation?	◯ Yes ◯ No
Item P.3	Given a framework to use daily, am I willing to verbally validate and affirm my students' cultural and linguistic behaviors?	◯ Yes ◯ No

Item P.1 Do I recognize the cultural behaviors of my students?

Anthropology can be defined as "the comparative study of human societies and cultures." So, when examining cultural behaviors, I turn to research in anthropology. Keep in mind that our focus is not on race. Race does not apply to behavior. Look at these cultural behaviors in a very broad sense, including the Rings of Culture, to avoid pigeonholing students. The best source for a general perspective of cultural behaviors is the Iceberg Concept of Culture (Fatiu and Rodgers 1984) shown in figure P.3.

Figure P.3 The Iceberg Concept of Culture

Like an iceberg, nine-tenths of culture is below the surface.

Surface Culture
More easily seen
Emotional level: low

Food, dress, music, visual arts, drama, crafts, dance, literature, language, celebrations, games

Shallow Culture
Unspoken rules
Emotional level: high

courtesy, contextual conversational patterns, concept of time, personal space, rules of conduct, facial expressions, nonverbal communication, body language, touching, eye contact, patterns of handling emotions, notions of modesty, concept of beauty, courtship practices, relationships to animals, notions of leadership, tempo of work, concepts of food, ideals of childrearing, theory of disease, social interaction rate, nature of friendships, tone of voice, attitudes toward elders, concept of cleanliness, notions of adolescence, patterns of group decision making, definition of insanity, preference for competition or cooperation, tolerance of physical pain, concept of "self," concept of past and future, definition of obscenity, attitudes toward dependents, problem-solving roles in relation to age, sex, class, occupation, kinship, etc.

Deep Culture
Unconscious rules
Emotional level: intense

(Fatiu and Rodgers 1984)

The Iceberg Concept of Culture is invaluable when looking at culture broadly, because it gives us a way to talk about culture without being stereotypical. To recognize cultural behaviors, you have to scan the figure to first recognize these behaviors as cultural rather than fictitious or random. Note that there is a superficial perspective of culture in the figure, which is not the essence of cultural and linguistic responsiveness. For example, having an annual International Food Day in your classroom where you serve foods from various ethnic groups does not truly validate and affirm your students' cultures or make your teaching culturally responsive. While the students may enjoy tasting various ethnic foods, this type of activity does not actually help students achieve academic success by building and bridging to the mainstream and academic cultures. Your focus should be on the behaviors below the surface. All of the behaviors are worth examining, though analysis of each one is beyond the scope of this book. Here are recommended steps for developing deeper understanding of cultural behaviors:

1. Peruse the list, focusing on the Shallow Culture section. You will see these shallow behaviors often in your classroom. Be sure to keep the cultural behaviors in mind and do not ignore them at this stage.

2. Focus on the behaviors listed in the Deep Culture section. Reflect on the role these behaviors play in your classroom.

3. Choose one behavior and see if you can give a layperson's definition of it as well as an anthropological definition. For instance, the layperson's definition of "courtesy" might be "acting politely," while the anthropological definition might be "a cultural behavior that communicates respect, cooperation, and consideration."

4. Apply the behavior to a student's culture in your setting. Evaluate if the behavior is of high or low importance in that student's culture compared to the school's culture. The following steps will help you reflect on how to identify these cultural behaviors.

Identifying Cultural Behaviors

1. Note the primary nonverbal communication methods your students display, such as eye contact, hand gestures, body movement, and facial expressions.

2. Ask yourself:

   ◆ What nonverbal communication behaviors do you notice?

   _____

   _____

   ◆ Which students show these behaviors?

   _____

   _____

   ◆ How do you define the significance of these behaviors in terms of culture?

   _____

   _____

3. How has this activity helped your understanding of your students' nonverbal communication? What do you think you will do to validate and affirm the student's culture?

   _____

   _____

For the sake of example, we will look at Hmong culture (Yang 2013). The Hmong people originate from the mountains just south of China. In general, nonverbal communication is of low importance in the Hmong culture, and their language relies on tonal changes (Shade, Kelly, and Oberg 1997). An awareness of Hmong nonverbal communication styles supports validating and affirming them, especially in the context of school culture where nonverbal communication is important. For example, giving clear verbal explanations of expectations, especially regarding nonverbal behavior, would benefit Hmong students and help avoid potential misunderstandings between Hmong students and students of other cultures. Hmong students would also benefit from role-playing situations that often include nonverbal communication in the mainstream culture, such as shaking hands to indicate agreement or reading facial cues that communicate emotions. Validation and affirmation may come from a deeper understanding and sensitivity that moves you toward building and bridging these students to the nonverbal norms of school culture.

Figure P.4 hones in on sixteen cultural behaviors that are least likely to be validated and affirmed in the milieu of school culture, which are, therefore, the focus behaviors for cultural and linguistic responsiveness. The behaviors/skills are listed from the least nuanced (simpler to understand and easier to recognize) to the most nuanced (more difficult to grasp conceptually and more difficult to recognize). Each behavior is briefly defined.

Figure P.4 Sixteen Most Commonly Misunderstood Cultural Behaviors

1.	**Eye Contact**	We communicate with our eyes. Depending on our cultural identity, we can show disrespect/respect, attention/lack of attention, and intrigue/non-intrigue by how long eye contact is maintained (known as *maintenance*).
2.	**Proximity**	The physical distance between two people is often a culturally dependent way of showing respect, rapport, and relationship. The appropriate distance can be culturally determined. Whether a person is asking a question, is seeking information, or simply wants to relate through conversation affects their proximity. The distance and purpose vary from culture to culture.
3.	**Kinesthetic (high movement)**	This refers to an orientation/preference to high levels of movement, especially while learning. It includes gross motor skills (movement of large muscles) and learning through physical activities. High levels of movement while learning are more engaging for some cultures, which can lead to better learning for members of those groups.
4.	**Cooperation/ Collaboration (shared work/dependence on the group)**	The value and practice of working together and sharing responsibility are integral to some cultures. Doing so can contribute to a richer overall experience as a group—"We work better together."
5.	**Spontaneity (unplanned, impromptu, impulsive)**	Some cultures create greater comfort levels in environments and contexts that are marked by impulse and improvisation. This includes responding immediately or from a natural impulse.
6.	**Pragmatic Language Use (nonverbal cues)**	Eye contact, hand gestures, facial expressions, and body language can sometimes communicate more effectively than verbal language. In some cultures, nonverbal cues are emphasized and seen as more meaningful, depending on the context and what needs to be communicated.

7. **Realness (frank, direct, upfront)**	Realness is the level of truthfulness, authenticity, and directness we utilize in our communications. Different cultures value different levels of directness. *How* truth and authenticity are communicated to others can also be culturally based.
8. **Conversational Patterns (verbal overlap, circular discourse)**	Talking or interjecting while someone else is speaking is known as verbal overlapping, and for some it shows respect because it demonstrates active listening. Nonlinear discourse includes the ability to offer tangential information while storytelling or providing information. In some cultures and languages, the ability to communicate in a nonlinear way shows authenticity, engagement, and connection, so talking while someone else is speaking indicates participation and focus.
9. **Orality and Verbal Expressiveness (verve, or expressiveness with verbal and nonverbal cues)**	It's not what you say but how you say it. Verve happens when emphasized use of nonverbal and verbal cues occurs simultaneously. Verve is valued in some cultures as a sign of enthusiasm, engagement, and passion.
10. **Sociocentrism**	The act of social interaction is a contributing variable to the learning. Sometimes known as learning by talking, socializing is as important as the learning itself.
11. **Communalism**	"We" is more important than "I." The success of the whole (community, family, class, collaborative group) outweighs and is more valued than the success of the individual.
12. **Subjectivity**	The essential understanding of a topic or concept lies in the relativity, perspective, and granularity, not simply about what's "right" or "wrong." Multiple perspectives are allowed and valued.
13. **Concept of Time**	Time can be seen conceptually as precise, meaning the beginning and ending of an event or occurrence is controlled by the clock. Or time can be seen as relative, meaning the event and occurrence are controlled by the human interaction (what is going on in the moment), not by the clock.
14. **Dynamic Attention Span**	This refers to a demonstration of varied ways to show focus and task orientation. There are different ways to pay attention.
15. **Field Dependence**	In some cultures, teaching and learning are best done in the context of groups' social and cultural experiences. Relevance is determined by contextualizing the learning, which is highly valued.
16. **Immediacy**	Immediacy is actions that all at once communicate warmth, acceptance, closeness, and availability. Connectedness and sense of immediacy can sometimes be interpreted through a lens of urgency (students who need something "now"; waiting creates stress due to their perception of what immediacy looks like).

Here are examples of some of cultural behaviors and how they play out in the classroom:

1. Communalism: Collective success is more important than individual success. Culturally, students are more invested in the success of the whole class or of their small group than they are in individual accomplishments. In the classroom, students practicing communalism are sometimes thought to be unfocused or "worrying about everybody else."

   ◆ **Example:** While in a collaborative group, a student is paying attention to a friend in another group to make sure the friend is succeeding.

2. Eye Contact: Telling students from a culture that does not maintain eye contact to focus by looking at the teacher sends a message that their cultural norm is unacceptable.

   ◆ **Example:** The teacher is giving direct instructions, and a student is looking down or away but paying attention.

3. Realness: In some cultures, directness is considered polite and expected, while in others, indirectness is more appropriate. In school culture, being direct is typically not preferred.

   ◆ **Example:** A student from a culture that values direct communication tells the teacher that a lesson is boring. The student's attention is redirected by the teacher, who asks the student what they are supposed to be doing at that moment instead of commenting on the lesson.

4. Orality and Verbal Expressiveness: Reliance on nonverbal communication sometimes is labeled as being too dramatic or emotional in the context of school.

   ◆ **Example:** During a heated discussion, a student assertively makes her point verbally and with nonverbal expressions such as hand gestures, body language, and eye contact.

5. Proximity: It is important to understand the proximal space of your students and teach them what is appropriate for school.

   ◆ **Example:** To show rapport with the teacher, a student stands very close (less than arm's length) to ask a question about the lesson or to share an idea.

6. Concept of Time: Students from cultures that embrace the relativity of time can be seen as disrespectful when they're tardy or viewed as lazy when they don't finish assignments on time. Of course, they should be on time and finish assignments promptly. However, understanding why they may be late and not immediately assuming it is a matter of disrespect goes a long way.

   ◆ **Example:** A middle school student shows up to class a minute or so late because she was finishing up an assignment in another class.

7. Conversational Patterns: In some cultures, interrupting or jumping in while someone is talking is acceptable or even expected. The timing of the jump-in is culturally or linguistically based. Clearly, in the school culture this is not usually considered acceptable. Students who come from "jump-in" cultures are confused when they are chastised for interrupting frequently, given that their conversations at home include regular jump-ins.

   ◆ **Example:** While the teacher is reading a very engaging story to the class, some students are chiming in with comments, questions, and praise about the story.

As you can see, a wide variety of cultural behaviors influence personal interactions and learning styles. The process here is to recognize the behavior as cultural, practice validation and affirmation, and teach the situationally appropriate behavior. By acknowledging these cultural behavior differences, and teaching students about the situational appropriateness of certain behaviors, teachers help students learn to effectively navigate different situations in the mainstream culture or macro society.

REFLECTIVE THOUGHT

The primary cause of biased thinking is ignorance. By beginning this process toward CLR, you automatically work toward lessening your biased thinking by increasing your knowledge about your students' cultures. What cultures are present in your classroom? How are these cultures expressed through your students' behavior patterns? What is your own cultural background? How are your thoughts and expectations regarding students' behavior affected by your cultural background?

Thought-Provokers: A Mindset for Moving Forward

1. I am ready for a homework assignment. I will select a culture and/or cultural behaviors in my classroom. I commit to a deep study by spending time with people of this culture and/or learning more about the cultural behavior, reading books that authentically portray this culture, and discussing cultural issues with my students.

2. I see my students as my best sources for learning about every culture and cultural behavior in our room. I ask about my students' cultural practices at home, spend time with my students and their families outside of the classroom, and engage in meaningful discussions about cultural practices with the caregivers of my students.

Thought-Blockers: A Mindset for Staying Stagnant

1. I assert that I know everything there is to know about each culture and the cultural behaviors in my classroom at this time and do not see the point in learning more or seeking confirmation of that knowledge.

2. I am unwilling to seek out additional information about the cultures and the cultural behaviors represented in my classroom in a given school year.

Item P.2 Do I reactively use teachable moments to have my students be linguistically or culturally appropriate depending on the situation?

This item comes down to one simple question that must be answered in the moment: Is the student's behavior cultural or not? To respond, you must follow these four steps:

1. Is the behavior cultural or not?
If yes, go to step 2. If not, go to step 4.

2. YES: Validate and affirm the behavior.

4. NO: If the behavior is not cultural, go to your classroom management system.

3. Build and bridge to the culturally appropriate behavior.

Let's walk through another example by picking a behavior that could happen at school. Imagine that your students are attending an assembly, and they have been told to be absolutely quiet during the performance. About mid-performance you see two students turn to each other and talk briefly, laugh quietly, and then turn right back to watch the show. You are watching the students, noticing it as a cultural behavior. The students see you, but they note to themselves that you ignored their behavior (validate and affirm). You give them "the look" to indicate the behavior was situationally inappropriate (build and bridge), not a wrong behavior.

REFLECTIVE THOUGHT

Our goal is to teach students the situationally appropriate behavior, regardless of the context—at school, at home, at work, and in society. In order to do so, students need to practice distinguishing between cultural behaviors and other behaviors. Is your understanding of your students' culture deep enough to allow you to distinguish between cultural and other behaviors? What are some methods you can use to help you gain a better understanding of your students' cultural behavior patterns?

Thought-Provokers: A Mindset for Moving Forward

1. I recognize that culturally appropriate behavior is situational. I accept that CLR does not mean that all behavior will be accepted or that students will not be held accountable. For example, a student should never be allowed to use violent or aggressive behavior in the classroom, regardless of their cultural background.

2. I limit my teachable moments for being linguistically or culturally appropriate in the situation to less than two minutes. This means I validate, affirm, build, and bridge, and move on.

Thought-Blockers: A Mindset for Staying Stagnant

1. I do not distinguish cultural behavior from misbehavior.
2. I employ CLR sporadically and am not consistent in my handling of teachable moments for being linguistically or culturally appropriate in the situation.

Item P.3 Given a framework to use daily, am I willing to verbally validate and affirm my students' cultural and linguistic behaviors?

A logical question to ask is, "What do I say that is validating and affirming in the moment?" The answer is a VABB statement: validate and affirm in the first sentence and then immediately build and bridge. Here is the structure and some examples:

Validate and Affirm (VA)

Use an Affirming Verb (love, appreciate, honor, relate to, value) and name the cultural behavior.

Examples for Cultural Behaviors

- Verbal Overlap: "I appreciate how engaged you are in this conversation."
- Directness: "I love your honesty."

Important Rule: Do not use *but*, *however*, or *although* in between the VA statement and the BB statement.

Build and Bridge (BB)

Put this part of your response in the form of a question (not a yes/no question) and use terms like *classroom culture*, *school culture*, or *situationally appropriate*—or any other term that contextualizes the behavior.

Examples for Cultural Behaviors

- Verbal Overlap: "In our classroom culture, how do we engage in a conversation when someone has the floor?"
- Directness: "When do we express our opinions, based on our established norms?"

VABB for Verbal Overlap: "I appreciate how engaged you are in this conversation. In our classroom culture, how do we engage in a conversation when someone has the floor?"

VABB for Directness: "I love your honesty. When do we express our opinions, based on our established norms?"

The key to a successful VABB statement is to avoid value and judgment. Words like *better*, *good*, and *respectful* are judgmental and imply that one type of behavior is better than another behavior. The goal is the proverbial leveling of the playing field, allowing the context to be the determinant of the appropriate behavior, not you or your bias.

Concluding Thoughts

Asking the question "Is it cultural or not?" will make a difference in your view of your students. Even better, your teaching will be liberated, empowered, and more fun, because you will be less focused on classroom management issues. The focus on cultural behaviors is reactive. Being proactive in your responsiveness begins when you plan your instruction to be culturally responsive, which is the focus of the remaining sections and chapters in this book.

Use these scenarios and exercises to assist you in processing, practicing, and applying the concepts from the chapter.

Behavior—Cultural or Misbehavior?

Read each statement in figure P.4 and indicate whether you believe it is a cultural behavior or a misbehavior. Remember, students can be taught to bridge cultural behaviors to mainstream or academic behaviors that serve the same purpose. Misbehavior that is not cultural needs to be addressed using your classroom management system. Use the Rings of Culture (page 14) to assist you.

Figure P.4 Cultural Behavior or Misbehavior?

Situation	Cultural Behavior or Misbehavior?
1. A teenage boy wears sagging jeans.	Answer: Reason:
2. A student looks down while being reprimanded.	Answer: Reason:
3. A student persistently answers questions or provides comments in class discussions without waiting to be called on.	Answer: Reason:
4. A student calls a teacher an expletive.	Answer: Reason:
5. Students talk to one another as they work to complete a classroom assignment.	Answer: Reason:

Answers:

1. Cultural behavior; wearing sagging jeans is accepted and expected among his peers.
2. Cultural behavior; in the child's experience, it shows respect to an elder.
3. Cultural behavior; at home, jumping in is the norm.
4. Misbehavior; it is disrespectful regardless of cultural background.
5. Cultural behavior; dialoguing and collaborating is acceptable and expected at home to engage in learning.

In summary, many of the behaviors that we see in the classroom every day have a cultural background. However, just because a behavior is cultural does not mean that it is acceptable in the school environment. For this reason, it is important to incorporate instruction about the situational appropriateness of cultural behaviors into the CLR classroom. Furthermore, it is important to acknowledge that some behaviors, such as the use of profanity to show disrespect or to degrade someone, are simply inappropriate regardless of the student's cultural background.

Classroom Applications

Consider your own classroom and teaching practices. Use the following prompts to reflect on your past experiences and consider how you can effectively differentiate between cultural behavior and misbehavior in your classroom.

1. Think about one of the students in your class who requires frequent attention because of their behavior. What is the student's cultural background? Do their behaviors reflect their culture?

   _____

   _____

2. What type of adjustments can you make to your classroom policies or procedures to accommodate your students' cultural behaviors?

   _____

   _____

Proactive or Reactive 1

Read the example in figure P.5. Is the teacher using proactive or reactive teachable moments to address students' observed cultural behaviors? Underline evidence to support your claim. Compare your answers to those given in figure P.6.

Figure P.5 Proactive or Reactive 1

Observed Cultural Behavior	Responsive Instructional Approach	Proactive or Reactive
Conversation Patterns	Mr. Thomas observed that some of his students talk really loudly when they are placed in small collaborative groups to complete assignments or conduct small-group discussions. Mr. Thomas began playing different kinds of music while students worked in collaborative groups requiring discussion. The level of the music was intended to act as the noise gauge. The music was not extremely loud or soft. Mr. Thomas told students that they could talk in their small groups, but they could not talk louder than the music playing. When the level of their voices got louder than the music, he used the "Aloha/Aloha" attention signal to get students' attention and indicate that they should lower their voices.	

Figure P.6 Answers to Proactive or Reactive 1

Observed Cultural Behavior	Responsive Instructional Approach	Proactive or Reactive
Conversation Patterns	Mr. Thomas observed that some of his students talk really loudly when they are placed in small collaborative groups to complete assignments or conduct small-group discussions. Mr. Thomas began playing different kinds of music while the students worked in collaborative groups requiring discussion. The level of the music was intended to act as the noise gauge—it was not extremely loud or soft. Mr. Thomas told students that they could talk in their small groups, but they could not talk louder than the music playing. When the level of their voices got louder than the music, he used the "Aloha/Aloha" attention signal to get students' attention and indicate that they should lower their voices.	Proactive

In this example, Mr. Thomas recognized that his students' tendency to use loud voices when placed in small collaborative groups was an example of a cultural behavior. The students were not using loud voices to show disrespect for the classroom rules, but rather because they were engaged in the activity. However, the students' continually rising voices made it difficult for everyone to converse. This behavior pattern needed to be changed in a culturally responsive way. In order to make his students aware of their voice levels, Mr. Thomas employed a culturally responsive attention signal to notify them when their voice levels passed an acceptable volume. The response signal made the students aware of their voice levels and allowed them to lower their voices in a positive, constructive environment. In this scenario, Mr. Thomas helped his students recognize and consciously implement the appropriate voice level to use in this particular situation (small-group discussions in a classroom setting).

Classroom Applications

Think about your own classroom and teaching practices. Use the following prompts to reflect on your past experiences and consider how you can proactively plan for and use reactive culturally responsive instruction in your classroom.

1. List two specific cultural behaviors that you see in your classroom. How do these behaviors affect the classroom environment?

   _____

   _____

2. Reflect on a situation where you reacted to a student's cultural behavior in a negative way. How did the student react? What would you do differently next time?

   _____

   _____

Proactive or Reactive 2

Read the example in figure P.7. Is the teacher using proactive or reactive teachable moments to address students' observed cultural behaviors? Underline evidence to support your claim. Compare your answers to those given in figure P.8.

Figure P.7 Proactive or Reactive 2

Observed Cultural Behavior	Responsive Instructional Approach	Proactive or Reactive
Loud tone of voice when speaking to other students in collaborative groups	Sean's class is participating in classroom conversation. Sean's teacher has been working with him because the tone of his voice gets louder when he speaks passionately about a topic. In today's lesson, the class is participating in a debate. Sean's group selected Sean to be the one who would present their ideas after their group collaborated. While Sean was presenting his opening argument, he looked at the teacher, who discreetly used a hand signal that indicated that his voice had gotten too loud. He saw the signal, lowered his voice, and continued his presentation.	

Figure P.8 Answers to Proactive or Reactive 2

Observed Cultural Behavior	Responsive Instructional Approach	Proactive or Reactive
Loud tone of voice when speaking to other students in collaborative groups	Sean's class is participating in a classroom conversation. Sean's teacher has been working with him because the tone of his voice gets louder when he speaks passionately about a topic. In today's lesson, the class is participating in a debate. Sean's group selects Sean to be the one who will present their ideas after their group collaborates. While Sean is presenting his opening argument, he looks at the teacher, who discreetly uses a hand signal that indicates that his voice had gotten too loud. He sees the signal, lowers his voice, and continues his presentation.	Reactive

This is an example of reactive responsiveness because Sean's teacher uses a hand signal to indicate situational appropriateness during, rather than before, the activity. In this way, both Sean and his teacher are reacting to the situation as it unfolds during the debate and adjusting behavior in a culturally responsive way. The teacher's reactive responsiveness in this example allows Sean to use the feedback about the situational appropriateness of his tone to modify his behavior on the spot to make it more appropriate for the classroom environment.

Building and Bridging Through Cultural Behaviors

Read the example provided in figure P.9. Note how Mrs. Smith adjusts her management techniques to incorporate cultural behaviors. Also, pay attention to how the teacher uses her policies for walking in a line to help the students learn about the situational appropriateness of when it is acceptable to talk while in line. After reading the scenario, respond to the questions.

Figure P.9 Classroom Management Using Cultural Behaviors

Walk in a Straight Line
Mrs. Smith understands the need for students to walk in an orderly fashion as they travel to different places on the school's campus. She also understands the sociocentric nature of her students and does not mind when they talk to one another as they walk in line. Mrs. Smith gives her students these rules for walking in line: 1. Do not run in line. It is not safe. 2. It is acceptable to walk next to one partner and talk, as long as you and your partner stay with the group and make it to where you need to be. 3. It is not acceptable to talk while in line in the hallway because it will disturb students in other classes. 4. When you see a school administrator, get silent, fall into a single-file line, and proceed to your destination.

Provide evidence from the scenario to answer the following questions:

1. What cultural behavior is Mrs. Smith supporting with her rules for walking in a line?

   _____

   _____

2. How is she validating and affirming this cultural behavior for her students?

   _____

   _____

3. How is she building and bridging her students' capacity to acquire the expected behavior for walking in a straight line?

   _____

   _____

Answers:

1. Sociocentric behavior allows for talking to a partner while walking in a line.
2. Mrs. Smith allows them to talk and walk next to a partner, as long as it does not impede their progress, cause danger by running, or disturb students in other classes.
3. Mrs. Smith builds and bridges by giving students cues about situationally appropriate times to display the cultural behavior.

In this scenario, Mrs. Smith adjusts the traditional expectation of having students walk silently from one location to the next to allow for the sociocentric nature of her students. She structures her guidelines so that her students can be sociocentric in line while still being safe and respectful. By doing this, Mrs. Smith is validating and affirming her students' cultural identities. In addition to validating them, Mrs. Smith uses this activity to teach her students the situations when it is appropriate and when it is not appropriate to talk quietly while walking in line.

Classroom Applications

Consider your own classroom and teaching practices. Use the following prompts to reflect on your past experiences and consider how you can effectively use cultural behaviors to build and bridge to academic or mainstream expectations regarding behavior.

1. Think about a specific cultural behavior you see in your classroom. How can you use this behavior to bridge to an academic or mainstream objective?

   _____

   _____

2. Reflect on your own cultural background. Describe a specific personal behavior that would be culturally appropriate in one situation but not in a different situation.

_____

_____

Sample Lesson—Role-Playing Using Cultural Behaviors

Role-playing is one effective way to teach students about the situational appropriateness of certain cultural behaviors. The following lesson demonstrates how to use role-playing to teach students about the situational appropriateness of making direct eye contact.

Procedure

Before planning a role-play lesson, survey your students' behavior and identify a specific cultural behavior that is only appropriate in certain situations.

1. Begin by asking students to share cultural practices regarding the target behavior in their home cultures. Students may never have consciously considered their use of this behavior so you may need to prompt them with questions. The following examples help students think about when they make or avoid direct eye contact:

    ◆ When you greet an old friend, do you look them directly in the eye?

    ◆ How about when you meet someone new for the first time?

    ◆ Does it matter if the person you are talking to is older or younger than you?

    ◆ When your parents are upset, do they want you to look directly at them when they're speaking to you?

2. After identifying how this behavior is used in their home cultures, ask students to think about different ways this behavior may be interpreted in the mainstream culture. Discuss various scenarios where this behavior might involve two people from different cultures, such as a classroom, the workplace, or during an extracurricular activity.

3. Place students into small groups of three to four students. If the class has a variety of different cultural backgrounds, make sure that the groups are heterogeneous, with different cultures in each group.

4. Introduce a scenario where the cultural behavior would be considered appropriate. For instance, in the scenario "a father discussing a disappointing report card with his child in a Latino household," the child would be expected to avoid eye contact as a sign of respect for the authority of the father.

5. Have the groups designate two people to role-play the scenario. For example, one student would play the father and another student would play the child while the remaining group members watch. Have students act out the scenario.

6. After the groups have a chance to complete their role-play, ask students what they observed about eye contact during the activity. Discuss how, in this particular situation, the target behavior was appropriate.

7. Give the groups another scenario where the same behavior would not be considered appropriate. For example, a lack of direct eye contact during a job interview with an interviewer from a mainstream American cultural background would be considered rude or inattentive.

8. Provide time for students to act out the second scenario in their groups. The students who did not have roles in the first role-play should be given roles in the second scenario.

9. As a class, discuss the situational appropriateness of the target behavior in the second scenario. Ask, "Why is this same behavior appropriate in one situation but not in another? Why is it important for a person to understand the situational appropriateness of certain cultural behaviors?" Review how the exact same behavior can have very different interpretations and implications depending on the situation.

To extend the activity, ask students to write a paragraph describing one specific cultural behavior that is acceptable in their home culture but not in another situation. When they are finished, allow students to share their writing with partners or in small groups.

Post-Reading Assessment

Now it is your turn to start "swimming" toward cultural responsiveness. Start today. As you plan your next lesson, think about when you can ask, "Is it cultural or not?" Be intentional and strategic. Allow yourself the time and space to fail, to make mistakes, and to be uncomfortable. After two weeks of implementing CLR, come back to this chapter and complete figure P.10 on cultural behaviors.

Figure P.10 Focusing on Cultural Behaviors Survey: After Infusing the CLR Principles

0: *Never Emerging* 1: *Rarely Splashing* 2: *Sometimes Floating* 3: *Mostly Kicking* 4: *Always Freestyling*					
I recognize the cultural behaviors of my students.	0	1	2	3	4
I reactively use teachable moments to help my students be linguistically or culturally appropriate depending on the situation.	0	1	2	3	4
I verbally validate and affirm my students' cultural and linguistic behaviors daily.	0	1	2	3	4

STUDENT VOICE

Allowing Your Students to Be Engaged in Their Own Way, or "BeYou": Dynamic Attention Span

BeYou is a call to action, reminding teachers to adjust instruction and classroom practices, ensuring students can be themselves at school culturally and linguistically. Here we consider how students might express the importance of being validated and affirmed when demonstrating dynamic attention span at school.

What's dynamic attention span like in the classroom? I feel most comfortable and can be the most successful when I can engage and sometimes multitask in nontraditional ways. This may mean I don't make eye contact with you, or I draw while the teacher is talking, or I might need to stand up and move my body while listening to stay engaged.

How might it be viewed if not understood? In the classroom, this can look like I am restless, off task, not doing what I am asked, or interrupting. It has also been received as defiance and disruption. Some say I am not paying attention, but it just isn't true. I simply check out when I am asked to engage in <u>only</u> traditional ways or <u>for periods of time that are too long</u>.

What do I need to be myself? I feel validated when I can engage in my own way, multitask, and/or vary the ways I stay connected to the learning. If you see me doodling during a lesson, or standing and swaying during group work time, you know I am doing what I need to do to focus and engage. I am affirmed when you see my dynamic attention span and recognize it as cultural, and then look for ways to bring those opportunities into the learning that happens in the classroom.

> **What CLR activities validate and affirm dynamic attention span?** Students excel in activities such as Merry-Go-Round, Who's the Stray, and Answer Chairs because they invite students to show focus in nontraditional ways.

Build CLR Community and Collaboration

This group activity helps staff members separate cultural behaviors from unacceptable behaviors. Staff cannot mistake cultural behaviors for unacceptable behaviors and vice versa. The objective is to reach consensus on specific cultural behaviors that most of the staff will agree to validate and affirm. That means no punishing, no negativity, no consequences. Unacceptable behaviors will also be identified. These behaviors are treated differently, meaning they are not validated and affirmed at all. There is also a third category of behavior: egregious. These behaviors require an immediate institutional response from the administration because they involve issues of safety or illegalities.

Procedure

1. Create a three-column chart with headers as shown on the next page.

2. Discuss the idea that *culturally inappropriate* does not mean bad or wrong. It means that "situationally" the cultural behavior is not "appropriate" for the context. It is not appropriate for the time and the place. Discuss the sixteen cultural behaviors (page 17) to ensure everyone is familiar with them.

3. Decide which two behaviors you want to focus on as a staff. (Aim for 60–80 percent agreement.) There must be a commitment to validate and affirm those cultural behaviors and not view them as negative or requiring consequences. Record these in the left column.

4. In the Unacceptable column, list two different behaviors that are unacceptable, which require managing using your classroom management/discipline system (or, in PBIS terms, major/minors). Discuss your progressive discipline plan and ask, "Is it consistently, equitably applied?"

5. In the last column, list two behaviors that are unmistakably out of bounds and require administrative support to handle. These behaviors are illegal and/or safety and health issues.

This activity is meant to challenge mindsets and blind spots. That's the whole point.

Culturally Inappropriate Behaviors	Unacceptable	Egregious
Example: Conversational Pattern—Verbal Overlap	Example: Eloping (leaving the class without permission)	Example: Vaping in the restroom

Culturally and Linguistically Responsive Management

Culturally and Linguistically Responsive Management Overview

Effective classroom management has always been a staple of any teacher's recipe for success. For students to have success as they matriculate through school, they must be able to understand and to accept the school's institutional culture, the varied classroom expectations and procedures, and the ever-changing unspoken rules. For maximum learning to occur, both students and teachers need to value a well-managed classroom.

How does cultural and linguistic responsiveness (CLR) apply? It relates to classroom management in three ways. The first way is to support increased student engagement (Marzano and Pickering 2010). CLR pinpoints increased student engagement as evidence that positive classroom management exists. The objective of CLR as it applies to classroom management is to increase student engagement and decrease management issues using responsive strategies and activities. The second way cultural responsiveness applies to effective classroom management is related to issues of race and equity. Typically, a disproportionate number of African American and Latino students are given referrals, suspensions, and expulsions (Gregory, Skiba, and Noguera 2010; Safir and Dugan 2021). By becoming responsive in classroom management, student engagement will increase and referrals, suspensions, and expulsions, especially among the aforementioned groups, will decrease (Hollie 2018). The third aspect of classroom management is what was covered in the prologue: Educators need to increase their ability to differentiate cultural behaviors from unacceptable ones.

How will student engagement increase? Section 1 describes and is organized by four categories that lend themselves to cultural responsiveness or teaching in a validating and affirming way.

- Chapter 1 centers on the use of effective attention signals, which allow for extensive use of Call and Response.

- Chapter 2 focuses on the importance of response and discussion protocols, which connect to underserved cultural behaviors such as sociocentrism, which acknowledges that in some cultures, social interaction is at times more important than the content being taught.

- Chapter 3 highlights the importance of movement in the learning, focusing on high-movement contexts—culturally and kinesthetically.

- Chapter 4 is about providing extended collaboration opportunities, which emphasize community, communalism, and interdependence—all cultural elements.

A variety and mix of strategies, guidelines, activities, scenarios, examples, and samples in each chapter give you what you need to dive into the CLR pool.

CHAPTER 1

Small Steps, Big Gains: Effective Use of Attention Signals

Understanding the Context

Effective use of CLR attention signals is not as easy as it first appears. What most teachers miss are the necessary nuances, as well as the intentional and strategic use of these signals. If teachers neglect these important subtleties in or during lesson planning, the desired outcome—increased student engagement—will remain elusive. Remember, small steps can produce big gains. In this chapter, you will discover a set of readiness questions and a checklist to determine your willingness and ability to use Call and Response attention signals. Below each readiness question are suggestions or things to think about for moving forward and possible hindrances that may keep you stagnant. Following the readiness questions is a sample list of effective attention signals organized by appropriate use. The chapter ends with practice exercises, lesson examples, and a survey for your reflection.

Considering the Research

Call and Response attention signals are an effective method to enhance classroom management techniques and to create a culturally responsive classroom.

- The advantages of Call and Response have been linked to neuroscience and the learning process in three ways: attention activation, firing and wiring, and mirroring neurons (Hammond 2013). With Call and Response, students can memorize *and* understand content, as it allows them to move from rote memorization to active participation (Adjapong and Emdin 2015).

- Call and Response has been shown to improve teaching and learning (Adjapong and Emdin 2015), along with literacy and language skills (Foster 2001). Its success is dependent on teachers' knowledge and the kind of questions that students are asked (Troyer 2023).

- Call and Response is connected to teachers demonstrating that they know who their students are (Toney and Rodgers 2011; Sosa 2017) and showing that their aim is creating social justice–centered spaces for student learning (Beltrano 2023). Further, when using Call and Response, students' contributions, especially those that reflect their experiences, literacies, and identities, should be met with respect from the teacher (Sosa 2017).

Pre-Reading Assessment

Before reading the rest of this chapter, survey your use of attention signals using figure 1.1. Begin the reflective process by asking yourself these questions:

- Do I understand why attention signals are important for my classroom management?

- Do I believe that some students may respond better if I use attention signals more effectively?

Figure 1.1 Effective Uses of Attention Signals Survey: Before Infusing the CLR Principles

0: *Never Emerging* 1: *Rarely Splashing* 2: *Sometimes Floating* 3: *Mostly Kicking* 4: *Always Freestyling*					
I use responsive attention signals consistently and strategically.	0	1	2	3	4
I use responsive attention signals for clarification/further instruction.	0	1	2	3	4
I use responsive attention signals for transitioning.	0	1	2	3	4
I use responsive attention signals for ending the lesson.	0	1	2	3	4
I use responsive attention signals for other purposes: praising, shout-outs, check-ins.	0	1	2	3	4

Beginning the Reflective Process

Learning happens when we reflect on what we have experienced. Critical reflection "*generates* learning (articulating questions, confronting bias, examining causality, contrasting theory with practice, pointing to systemic issues), *deepens* learning (challenging simplistic conclusions, inviting alternative perspectives, asking 'why' iteratively), and *documents* learning (producing tangible expressions of new understandings for evaluation)" (Ash and Clayton 2009, 27). Are you ready to respond and use attention signals in your classroom?

Use the following checklist to gauge your readiness and ability to effectively integrate attention signals into your teaching. Each item represents an important aspect of understanding and using attention signals in a culturally and linguistically responsive classroom. After completing the checklist, read the detailed descriptions of the items and reflect on how you plan to implement or increase your use of responsive attention signals.

☑ The Use of Attention Signals Reflection Checklist

Item 1.1	Do I know the technical definition and the purpose of an attention signal?	○ Yes ○ No
Item 1.2	Do I have something that is worthy and meaningful to bring students back into focus for?	○ Yes ○ No
Item 1.3	Do I use attention signals for instructional value and not for classroom management purposes only?	○ Yes ○ No
Item 1.4	Do I acknowledge that responsive attention signals are not just about getting students to be quiet?	○ Yes ○ No
Item 1.5	Do I have at least one signal in each of the instructional range categories (traditional, responsive, culturally responsive)?	○ Yes ○ No
Item 1.6	Do I have a Stop-on-a-Dime signal for classroom management purposes that I have procedurally contrasted from the other attention signals?	○ Yes ○ No

Item 1.1 Do I know the technical definition and the purpose of an attention signal?

An attention signal is an agreed-upon verbal or nonverbal cue used to bring the students back to focus when they are engaged. A special emphasis is placed on the word *engaged*, as opposed to when they are sleeping, when they are working individually, or when they are off task. The definition of an attention signal cannot be assumed or taken for granted, especially from a classroom management perspective. Unfortunately, many teachers miss the importance of the attention signal and do not realize that the skill of using an attention signal is a small step that can yield huge results. These cues are only to be used during three specific contexts:

◆ to clarify directions already given or to give further direct instruction

◆ to transition during the lesson from step one to step two and so on

◆ to bring the lesson, activity, or class time to a close

Understanding the definition and purpose of the attention signal assists in its strategic and frequent use, increasing student engagement and decreasing classroom management issues.

REFLECTIVE THOUGHT

Break down your current use (purpose) of attention signals by percentage (numbers must add up to 100 percent):

Clarifications _____   Transitions _____   Terminations _____   Other _____

Thought-Provokers: A Mindset for Moving Forward

1. Attention signals are conceptually social cues. I value using them to give students the opportunity to learn a necessary life skill for success in the world beyond the classroom.

2. I value validating and affirming students' culture by using Call and Response cues. Call and Response is a cultural norm with deep relevance for many cultures. Call and Response is defined as the mandated response to a call in a social or cultural setting, like in church where *amen* can be said anytime during the service as an affirmation.

> Engagement exists when students and the teacher equally feel the need for a cue to come together and refocus.

Thought-Blockers: A Mindset for Staying Stagnant

1. I use responsive attention signals when my students are not engaged, expecting the signals to work successfully. I do not believe that engaged students respond best to attention signals.

2. I do not believe that students need to be validated and affirmed culturally with Call and Response. I believe that students are in school to comply with the school's cultural norms.

Item 1.2 Do I have something that is worthy and meaningful to bring students back into focus for?

Over time, students lose confidence in "what comes next" if the teacher repeatedly brings them back to focus without a good reason. Students assume an attitude of "Why should we focus when nothing is being offered instructionally?" This attitude, however, is very different from when students are unfocused or off task "just because." The teacher blames the students for the former as if it were the latter, which then becomes a classroom management issue.

REFLECTIVE THOUGHT

Remember a time when you brought your class back to order without a "good" reason. How did students respond?

Thought-Provokers: A Mindset for Moving Forward

1. I check the validity of my reason to bring the students back together.
2. I remind myself of the three reasons to use responsive attention signals, and I hold myself to those.

Thought-Blockers: A Mindset for Staying Stagnant

1. I believe that students should come to focus regardless of the reason.
2. I do not consider it instructionally valuable to strategically plan for use of the responsive attention signals.

Item 1.3 Do I use attention signals for instructional value and not for classroom management purposes only?

When using responsive attention signals, do not expect that students will be completely quiet all at once and at a given moment. The purpose of the attention signal is the acknowledgment that students will quiet down shortly but not instantly. Waiting for all students to be quiet at once defeats the purpose. If done correctly and with student buy-in, once you start redirecting or giving the instruction, all students should quiet down within three to five seconds. If you want all students totally quiet at once, then use your Stop-on-a-Dime or traditional attention signal.

REFLECTIVE THOUGHT

When it comes to using attention signals for instructional value, which of the following classroom management schools of thought are you more likely to agree with?

a. Authoritarian: Teacher is an authority figure, is in control, and bases discipline around stimulus-consequence.

b. Permissive: Signals are not based on stimulus-consequence model; students are given more autonomy.

c. Collaborative: Teacher facilitates a process for management in collaboration with students; students have more choice and freedom.

Note: The collaborative classroom management school of thought supports CLR.

Thought-Provokers: A Mindset for Moving Forward

1. I trust that using attention signals will add instructional value and a positive layer to my classroom management. I ask myself, "When do I want my students to be totally quiet? When am I okay with a little noise?"

2. I acknowledge that it teaches me patience, which is key not only in cultural responsiveness but also in effective classroom management.

3. I find myself "managing less" over time and assuming more energy for instruction.

Thought-Blockers: A Mindset for Staying Stagnant

1. I instruct by managing, whereas responsiveness calls for collaboration.

2. I am impatient. I want it quiet now.

Item 1.4 Do I acknowledge that responsive attention signals are not just about getting students to be quiet?

The use of responsive attention signals goes far beyond quietness and your students simply listening to you. They signal community, harmony, vibe, energy, rhythm, and unity. They signal meaningfulness for those cultures that depend on Call and Response for connecting (validation and affirmation). They signal that you are with your students and your students are with you.

REFLECTIVE THOUGHT

How important is Call and Response in your home (ethnic) culture?

a. very important

c. not so important

b. important

d. not important at all

 ## Thought-Provokers: A Mindset for Moving Forward

1. Ask yourself, "What do I believe about the culture and the community of my students?"

2. Check your filter by asking yourself, "What has informed me to make me believe that way?" Make sure that you are listening to your deficit monitor, which should signal whether you are looking through a negative lens or a cultural lens.

 ## Thought-Blockers: A Mindset for Staying Stagnant

1. I do not believe that Call and Response is connected to culture and community.

2. I do not believe that there is a link between Call and Response and validation and affirmation, mental stimulation, lifted energy in the room, and student success.

Item 1.5 Do I have at least one signal in each of the instructional range categories?

The introduction explained the three general categories of instructional methodology: traditional, responsive, and culturally responsive. Remember that providing instruction in all three categories is what makes you culturally responsive. The point here is that you have at least one attention signal for each category and that you use them interchangeably.

Using a traditional attention signal, such as Give Me Five, over and over will bore the students (and you). However, the same is true for a culturally responsive signal, such as "Whoop!/Dere it is!" To engage students, you must change it up.

REFLECTIVE THOUGHT

Create a list of signals for each category here:

• Traditional_____

• Responsive_____

• Culturally Responsive_____

Thought-Provokers: A Mindset for Moving Forward

1. I see the advantage in variety. I not only believe that it is important to have different signals, but I also believe it is important that students understand the differences between them and why I use one type of signal versus another.

2. I allow my students to make suggestions and contributions, and I change up my signals regularly. Once I have a set of successful signals, I rotate them every month or so.

Thought-Blockers: A Mindset for Staying Stagnant

1. I have one or two signals that work and use those exclusively each time.

2. I expect every signal to work every time because they have worked in the past. I am not willing to step out of my comfort zone and try new signals.

Item 1.6 Do I have a Stop-on-a-Dime signal for classroom management purposes that I have procedurally contrasted from the other attention signals?

When all else fails, you can always use your Stop-on-a-Dime signal. A Stop-on-a-Dime signal is when the students know to come to complete quiet. What is key is that the students understand that your Stop-on-a-Dime signal is for urgent times and for when you need it absolutely quiet for whatever reason.

REFLECTIVE THOUGHT

What are some of your Stop-on-a-Dime signals?

_____

 ### Thought-Provokers: A Mindset for Moving Forward

1. Before I deem responsive attention signals ineffective, I acknowledge that I use some type of attention signal and I assess whether it is working.

2. I acknowledge that responsive attention signals are different from Stop-on-a-Dime signals.

 ### Thought-Blockers: A Mindset for Staying Stagnant

1. I simply do not have a Stop-on-a-Dime signal, or I have used it in place of an attention signal.

2. I am using one signal for all situations. As a result, I am missing opportunities to teach social cues and situational appropriateness.

Building Your Attention Signal Quantity

Whether you checked yes or no for the six items in the Use of Attention Signals Reflection Checklist, the biggest challenge for most teachers is not having attention signals at all. Remember that our formula for infusing CLR into your teaching is Quantity + Quality + Strategy. The first step to successfully using attention signals is to have enough choices (Quantity) to work with at the start. The second step is Quality. This is the fine-tuning process, and it takes time, practice, and patience. Like teaching in general, it begins with trial and error. The last step is Strategy. This step takes place when you are able to strategically use an attention signal with a specific purpose for an instructional advantage for your students. The Use of Attention Signals Reflection Checklist is a guide to implementing Quality and Strategy. On pages 45–47 is the Quantity, a sampling of successful attention signals from classrooms all over the United States. This list is a combination of responsive and culturally responsive signals. As you are reading through the following list, mark the ones that are culturally responsive with a C. Another important consideration is the purpose of the signal. The signal should tell students what exact behavior or next action is expected. Looking at it this way keeps the attention signals from being used randomly or without intention.

Examples of Successful Call and Response Attention Signals

Beginning Lesson

1. Aye go/Aye may
2. Let's get it started/In here
3. Aloha!/Aloha!
4. Show up! Show up! Bet you, I'll see stars, bet you, I'll go far!
5. Throw up! Throw up! (*hands in the air*)
6. Spider-Man/ppsshh (*students hold up web slinger hands*)
7. Tootsie Roll/Lollipop
8. Let me see you go to work, let me see you go to work/Go to work, go to work, go to work
9. Let me hear you say, "Oh we oh, Oh we oh"/Now step this way, step that way!

10. Tell 'em I'm, Tell 'em I'm best/Tell 'em, tell 'em, I'm way too fresh (*students pop their collars*)
11. Fortnite/Battle pass
12. It's me, hi/I'm the problem, it's me
13. Andy's coming/(*students go limp and collapse*)
14. Yo Yo/Let's Go
15. Rollin'/Down the Highway
16. Never back down never what?/Never give up!
17. I don't know about you/I'm feeling 22
18. Hands on top/That means stop

Transitioning

19. Don't just stand there/Bust a move
20. Get up, stand up/Stand up for your right
21. Bottoms up, bottoms up/Get your bottoms up

22. I like to move it, move it/Move it
23. Tell me when to go/Go, go, go, go

Movement

24. Tell me why/Ain't nothin' but a heartache
25. Scooby-doo be do/Where are you?
26. Stop/Collaborate and listen

27. Who lives in a pineapple under the sea?/SpongeBob SquarePants
28. Hot fudge/Sundae
29. It's cool when they do it/It's a problem when I do it...BUMP!

Continued →

Clarification/Further Directions

30. My turn/Your turn

31. When I say _____, you say_____

32. When I say "holla," you say "back." Holla/Back

33. It's like that/And that's the way it is

Focusing/Coming to Attention or Quiet

34. When I say "listen," you say "up." Listen/Up

35. A little bit softer now/Shout/A little bit louder now/Shout

36. Do your work/I know

37. Are you ready?/Yes, I'm ready, ready to learn

38. Hocus Pocus/Everybody focus

39. Macaroni and cheese/Everybody freeze

40. Peace/Quiet; Clapping/Clap back

41. R.E.S.P.E.C.T./Find out what it means to me, Shhh!

42. When I say "holla," you say "back." Holla/Back

43. If you can hear me clap once…clap twice

44. 1, 2, 3, eyes on me/4, 3, 2, looking at you

45. Eyeballs/Click

46. The snack that smiles back/Goldfish

47. Do you wanna build a snowman?/No

48. Zip it, lock it/Put it in your pocket

49. Banana split/Now we sit

50. Hands on top/Everybody stop

51. What sound does a tire make?/Shhhhhhhhh

52. When I say "dream," you say "big." Dream/Big

53. When I say "work," you say "hard." Work/Hard

54. Uno, dos, tres!/¡Estamos listos otra vez!

55. Bring it back/On track

56. What's poppin'?/Don't mind me, just watchin'

Ending Lesson

57. Time for/Lunch

58. Time to/End

59. Whoop!/Dere it is!

60. Lean wit it/Rock wit it

61. McDonald's/I'm loving it!

62. Bring it back now/I'll show you how

63. M-I-C/K-E-Y/M-O-U-S-E

64. Take it to the bank/Cha-ching

65. I got that boom boom/Pow

66. Zip it, lock it/Put it in your pocket

67. All set?/You bet

Just For Fun/Community Builders/Praise

68. Teach me how to/Teach me how to multiply

69. Se puede/Sí, se puede

70. School name (e.g., Hawthorne)/Mascot (e.g., Eagles)

71. The title of a book/Repeat or complete the title

72. Learn it up kids/I'm about to; Learn it up kids/'Cause that's what I was born to do

73. What's/Up?

74. Chicka Chicka/Boom-Boom

75. You are smart/And we know it/You are smart/So let's show it

76. Who's got it better than us?/Nobody

77. Call me/Maybe/Call me/Maybe

78. Red Robin/Yum

79. Power/to the People

80. Can I get a whoop, whoop?/Whoop, whoop!

81. The more you do/The better you get

82. Do your best and/Forget the rest

83. Readers are/Leaders

84. Math is/Cash

85. You know you're a firework/We make 'em go aye, aye, aye

86. It's gettin'/Smart in here

87. Yeah buddy/Rollin' like a big shot

88. I got that boom boom/Pow

Celebration

89. Chugga Chugga/Choo! Choo!

90. My, my/That's some hard work

91. Zoom, Zoom, Zoom/Make my heart go boom, boom, boom

92. Don't lose your head/Use your head, mane

93. Hear ye, hear ye/All hail the King (or Queen)

94. Period I/Period uhhhh

95. Romeo/Juliet; Montagues/Capulets

96. Multiply/Repeated Addition

97. Ba dah dah da dahhh/I'm lovin' it

98. Avengers/Assemble

99. Wakanda/Forever

For Eye Contact

100. Tupac says/"All Eyez On Me"

Thank you to the following teachers and students who contributed to this list: Miss Baker, Kendra Black, April Britt, Destiny Renee, Erica Doty, Carolyn Gildehaus's students, Sarah Gunn, Shannon (Leading Little Lights), Jennifer Hutchinson, Yasmin Jackson, Srta. Kendrick, Teacher Robi, Monica Veira, Sonja White.

The following example illustrates how to use an attention signal to refocus the students' attention on the teacher after a discussion or activity.

> Teacher: When I say 'listen,' you say 'up!' Listen
>
> Students: up!

The list goes on. If you have a successful attention signal, post it on social media and tag us @validateaffirm.

Now that you have a selection of attention signals, create your instructional range. Add your signals to figure 1.2. Aim for at least three in each category. I gave you one to start, so you will have a total of at least four.

Figure 1.2 Creating Instructional Range with Attention Signals

Traditional	Responsive	Culturally Responsive
High Five	School name/Mascot	When I say peace, you say quiet (with rhythm)
Add Stop-on-a-Dime signals here:		

Other Uses for Attention Signals

Once you have mastered the use of attention signals in general, you can begin Freestyling. Freestyling shows how CLR can be applied beyond its original parameters. There are many teachers who Freestyle. However, Freestyling is only recommended after you have conquered the strategy component of the CLR formula. Here are three other possible uses for attention signals once you're ready to Freestyle:

1. **Check-Ins for Understandings/Active Listening**

   There are times when you want to know that your students are with you in the lesson. Instead of asking the traditional "Do you understand?," you can now use Call and Response. For example, say, "Are you with me? Let me hear you say 'I got it!'" "If you understand, thumbs up. Thumbs down if you do not understand." "Tell your face to make an expression that shows you understand or that shows you do not understand."

2. **Praise and Affirmations**

   These are best used for the whole group, praising when students have been exceptionally well-behaved or working hard. These are some examples:

   ◆ Throw your hands in the air and wave them like you just don't care.
   ◆ Give me a high five from afar.
   ◆ Pat yourself on the back.
   ◆ Tell your neighbor, "Great job!" or "You are awesome!"
   ◆ Show yourself some love.

3. **Rallying or Pumping It Up**

   Sometimes the energy is low in the room, or you need to get the juices flowing before the lesson starts. Call and Responses work well for these moments too. Try calls like these:

   ◆ Are you ready to throw down?/Yes, we are!
   ◆ Let's get it started/In here!
   ◆ When I say "ready," you say "let's go."

Use these scenarios and exercises to assist you in processing, practicing, and applying the concepts from the chapter.

"I Am" Call and Response

The students are working in cooperative groups to complete an assignment. While working with one group, the teacher hears adult voices rising outside of the classroom. The teacher assertively calls out, "I am!" The students respond, "Ready!" and immediately get quiet. Their eyes find the teacher and wait for further direction. During the silence, the teacher is able to assess the situation outside of the classroom in order to determine the actions that need to be taken.

The Call and Response protocol employed by the teacher was used:

  a. to clarify directions already given.

  b. to give further directions.

  c. to transition during the lesson.

  d. as a Stop-on-a-Dime attention signal.

Answer: d. as a Stop-on-a-Dime attention signal.

This teacher's Stop-on-a-Dime attention signal is a much-abbreviated version of a Call and Response attention signal used during instruction. When the teacher assertively calls out, "I am" just once as opposed to repeating it two or three times, her students understand the difference and immediately respond, "Ready!" They come to attention because they understand that there will be no second call. They know that they need to get quiet to allow the teacher time to assess the situation and that their eyes need to find the teacher to wait for further directions.

Classroom Applications

Think about your own classroom and teaching practices. Use the following prompts to reflect on your experiences and consider how you can effectively use a Stop-on-a-Dime attention signal with your students.

  1. List some situations when you needed to immediately call students' attention. What did you try in those situations? Was your use of a Stop-on-a-Dime attention signal appropriate in those situations?

  _____

  _____

  2. Choose a Stop-on-a-Dime attention signal you would like to use in your classroom. Describe how you plan to implement the use of this signal with your students.

  _____

  _____

Sample Lesson—Introducing an Attention Signal

Attention signals can only be used successfully if they are taught well and used appropriately. Before attempting to use an attention signal for an instructional purpose, be sure to take the time to deliberately introduce the attention signal to the class and practice the desired response. The following lesson provides one method for introducing a Stop-on-a-Dime attention signal.

Procedure

1. Before beginning the lesson, choose a Call and Response that you plan to use as your Stop-on-a-Dime attention signal. Since the students need to respond to the signal immediately, the Call and Response should not involve multiple repetitions. You may also want to choose an attention signal that reminds students to stop moving as they focus their attention on the teacher.

2. Say, "There are times when I need your attention immediately, such as when a fire alarm goes off, when the principal needs to make an announcement, or when the daily news is being announced over the loudspeaker. I am going to use the 'Macaroni and cheese/Everybody freeze!' signal to let you know when I need your attention immediately. Let's practice what that would look and sound like. When I say 'Macaroni and cheese,' you immediately stop what you are doing, freeze your body, turn your eyes to me, and reply 'Everybody freeze!' Now, let's try it."

3. Practice calling the attention signal and having students respond several times. If students get distracted or begin to lose focus, remind them about the importance of the Stop-on-a-Dime signal and reinforce your expectations that they immediately give you their full attention when they hear it.

4. Role-play different scenarios from the list of situations when you might use the Stop-on-a-Dime attention signal. For instance, have students move around the room and converse with each other. Imitate the sound of the fire alarm going off and practice using the attention signal to get students' attention.

5. Throughout the rest of the day, practice using the attention signal to call students' attention at random times. Once they have mastered the designated Call and Response, only use the Stop-on-a-Dime signal when it is imperative to get the students' complete attention immediately.

Ineffective Use of Attention Signals

A middle school teacher is conducting a lesson. While the content has the potential to be the basis of a great lesson, the teacher's delivery of the content does not have the students' attention or buy-in. On the other hand, the students are very interested in their own personal conversations.

Determined to make it to the end of the lesson, the teacher presses forward as planned. Throughout the lesson, the teacher uses a variety of attention signals to bring the students back to focus. The teacher rings a bell to quiet students down, uses a rain stick to signal that they are talking too loudly, and even uses a variety of Call and Responses. The lesson comes to a close, the class period is over, and the students move on to their next class.

In this scenario, the teacher did not use attention signals:

a. to stop students from engaging in off-task behavior.

  b. to encourage students to pay attention during the delivery of the lesson's content.

  c. to have the students engage in instructional activities designed to help them access the content.

  d. to "get the kids quiet."

Answer: c. to have the students engage in instructional activities designed to help them access the content.

Kudos to the teacher for using both responsive (the rain stick) and culturally responsive (Call and Response) attention signals, in addition to the more traditional one (the bell). The use of attention signals in this scenario does, however, demonstrate a misunderstanding of how to strategically use these pedagogical tools. As answers a, b, and d suggest, the attention signals were being used as classroom management tools. This is not their intended use and can lead to overuse of the protocols. Attention signals can be effectively used when students are working in collaboration or in discussion (Hollie 2018); both of these uses could have helped increase the students' engagement with the lesson.

Classroom Applications

Think about your own classroom and teaching practices. Use the following prompts to reflect on how you have used attention signals in the past and the types of changes you would like to make in your classroom.

  1. Reflect on a lesson that did not go as planned. What strategies did you use to refocus students' attention? Were they effective? Why?

  _____

  _____

  2. If you were the teacher in the example above, what could you have done to avoid the overuse of the attention signal protocol?

  _____

  _____

Sample Lesson—Using Attention Signals to Increase Collaboration

The following lesson demonstrates how a teacher can use attention signals as an effective tool to engage students in instructional material. This lesson shows how to use the "The more you do/The better you get" attention signal to facilitate collaborative group learning and transitions.

Procedure

  1. Before beginning the lesson, select an array of instructional artifacts related to a current area of study, such as the Great Depression. For example, artifacts related to the Great Depression might include newspaper articles, photographs, postcards, and letters. Divide the artifacts into four groups and place them at centers around the classroom.

  2. Place students into four groups. Assign each group to one of the artifact centers.

3. Say, "I am going to use a Call and Response signal to let you know when it is time to rotate artifact centers. When I say 'The more you do,' you reply 'The better you get!' When you hear the attention signal, you will have 30 seconds to finish what you are doing. After 30 seconds, I will repeat the signal, and you will need to have your complete attention on me. I will know that I have your attention when your eyes are on me, your hands are folded on your desk, and your mouth is quiet. When I have everyone's attention, I will tell you how we are going to rotate to the next center."

4. Practice calling the attention signal and having the students respond several times.

5. Have students examine the artifacts in their groups. Before small-group discussions begin, ask the class, "How are the artifacts related to each other? How do they relate to the concepts we have been studying?" If appropriate, provide students with graphic organizers, so they can take notes on the various artifacts at each station.

6. After the allotted amount of time, use the attention signal to notify students that it is time to rotate centers. Direct them on how to move to the next artifact center.

7. Instruct students to repeat the process of examining and discussing the artifacts at the new center.

8. Continue rotating until all four groups have been to all four artifact centers.

9. Ask students to return to their seats. Have volunteers share their ideas and notes about the artifacts with the rest of the class. Discuss the similarities and differences between the groups of artifacts.

Math Lesson

Students are learning how to use multiplication to evaluate exponential expressions. The teacher observes several students who have confused the meaning of the exponent when using multiplication to calculate the value of exponential expressions.

For example, students are computing 3^3 as (3×3) instead of $(3 \times 3 \times 3)$ and 5^3 as (5×3) instead of $(5 \times 5 \times 5)$. The teacher should use an attention signal to:

   a. clarify directions already given to the students.

   b. give further directions.

   c. transition from one step to another during the lesson.

   d. close out the lesson and prepare to transition into another activity.

Answer: Although all of these are valid reasons to use attention signals in a lesson, the answer is: **a.** clarify directions already given to the students.

Classroom Applications

Think about your own classroom and teaching practices. Use the following prompts to brainstorm different ways to integrate the use of attention signals into your instruction.

   1. Think about the specific students in your classroom. What type of culturally responsive attention signals might work best with them?

   _____

   _____

2. List three different purposes for using attention signals in the classroom. Which of these purposes do you see as being most relevant to your classroom? Why?

_____

_____

_____

Sample Lesson—Using Attention Signals to Explain and Clarify

The following lesson demonstrates how a teacher in the math scenario could use an attention signal to aid students' comprehension.

Procedure

1. When you realize that some students are having difficulty with the new math concept, use a pre-taught attention signal, such as hand-clapping repetitions, to call students' attention to you.

2. To use the hand-clapping attention signal, clap your hands in a pattern, such as clap, clap, clap-clap-clap. Students should respond to the signal by repeating the same clapping pattern. In order to do this, they must refocus their attention (to remember the clapping pattern) and put down their pencils, so they can use their hands to clap.

3. If necessary, repeat the Call and Response signal using a different clapping pattern to ensure that you have all students' attention. It is up to the individual teacher to define what it means to have students come to attention. For some teachers, it is acceptable for students to finish their work after an attention signal is given as long as their mouths are quiet. Be sure to clearly define your expectations and consistently reinforce them when using an attention signal with your students.

4. Once the students stop working, say, "I stopped you because I noticed that some of you are having difficulty understanding the difference between multiplication and exponents. Let's review this difference again as a class, so we can make sure that everyone understands how to use exponents." Address students' confusion by reviewing the new concept and demonstrating how to solve several practice problems on the board.

5. After engaging in guided practice with the new concept, have students return to their independent work. You can restart the students with another signal, such as "Time to/Start." Continue to monitor their progress and comprehension.

Reading Comprehension Lesson

In a reading comprehension lesson, students conduct a close read of a text to determine why the author included particular facts and details. First, students are allotted a certain amount of time to read the text silently, annotating it to find support for their ideas about the text. When time is up, the teacher calls out, "When I move, you move" ("Stand Up" by Ludacris). The students respond, "Just like that" and move to meet up with a partner or group to compare notes and discuss their ideas. After a predetermined amount of time, the teacher repeats the same Call and Response protocol two times, allowing students to move into different partnerships as they discuss their ideas about the text with one another.

In this scenario, the teacher used a Call and Response attention signal to:

a. integrate movement into a reading comprehension lesson.

b. facilitate small-group discussions in the class.

c. transition from one step to another during the lesson.

d. All of the above

Answer: d. All of the above

This scenario demonstrates how attention signals can be used to facilitate the use of movement and discussion in a classroom lesson. Students engage in collaborative discussions to compare the information they collected from their reading of a text. The teacher's use of the Call and Response attention signal incorporating a song ("Stand Up" by Ludacris) that is responsive to youth culture provides the students with something they can relate to while bringing them to attention before moving on to the next step within the lesson.

Classroom Applications

Think about your own classroom and teaching style. Use the following prompts to examine different ways to integrate attention signals into your daily classroom practices.

1. Reflect on your daily classroom schedule. How can you use attention signals to add movement to your daily routine in a way that would benefit instruction and comprehension?

   _____

   _____

2. Think about problems that arise during times of transition in your classroom. How can you utilize attention signals to help students move more smoothly from one activity to the next?

   _____

   _____

Sample Lesson—Adding Movement with Attention Signals

While most teachers find it relatively easy to integrate movement into their instruction generally ("Everyone stand up and give me five jumping jacks"), adding movement that deliberately supports the instructional objectives of the lesson can be more challenging. Teachers often worry that students will "get out of hand" while doing movement activities and that they will not be able to refocus their students' attention when necessary. The following lesson illustrates one way to use attention signals to ensure that a movement activity (Inner-Outer Circle) about the elements of the Periodic Table occurs responsively.

Procedure

1. As a whole class, discuss the elements of the Periodic Table that will be reviewed using the Inner-Outer Circle activity. Provide students with review questions about the content or have them develop their own questions before beginning the activity.

2. Split the class in half. Have half of the students form a circle in the middle of the room facing outwards. Help the remaining students form an outer circle, facing inwards. With both circles in place, each student on the inner circle should be facing one student in the outer circle.

3. Say, "To start this activity, those of you in the outer circle are going to be asking review questions to those of you in the inner circle. After each question, the students in the outer circle will rotate one person to the right. I am going to use the 'Whoop!/Dere it is!' attention signal to tell you when it is time to rotate. When I say 'Whoop!' you respond with 'Dere it is!' When you hear the attention signal, stop talking, freeze your body, and turn your eyes to me so we can make sure to rotate at the same time."

4. Begin the activity by having the students in the outer circle ask their partners in the inner circle a review question about the content. For example, one student might ask, "What type of metal is copper?" Provide time for the students in the inner circle to try to answer the questions.

5. Call out the attention signal, wait for students to respond, and then have students in the outer circle rotate one person to the right. After rotating, have students in the outer circle ask a question to their new partners in the inner circle.

6. Continue to have the students in the outer circle rotate and ask questions until a full rotation is complete.

7. Switch roles and give the students in the inner circle the opportunity to rotate and ask review questions while the students in the outer circle remain still and respond to the questions.

Post-Reading Assessment

Now it is your turn to begin "swimming," or infusing these activities into your practice. Start now. As you plan your next lesson, look for times and ways that you can use responsive attention signals. Be intentional and strategic. Allow yourself the time and space to fail, to make mistakes, and to be uncomfortable. After a couple of weeks of implementing CLR, come back to this chapter and complete the survey (figure 1.3) on your use of attention signals.

Figure 1.3 Effective Uses of Attention Signals Survey: After Infusing the CLR Principles

0: *Never Emerging* 1: *Rarely Splashing* 2: *Sometimes Floating* 3: *Mostly Kicking* 4: *Always Freestyling*					
I use responsive attention signals consistently and strategically.	0	1	2	3	4
I use responsive attention signals for clarification/further instruction.	0	1	2	3	4
I use responsive attention signals for transitioning.	0	1	2	3	4
I use responsive attention signals for ending the lesson.	0	1	2	3	4
I use responsive attention signals for other purposes: praising, shout-outs, check-ins.	0	1	2	3	4

STUDENT VOICE

Allowing Your Students to Be Engaged in Their Own Way, or "BeYou": Spontaneity

BeYou is a call to action, reminding teachers to adjust instruction and classroom practices, ensuring that students can be themselves at school culturally and linguistically. Here we consider how students might express the importance of being validated and affirmed when being spontaneous at school.

How can spontaneity be expressed and culturally misunderstood in the classroom? I thrive when I am free to jump in on the fly and don't have to wait to be prompted. This is my natural way of engaging with you and it makes learning more exciting. If I get out of my seat or shout out during a lesson, some may call me impulsive, or even disruptive. That impulse really means I want to connect with you or what you are teaching.

How does it feel to be misunderstood? Being told I am too impulsive, when it is viewed negatively, is rough. My impulse to jump in can be seen as being disrespectful or rude, but it is actually the opposite! When I participate on the spot or can improvise, instead of having to be planned or prompted, I am showing my comfort with or connection to whatever is going on. It means I am into it and enjoying the learning!

What do I need to be myself? I feel validated when I can participate, respond, or move without being prompted or given a standard way to participate. I am affirmed when you see my impromptu participation as my natural way of engaging and recognize it as cultural.

> **What CLR activities validate and affirm spontaneity?** Students shine in activities like Give One, Get One, Shout Out, and Find Someone Who…, because they are free to connect and participate in unplanned and impromptu ways.

Build CLR Community and Collaboration

Go Four Deep: Moving from Student Generalization to Validation and Affirmation

This group activity helps staff reach consensus on the students who are being underserved as defined by CLR (see Hollie 2018, 45). The key is to avoid the pitfalls of institutionalized generalizations that are primarily racialized only. The first objective is to dig below any generalizations and define three to four narrower variables that speak to a specific student profile and a probability of who is most likely to be underserved. The second objective is to discuss and discover validating and affirming ways to support the specific student population (action-research).

Procedure

1. Start with a generalized student population using data that is provided by your district, state, or the federal government. This data will be generalized racially, economically, linguistically, or according to special needs. Do not simply express your opinions! Start with the actual data. Record this group in the top layer of the inverted pyramid organizer.

2. Ask, "Are there any students in this group who are having success?" If yes, then go to the next question.

3. Ask, "Among the students who are NOT having success, who is most likely to be underserved?" Your answer is the second variable. Record this group in the second level of the inverted pyramid organizer.

4. With the two variables in play, ask question 2 again. If yes, then ask question 3 again. Record this group in the third level of the inverted pyramid organizer. You should have three variables now.

5. Do a round of questions one more time, and end with four variables.

6. Discuss how to effect change with the students culturally and linguistically. End your discussion by developing a plan of action.

Are there any students in this group who are having success? If yes, then go to the next question. If no, stop here.

Among the students not having success, who is most likely to be underserved?

Of that group, are there any students who are having success? If yes, go to the next question. If no, stop here.

Among the students not having success, who is most likely to be underserved?

English Learners

boys

non-Spanish language

very low socioeconomic

Break the Code: Go Four Deep

Use this organizer to identify underserved students. See the directions on pages 57–58.

CHAPTER 2

Talking Is Good: The Importance of Response and Discussion Protocols

Understanding the Context

The explicit use of defined structures for students to respond to questions and conduct discussions is essential in the CLR classroom. These structures are known as *protocols*. According to David Allen and Tina Blythe (2004), protocols provide structures for conversation or response and specify roles for participation in specific types of discussions. They are meant to encourage conversations about content within a productive, inclusive, positive, and safe environment. Allen and Blythe point out that protocols may seem deceptively simple to use, but the reality is they can be very complex. When used effectively, protocols foster experiences through which individuals and groups are strengthened as learners. In short, protocols sustain the notion that talking is good. When defined this way, frequent and strategic use of protocols provides three windows for teachers to be CLR.

> A *protocol* is a guided conversation or response aimed at enabling students to learn content more deeply.

1. **Protocols provide opportunities for students to be validated and affirmed as sociocentric learners—learners who see the act of socializing as central to the learning experience.** Students can freely talk, while still discussing the content with focus. This is not seen as bad, off task, or talking too much. The Give One, Get One activity allows students to share and learn information by interacting socially with one another. After thinking or journaling about a topic, students are asked to get out of their seats and share their thoughts or answers with a classmate. Students take turns explaining their ideas and listening to their partners' thoughts and ideas. Students are thus receiving an idea in exchange for giving one.

2. **Protocols provide an opportunity to teach situational appropriateness by juxtaposing a validating and affirming protocol with a building and bridging protocol through strategic teaching.** By participating in collaborative discussions related to specific learning objectives, students learn the value of contributing to a group through verbal and social means. Not only do they receive validation as sociocentric learners, but they also engage with academic content in a meaningful and purposeful way.

3. **The use of protocols increases student engagement by default, because they force the teacher to talk less and make the learning process more student centered.** Rather than depending on teacher-centered lectures to explain material, structured group activities and discussions allow students to participate in both learning and teaching. One example of this type of protocol is the Jigsaw activity. In this activity, the teacher places the students into several small groups and assigns each group a section of material or text to learn. After

groups study the material, the teacher forms new groups with one member from each of the original groups. In their new groups, students take turns teaching one another the material they learned in their original groups. This activity fosters a sense of interdependency and accountability within the class by making the students responsible for both learning and teaching new material.

Considering the Research

Research supports the use of discussion protocols as an effective method to enhance collaboration and create a culturally responsive classroom.

◆ Verbally processing a topic as well as mentally processing it increases learners' understanding (Allen 2008; Shea and Ceprano 2017).

◆ Students need to debate issues or participate in discussions around topics that are relevant to them (Caine et al. 2004; Shea and Ceprano 2017).

◆ Structured discussions allow students to own the learning (Mohr 2007; Shea and Ceprano 2017).

◆ Some researchers assert that interaction stresses collectivity rather than individuality (Shade, Kelly, and Oberg 1997). More recently, frameworks have encouraged a balance between individuality and collectivity, especially in culturally responsive approaches to teaching (Howard 2017).

Pre-Reading Assessment

Before reading this chapter, reflect on your current use of protocols for responding and discussing. Complete the survey (figure 2.1) and as you rate yourself, consider how to use these protocols more effectively. Chances are that you are already using some protocols for responding and discussing. The overall reflective question is: How effectively are you using them and how responsively?

Figure 2.1 Effective Uses of Response and Discussion Protocols Survey: Before Infusing the CLR Principles

0: *Never Emerging* 1: *Rarely Splashing* 2: *Sometimes Floating* 3: *Mostly Kicking* 4: *Always Freestyling*					
I use protocols for responding and discussing at least two to three times per instructional block.	0	1	2	3	4
I use protocols for responding and discussing with purpose (pre-planned).	0	1	2	3	4
I use protocols for responding and discussing that are specifically for validating and affirming.	0	1	2	3	4
I use protocols for responding and discussing that are specifically for building and bridging.	0	1	2	3	4
I use protocols for responding and discussing for other purposes: praising, shout-outs, check-ins.	0	1	2	3	4

Beginning the Reflective Process

Learning happens when we reflect on what we have experienced. Critical reflection *generates*, *deepens*, and *documents* learning (Ash and Clayton 2009). Are you ready to respond and use discussion and response protocols?

Use the following checklist to gauge your readiness and ability to effectively integrate discussion and response protocols into your teaching. Each item represents an important aspect of understanding and using these protocols in a culturally responsive classroom. After completing this checklist, read the detailed descriptions of the items and reflect on how you plan to implement or increase your use of discussion and response protocols.

☑ **The Use of Discussion and Response Protocols Reflection Checklist**		
Item 2.1	Do I believe in the cultural value of the protocols and intentionally use them?	○ Yes ○ No
Item 2.2	Do I know how to design and structure a protocol?	○ Yes ○ No
Item 2.3	Do I know the strategic purpose of each protocol in my CLR pool?	○ Yes ○ No
Item 2.4	Do I know that my affect is effective?	○ Yes ○ No

Item 2.1 Do I believe in the cultural value of the protocols and intentionally use them?

Believing that the use of a protocol can be culturally valuable to the student directly links to the concept of validation and affirmation through instructional practice. This is shown in two ways. First, there is a belief in myriad cultural norms and nuances that exist at the deep cultural level with your students. Looking back at the sixteen cultural behaviors discussed in the prologue (see also figure 2.2), ask yourself these three questions:

1. Do I truly believe these to be cultural behaviors?
2. Will I know the cultural explanation of a behavior that I select?
3. Can I explain the behaviors in relation to the different cultural identities in my classroom?

Answering "yes" to these questions means that you have the prerequisites for applying the different protocols to the selected cultural behaviors.

If you answered "no" to any of the questions, you have some homework to do as you learn more about your students and their different cultural behaviors and backgrounds. Start by interviewing students' families or researching online. For example, personal space or proximity is culturally based. Different cultures find different distances appropriate when conducting a social interaction. Some cultures may want to be up close, others may not. Being aware of your students' proximal space can shape which protocols you use or do not use. A protocol such as Numbered Heads Together where the participants are required to get very close may not work for some of your students initially. They will need priming and patience from you to be eased into the close proximity the activity requires.

Figure 2.2 Sixteen Cultural Behaviors

1. Eye Contact
2. Proximity
3. Kinesthetic (high movement)
4. Cooperation/Collaboration (shared work/dependence on the group)
5. Spontaneity (unplanned, impromptu, impulsive)
6. Pragmatic Language Use (nonverbal cues)
7. Realness (frank, direct, upfront)
8. Conversational Patterns (verbal overlap, circular discourse)
9. Orality and Verbal Expressiveness (verve, or expressiveness with verbal and nonverbal cues)
10. Sociocentrism (socialize in order to learn)
11. Communalism (*we* is more important than *I*)
12. Subjectivity (relative to the person or situation)
13. Concept of Time (how precisely or relatively time is held)
14. Dynamic Attention Span (varied ways to show attention)
15. Field Dependence (learning is relevant to students' social and cultural contexts)
16. Immediacy (sense of personal connectedness, warmth)

The second way to demonstrate the cultural value of protocols is with intentional use. When a protocol is used randomly or without intention, it tends to sputter instructionally and not have the maximum effect. Typically, the protocol fails to support learning or a meaningful experience for the students or you. For some teachers, the unintended consequence of this failure is to abandon the use of the protocol, rather than look at using it with intentionality. Intentionality requires planning and forethought. In the planning phase, this means connecting specific protocols for increasing engagement to specific cultural behaviors to be validated and affirmed or built and bridged. Planning increases the likelihood of success tenfold.

REFLECTIVE THOUGHT

Choose three protocols that you know. See if you can match them to the behaviors in figure 2.2.

 ## Thought-Provokers: A Mindset for Moving Forward

1. I am prepared and expect to learn from my students, their families, and their communities about their cultural behaviors. I realize that I am not expected to know everything about every culture represented in my classroom.

2. I recall the differences between superficial culture and deep culture. The protocols I use validate and affirm deep culture in most cases.

🚫 Thought-Blockers: A Mindset for Staying Stagnant

1. I am stuck on how these cultural behaviors compare to what is expected of students within the school culture. In other words, I feel that I am letting my students off the hook when I validate and affirm. By validating and affirming, I believe that I am not holding my students up to a high standard.

2. I do not believe in the protocols beyond their traditional methodology. Teacher-centered is my preferred approach in the classroom no matter what.

Item 2.2 Do I know how to design and structure a protocol?

A well-designed protocol is more than a sum of its steps (Allen and Blythe 2004). In fact, how the protocol is designed determines how enriching the experience will be for the learner. Allen and Blythe provide three steps for a well-designed protocol:

1. **Define the context.** It is important for students to know why they are following a certain protocol, especially as it relates to situational appropriateness. Additional information that defines the context includes the nature of the assignment, levels of required participation, explicit directions, and partnership norms.

   ◆ Before using the My Turn, Your Turn protocol for taking turns, tell the class, "In this discussion, it is important for one speaker to be heard at a time. I'm going to use the 'My Turn, Your Turn' attention signal to let you know when it is appropriate for you to share your thoughts and ideas with the class. When I say, 'My Turn,' I need you to focus your attention on me by having a quiet mouth, a still body, listening ears, and watching eyes. When I say, 'Your Turn,' that indicates that it is your turn to share."

2. **Clarify the needed skills.** Students should know what is required of them to be fully engaged and to make a valuable contribution. Some of the protocols, particularly the discussion ones, require evaluation skills. Almost all need participants to use active listening skills, while some want students to be more interpretative, making hypotheses or drawing conclusions. Skills related to asking questions and knowing the difference between open-ended and closed questions are necessary overall.

   ◆ When using the I Got This! protocol, one student in the group starts as the team captain. The team captain reads a review question, and all group members independently answer the question on individual white boards or sheets of paper. When everyone in the group has put down their writing utensils, the captain calls out "I got this!" and checks everyone's answers. If everyone answered the question correctly, the team chooses a way to celebrate, such as high fives all around. If some group members did not get the correct answer, the group works together to help these students understand the material.

   ◆ Tell the class, "In order to participate in this activity, each group member needs to listen carefully when the captain reads the question. Then you need to use critical-thinking skills to answer the question. Be considerate of the other members in your group and refrain from discussing the answer until the captain says, 'I got this!' When it is time to discuss the answer, you need to work together to ensure that everyone understands the correct answer. You also need to use patience and be respectful when it is not your turn to be captain."

3. **Add structure and accountability.** This step assumes that the outcome of the protocol or interaction has been established. Identifying an explicit outcome could be another step in itself. In order to increase the likelihood of success, however, there must be structure (timed tasks, group roles, and tangible products) and accountability, such as exit tickets.

◆ The Post Your Thoughts protocol is an excellent example of an activity where you should clearly define the parameters and expectations before engaging students in the task. In this activity, students are given a prompt or question, and a timer is set for a specified amount of time, such as thirty seconds. During this time, students write as many responses as possible on individual sticky notes and stick them to the table. Before beginning this activity, it is important to specify exactly how long the students will have to respond. Discuss the expectations in terms of group participation, such as each student contributes at least three sticky note responses, and final outcomes, such as the group produces enough sticky notes to cover the table.

> An exit ticket provides students an opportunity to demonstrate their understanding of a lesson before leaving the room or moving on to another lesson.

As you plan with intention, keep these three steps in mind to ensure that your protocol use is well-designed and likely to be successful.

REFLECTIVE THOUGHT

Think-Pair-Share (TPS) (Lujan and DiCarlo 2006) is a discussion protocol used frequently by teachers. However, few think in terms of designing it as an activity. You try. Plan a use for TPS in an upcoming lesson. Remember to include the following:

- context for use
- needed skills
- structure and accountability

Thought-Provokers: A Mindset for Moving Forward

1. I accept that the context for use can change from activity to activity. I understand that I must be very explicit in some cases, especially at the beginning. As my use increases and the protocols become part of my classroom culture, I know that I will need to be less explicit.

2. I give myself time to make the protocols second nature to my teaching. I am patient with myself.

 ### Thought-Blockers: A Mindset for Staying Stagnant

1. I do not currently plan with design in mind, which makes implementing the protocols challenging.
2. I am unwilling to start. (Starting is the most difficult part. The lack of willingness to start can be the biggest blocker!)

Item 2.3 Do I know the strategic purpose of each protocol in my CLR pool?

The protocols were developed for broad use, beyond CLR contexts. Several programs and approaches promote the use of protocols. The most popular and effective of these approaches is known as the Kagan Structures (Kagan 2009). The Kagan Structures are comprehensive, with more than 100 options to explore. Though these protocols were not necessarily invented for CLR purposes, educators add the element of cultural relevance to their use.

What is the difference with CLR? The difference is in the strategic purpose, which links validating and affirming a cultural behavior via a specific protocol. Kagan, the Responsive Classroom approach (as offered by the Center for Responsive Schools), and other systems do not offer a specific link to culture. CLR ties specific protocols to specific cultural behaviors. For example, the Shout Out protocol relates to the cultural behavior of spontaneity. With this protocol, students are encouraged to shout out short answers (one word or phrase) in response to the teacher's questions. Rather than using the standard school protocol of a prompted response, the strategic purpose of this response activity is to tap into a specific cultural behavior trait, spontaneity, and use it to facilitate learning and responding.

A second strategic purpose is knowing when you are being traditional, responsive, or culturally responsive in your methodology. For example, Turn and Talk is a common discussion protocol. Students are given a prompt and asked to turn to their neighbors and share a comment. Turn and Talk is a quick, simple way to have students interact with one another and process information. For the CLR teacher, there is a strategic purpose, as well. Turn and Talk allows students to be sociocentric. In some ethnic cultures and certain age groups, talking while learning is highly valued, even to the point that the social activity itself may outweigh the topic or content.

In this example, the specific CLR purpose of Turn and Talk is to validate and affirm some cultures' and age groups' sociocentrism. While Turn and Talk at face value would be responsive methodologically, when you use it with this cultural purpose in mind, then Turn and Talk becomes culturally responsive. I call this Turn and Talk Plus. The *plus* is the strategy of validation and affirmation. The strategy aspect cannot be underestimated, because with strategy in mind, you have multiple teaching options. There are options in terms of the cultural purpose of a given protocol, and there are methodological options in terms of traditional, responsive, or culturally responsive approaches. When you plan with this type of strategic intentionality, your teaching is elevated, making it more purposeful and culturally responsive.

REFLECTIVE THOUGHT

For each of the following three protocols, provide a possible way that it can be made culturally responsive by validating and affirming a cultural behavior.

- Whip Around
- Somebody Who…
- Graffiti Talk

 ## Thought-Provokers: A Mindset for Moving Forward

1. I am continually adding protocols to my toolbox. I accept that the more tools I have, the more strategic I can be with my teaching.

2. I keep track of what works and what does not work. There is no perfect protocol, and each one has its pluses and minuses when considering the different cultures in my classroom. One protocol may validate and affirm some students but not others, which is why I have to have as many as possible to ensure I am meeting the needs of all of my students.

 ## Thought-Blockers: A Mindset for Staying Stagnant

1. My use of protocols is limited because I simply do not have enough.

2. I do not recognize the importance and effectiveness of teaching through all three methodologies—traditional, responsive, and culturally responsive.

Item 2.4 Do I know my affect is effective?

There is an affective component to using protocols that must be addressed. When I visit a classroom to conduct a CLR observation, the first element I look for is the affect of the room. For me, *affect* means the energy and the vibe, the mood and the flow, and the calmness and connectedness of the room. What I have noticed after observing thousands of classrooms is that the CLR classrooms have a very strong and positive affect, which lowers students' affective filter and thereby positively affects their academic success.

Without a doubt, the frequent and strategic use of protocols helps create a positive affective domain. There are three ways that protocols assist in creating positive affective classrooms:

1. They help teachers build positive relationships with students.

2. They ensure fair and equitable treatment of all students.

3. They enrich the learning experience for all students.

The best reason to use protocols is the intangible and immeasurable outcome of building positive relationships with your students, which is shown to impact student engagement and achievement

(Quin 2016; Sparks 2019) and is one of the five strategies employed by top-performing school systems (Darling-Hammond 2010).

Teacher-student relationships are key to ensuring that students feel good about being learners in your room (Marzano and Pickering 2010). The responsive use of protocols moves the relationship beyond words to actions and behaviors. You demonstrate your appreciation and value of your students culturally when you use the protocols frequently and strategically. Validation and affirmation are liberating for you and empowering for students. According to Marzano and Pickering, "By showing interest in and affection for students, and identifying positive information about them, teachers can forge positive relationships" (2010, 36). This is accomplished partly through the use of protocols.

> Think of the affect in places that you have visited, such as a medical office, an auto repair shop, or a restaurant. How did the place feel when you walked in? What did it feel like while you were conducting your business?

An advantageous result of using protocols is fair and equitable treatment of all students. The protocols allow for fair treatment by increasing the opportunities for students' voices to be heard and for them to own their learning. Joseph McDonald (2007) suggests that a facilitator (which should be the primary role of the teacher) is charged with three tasks: promote participation, ensure equity, and build trust. Participation reinforces that learning is social, and learning together actively and meaningfully "feels good." McDonald asserts, "We are smarter in the aggregate" (16).

Participation is a prerequisite to authentic student engagement, which is necessary for culturally responsive teaching and learning. Equity is challenging to accomplish in tangible ways. The fact that people discuss and interact in different ways, including in ways that speak directly to our cultural differences, makes it difficult to achieve equity. Culturally responsive use of the protocols promotes equity in a visible way and gives every student a fair chance to engage in the learning process. Trust matters in the classroom, and your students will trust in your teaching more when you allow for independence and freedom through the use of the protocols. I liken trust to "get-out-of-jail-free" cards. There will be times, such as when the flow of the class is ebbing, when your students have to trust you and vice versa. The process of using protocols builds trust.

Lastly, the most important effect of frequent and strategic use of the protocols is that they enrich learning. Protocols encourage an environment of learning that presumes the social construction of knowledge, where it is an accepted and desired norm that everyone is expected to speak and to listen, to diagnose and to speculate, and to discover and to explore (McDonald 2007). Protocols foster democracy and cognition in learning. They encourage learners, regardless of age or grade level, to appreciate the value of diverse ideas and the power of deliberative communications. McDonald sums it up best: "Students exercise their descriptive powers, intensify their listening, enhance their qualities of judgment, and facilitate their communication with one another" (8).

REFLECTIVE THOUGHT

> How would you assess the affective domain of your classroom now? What are your measures for energy and vibe, mood and flow, and calmness and collectedness?

Thought-Provokers: A Mindset for Moving Forward

1. I consider how the affective domain of my classroom allows for yet another strategic reason to plan with intention.

2. I think about which protocols are high energy compared to which ones are low energy. I strategically use them depending on what level of energy is needed.

 ## Thought-Blockers: A Mindset for Staying Stagnant

1. I do not consider the affect of the classroom important.

2. I might need external support and am afraid to ask for it. I feel vulnerable.

   Affective domain is very sensitive and sometimes we do not want others to know that the vibe and energy in our rooms is not where we want it.

Building Your Protocol Quantity

Classroom discussions should be an integral part of teaching and learning, but the logistics of designing, facilitating, and assessing discussions are often overwhelming for teachers. Using responding and discussion protocols encourages strategic connection with specific cultural behaviors and helps to organize classroom discussions. In general, classroom discussions align well with many cultural behaviors of underserved students. Discussions offer social and collaborative opportunities for students to express themselves and work together toward shared objectives. Furthermore, the strategic use of specific discussion protocols helps to utilize students' dynamic attention spans, relational learning styles, and spontaneous behavior traits to enhance classroom learning.

The next section of this chapter presents a comprehensive collection of discussion and responding protocols. The protocols have been adapted from many sources including Kagan (2009), Duplin County Schools (2008), and National School Reform Faculty (2015). The section includes a description of each protocol, the corresponding behavior, and directions for using the protocol. Use the section to choose behaviors that you want to validate and affirm, then decide what protocols would enhance your lessons and contribute to student success. Many protocols can also be used to build and bridge school-culture behaviors.

Discussion Protocols

CAMPFIRE

Validate and Affirm Cultural Behaviors: Spontaneity, Subjectivity, Sociocentrism, Collaboration

Build and Bridge Behaviors: Turn-taking, Autonomous (at first)

Description: Students read and respond to anonymous responses of classmates around a "campfire."

Most Effective Uses: Introducing or reviewing concepts and ideas for discussion

Process

1. The teacher places students into groups of four to five.
2. The teacher presents a prompt or a question.
3. Each student quietly writes an individual response to the prompt on a sticky note and places it around the "campfire" (a sheet of paper in the center of the group).
4. Students take turns reading aloud a sticky note other than their own. Each person in the group has an opportunity to question, agree, disagree, and respond to the sticky note.
5. Repeat until each has been read and discussed. This typically takes five minutes.

FAN AND PICK

Validate and Affirm Cultural Behaviors: Cooperation/Collaboration, Sociocentrism, Dynamic Attention Span

Build and Bridge Behaviors: Turn-taking, Objectivity

Description: Students review material collaboratively; each student has a defined role in the collaborative effort.

Most Effective Uses: Reviewing direct instruction, reading, content, and/or skills

Process

1. The teacher creates duplicate sets of cards with review questions; one set for each group of four students. Or, students can create cards with questions that review the content.
2. The teacher places students in groups, where they number off from one to four.
3. Student 1 fans out the cards and tells Student 2 to pick a card. Student 2 reads the question and Student 3 answers the question. Student 4 confirms the answer (praises if correct, clarifies if incorrect).
4. Students shift roles and repeat the process with the next card.

FISHBOWL DISCUSSION

Validate and Affirm Cultural Behaviors: Dynamic Attention Span, Immediacy, Cooperation, Sociocentrism

Build and Bridge Behaviors: Turn-taking

Description: Some students observe classmates discussing a given topic or question, and then roles are reversed and they're observed discussing the same topic or question.

Most Effective Uses: Reviewing and discussing theme, concepts, and ideas

Process

1. The teacher arranges chairs in two circles—an inner and an outer circle. Students are seated in the circles.

2. Students in the inner circle discuss a given topic or question.

3. Students in the outer circle are silent, taking notes on what they hear and observe.

4. Students in the outer circle move to the inner circle and continue the discussion, based on their notes and observations. Or, students in the outer circle can tap in when they want to add something and trade places with someone in the inner circle.

5. After each student has had an opportunity to share and discuss, the teacher allows approximately three to five minutes for the inner and outer circles to interact, ask for clarifications, and/or summarize the main points.

GRAB THAT SPOON

Validate and Affirm Cultural Behaviors: Sociocentrism, Kinesthetic

Build and Bridge Behaviors: Objectivity, Competition, Autonomous

Description: Learners review content in a gamified, student-centered way.

Most Effective Uses: Reviewing direct instruction, reading, content, and/or skills

Process

1. The teacher places students in small groups. Each student needs a pen/pencil and an index card. Each group needs one plastic spoon.

2. Each learner writes a review question and answer on an index card, as well as a point value (e.g., 1 point for a yes/no question; 3 points for a challenging question). Or, the teacher provides the group with a set of questions on index cards.

3. The teacher places the spoon within reach of all students in the group.

4. One person volunteers to be the first reader. The reader may not grab the spoon. The reader reads aloud a question. The first group member to grab the spoon answers the question. If they are correct, a point is earned. If not, the point is lost.

5. Group members take turns being the reader.

6. Once all the questions have been answered and discussed, students count their points.

7. The student with the highest points is the winner.

I GOT THIS!

Validate and Affirm Cultural Behaviors: Communalism, Spontaneity, Dynamic Attention Span

Build and Bridge Behaviors: Autonomous (at first), Objectivity

Description: Small groups support one another in answering objective questions.

Most Effective Uses: Reviewing for a test or quiz; discussing reading material or instructional content

Process

1. The teacher places students in groups of four to six. Each group has a set of question cards and whiteboards (or paper) to write responses.

2. The group's captain pulls a question card and reads it aloud to the group.

3. Group members work independently writing their answers.

4. After all students have responded, they share their answers.

5. When an answer is agreed upon, they yell, "I got this!" and celebrate with a cheer created by the group. Then they move on to the next question. Or, the teacher can come over and ask one person in the group to share the answer and the reasoning.

MERRY-GO-ROUND

Validate and Affirm Cultural Behaviors: Sociocentrism, Cooperation/Collaboration, Immediacy, Dynamic Attention Span

Build and Bridge Behaviors: Turn-taking

Description: In small groups, students share personal responses to a question or prompt in a brief time period.

Most Effective Uses: Responding to literature; expressing ideas

Process

1. The teacher places students in groups of three or four.

2. The teacher asks an open-ended question.

3. Students take turns sharing a thought or reaction with their groups.

4. Responses are concise, one to five words, keeping the rotation quick. (This should be fast like a Whip Around.)

5. Students keep the sharing going around until the teacher calls them back with an attention signal.

Strategies for Culturally and Linguistically Responsive Teaching and Learning—152468

NUMBERED HEADS TOGETHER

Validate and Affirm Cultural Behaviors: Cooperation/Collaboration, Communalism, Sociocentrism, Conversational Patterns

Build and Bridge Behaviors: Turn-taking

Description: Group members work together to form consensus, and then all are held individually accountable.

Most Effective Uses: Reviewing information; working in cooperative groups

Process

1. The teacher places students into groups of four to six.
2. Students number off in their groups.
3. The teacher asks a question, and the group members work together to find the best answer.
4. The teacher rolls a number cube or randomly chooses a number one to six. The students with that number stand.
5. Each student represents their group and reports the group's answer.

PARTNERS

Validate and Affirm Cultural Behaviors: Cooperation/Collaboration, Sociocentrism, Conversational Patterns

Description: This is similar to Turn and Talk but is useful for a deeper discussion. Students work with partners to review content, research information, or practice skills.

Most Effective Uses: Reviewing content and skills; researching information; practicing a particular skill, such as order of operations

Process

1. Partners can be random, based on student choice, or assigned by the teacher.
2. Partners discuss material on a given topic, teaching it to one another and quizzing each other. They become experts on the topic.
3. After partners have worked together, the teacher calls the class back together using an attention signal.
4. If desired, to shift to individual accountability, the teacher can use a response protocol such as Pick-a-Stick to hear from a few partnerships.

Addition: Partners Squared—Two sets of partners join to form a group of four ("squared") to strengthen the discussion and further teach and quiz one another.

POST YOUR THOUGHTS

Validate and Affirm Cultural Behaviors: Sociocentrism, Cooperation/Collaboration, Dynamic Attention Span, Subjectivity

Build and Bridge Behaviors: Written Communication, Autonomous, Turn-taking

Description: Students quickly share, clarify, brainstorm and generate ideas or answers about a topic or concept. This protocol creates a sense of excitement and urgency and gives everyone an opportunity to share ideas. It allows for individualism (writing on sticky notes) before it shifts to social, collaborative learning (discussion of sticky notes).

Most Effective Uses: Brainstorming ideas on a topic; generating a large number of responses to one or more questions

Process

1. The teacher places students in small groups of four to six.

2. The teacher provides a prompt or question, then sets a time limit (about two minutes) for students to each write as many responses as they can on sticky notes, trying to cover their table in a single layer with as many responses as possible.

3. When time is up, the teacher invites groups to Whip Around to share the most dominant or important ideas covering their tables.

4. Finally, the teacher uses a responding protocol (involuntary is best) to hear a few groups' ideas and to hold students accountable for the Whip Around discussion. This builds and bridges from the social, student-centered discussion to individual accountability.

PUT YOUR TWO CENTS IN

Validate and Affirm Cultural Behaviors: Spontaneity, Dynamic Attention Span, Subjectivity, Sociocentrism

Build and Bridge Behaviors: Turn-taking

Description: In small groups, students take turns sharing, questioning, and supporting opinions.

Most Effective Uses: Processing or reviewing information in any content area

Process

1. The teacher places students in groups of four. Each student has two tokens.

2. The teacher provides a prompt or question. Each student takes a turn responding by putting one coin in the center of the table and sharing their idea.

3. After everyone has shared once, students take turns putting their second coins in and responding to what another group member has shared (e.g., "I agree with ___ because…" or "I don't agree with ___ because…"). Alternately, each student can share twice; they decide when (e.g., they use their tokens right away or wait).

ROUND ROBIN BRAINSTORMING

Validate and Affirm Cultural Behaviors: Cooperation, Sociocentrism, Immediacy, Concept of Time

Build and Bridge Behaviors: Turn-taking

Description: Students quickly generate ideas or responses with equal opportunity for participation by all group members.

Most Effective Uses: Brainstorming ideas; generating a large number of responses to one or more questions

Process

1. The teacher puts students in groups of four to five. One person can serve as a recorder if desired.
2. The teacher asks an open-ended question. Students have about thirty seconds to think about their answers.
3. Team members share their responses with the group. If there is a recorder, they write the ideas.
4. A person may "pass" and provide a response on the next rotation (allowing them additional time to think).
5. The process continues for about five minutes (relative time, gauge by watching groups).

SEND A PROBLEM

Validate and Affirm Cultural Behaviors: Sociocentrism, Cooperation/Collaboration, Communalism, Subjectivity

Description: Students generate and answer questions or problems.

Most Effective Uses: Discussing and reviewing material or potential solutions to content-related problems

Process

1. The teacher puts students in groups of four or five. Groups collaborate to write review problems or questions.
2. Each group passes its question or questions (could be several in folder or one on a piece of paper) to another group for a response or solution. The groups have a set amount of time to discuss and write their answers or solutions.
3. The questions are then passed to the next groups; repeat until all groups have had time to find solutions to all questions.
4. The original group evaluates all of the solutions and picks the best one to share with the class.

SILENT CONVERSATIONS

Validate and Affirm Cultural Behaviors: Cooperation/Collaboration, Subjectivity, Communalism, Dynamic Attention Span

Build and Bridge Behaviors: Written Communication, Eye Contact

Description: Group members respond to one another in writing only; as an option, groups can shift into oral discussion at the end.

Most Effective Uses: Introducing or reviewing concepts or ideas for discussion

Process

1. The teacher prepares five to eight sheets of chart paper (one per group) with at least three images, lines of text, quotes, or questions related to the topic.

2. The teacher places students into groups of four to five. Each group is given one of the sheets of chart paper.

3. Groups silently read the information on their chart paper. Students find a spot on the chart paper to write or draw their thoughts.

4. Group members rotate the paper so they can read and respond to one another's answers.

5. Students continue rotating the paper until they are back to their original comments.

6. If desired, have groups orally share and discuss the ideas on their chart papers.

7. To close, use involuntary response to have one person from each group share the important ideas with the class (drawing from their group's communal ideas).

SIX-COLOR THINKING

Validate and Affirm Cultural Behaviors: Sociocentrism, Cooperation/Collaboration, Subjectivity, Dynamic Attention Span

Build and Bridge Behaviors: Prompted

Description: Students assume specific roles to participate in small-group discussions about open-ended topics.

Most Effective Uses: Discussing open-ended topics in history, science, current events, or controversial issues; responding to literature or texts

Process

1. The teacher places students in groups of six.

2. Each student in a group is given a different colored card (white, red, green, yellow, black, blue).

3. During the discussion, students assume the role assigned to their color.

   ◆ Neutrality (white): Questioner; seeks to affirm or gather new information

   ◆ Feeling (red): Feeler; provides instinctive reactions or emotional feelings without any justification

   ◆ Negative Judgment (green): Logician; seeks discrepancies in the discussion, applying logic to uncover inconsistencies or errors

   ◆ Positive Judgment (yellow): Harmonizer; seeks cohesion in the discussion using logic

   ◆ Creative Thinking (black): Motivator; keeps the conversation moving with thought-provoking statements or questions of investigation

   ◆ The Big Picture (blue): Facilitator; sets the objectives for the discussion; keeps the group on task

TEAM-PAIR-SOLO

Validate and Affirm Cultural Behaviors: Sociocentrism, Cooperation/Collaboration, Communalism

Build and Bridge Behaviors: Individual Success, Autonomous

Description: Students begin by supporting each other and gradually work toward being able to complete a task on their own.

Most Effective Uses: Reviewing content and skills; researching information; practicing a particular skill, such as order of operations

Process

1. Students work in teams to solve a problem or accomplish a task.

2. Teams break into pairs and each pair completes a similar problem or task.

3. Pairs break up and students work individually to complete another similar problem or task.

THINK-PAIR-SHARE

Validate and Affirm Cultural Behaviors: Cooperation/Collaboration, Sociocentrism, Conversational Patterns

Build and Bridge Behaviors: Individual Success, Autonomous (think), Turn-taking (share)

Description: Students generate ideas before being asked to share with the class.

Most Effective Uses: Accessing prior knowledge; sharing journal or quick-write responses; reviewing or summarizing information

Process

1. The teacher asks a question that students silently ponder.

2. Students then share their ideas with partners.

3. Using involuntary response, some students are selected to share with the group. To cultivate listening skills, each student explains their partner's ideas.

THREE-STEP INTERVIEW

Validate and Affirm Cultural Behaviors: Sociocentrism, Cooperation/Collaboration, Immediacy

Build and Bridge Behaviors: Turn-taking

Description: Students generate interview questions and listen carefully to one another's responses.

Most Effective Uses: Discussing and reviewing material or potential solutions to problems related to content information

Process

1. Students pair up.

2. The teacher poses a question.

3. Students interview their partners about their responses.

4. Each student shares their partner's response with another pair of students or the class.

TURN AND TALK

Validate and Affirm Cultural Behaviors: Cooperation/Collaboration, Sociocentrism, Conversational Patterns

Build and Bridge Behaviors: Turn-taking

Description: Students are asked a question or given a prompt and share their responses with partners sitting nearby. Turn and Talks should be brief, used to process socially.

Most Effective Uses: Processing or reviewing information for discussion

Process

1. The teacher asks a question.
2. Students discuss their response with someone sitting nearby.
3. The teachers calls students' attention back to the whole group with an attention signal.
4. The teacher can then use a response protocol such as Pick-a-Stick to hear from some pairs of students, thereby shifting to individual accountability.

TURNING WHEELS

Validate and Affirm Cultural Behaviors: Cooperation/Collaboration, Sociocentrism, Dynamic Attention Span, Subjectivity

Description: Students ask and answer teacher- or student-created questions about content covered in class or reading. This is a great variation on Fishbowl Discussion, Inner-Outer Circle, and Socratic Seminar.

Most Effective Uses: Reviewing direct instruction, reading, content, and/or skills

Process

1. The teacher prepares four to six questions on a studied topic. The questions are open-ended and/or require an explanation.
2. For the inside wheel, four to five chairs are placed in a circle with chair backs together. For the outside wheel, one chair is placed facing each inside chair.
3. Students sit in the seats of both wheels.
4. The teacher provides each student in the outside wheel with a different question and each student in an inside seat with paper and a pen to take notes.
5. The student sitting on the outside seat asks the student on the inside seat the question.
6. The student on the inside seat answers the question and both students discuss.
7. After three to five minutes, the students on the outside seats rotate to the right and repeat the process.
8. Students continue rotating and discussing until they get back to their original partners.
9. Students discuss their notes, questions, and comments with the whole class.

YESTERDAY'S HEADLINES

Validate and Affirm Cultural Behaviors: Sociocentrism, Cooperation/Collaboration, Communalism, Subjectivity

Description: Students review key concepts from yesterday's lesson in a nonthreatening way.

Most Effective Uses: Reviewing content, information, and skills; researching information; accessing prior knowledge

Process

1. The teacher hands each student a blank index card.

2. The teacher asks students to talk to two or three different people and share an important concept or headline from yesterday's lesson.

3. On their index cards, students write about one concept from the previous day's lesson. Students explain the concept and why it is important. This could be done in a "Who? What? When? Where? Why?" format.

4. When finished, the cards are collected and passed out randomly.

5. Students read the cards. If anyone has a card with a concept that they do not understand or think is wrong, they place it on a "Headlines" chart posted at the front of the room.

6. The teacher addresses any misconceptions or concepts that are confusing.

Response Protocols

BINGO RESPONDING

Validate and Affirm Cultural Behaviors: Spontaneity, Dynamic Attention Span

Build and Bridge Behaviors: Turn-taking

Description: Bingo Responding is an involuntary response protocol that works well in combination with a discussion or movement protocol to bring accountability, which in turn heightens engagement.

Most Effective Uses: Randomly sampling students to assess prior knowledge or assess understanding; maintaining whole-group engagement during direct instruction

Process

1. If the teacher has multiple classes each day, they number the desks in the classroom. As students enter, they pick a Bingo number. That is their number for the class period.

2. If the teacher has a self-contained classroom, desks are not numbered. Instead, students pick a different Bingo number each day.

3. After a discussion protocol or movement protocol, the teacher randomly selects numbers to hear responses from a few students.

MOMENT OF SILENCE

Build and Bridge Behaviors: Autonomous, Prompted, Individual Success

Description: Moment of Silence is used for activities such as journal writing, silent reading, and reflection. When juxtaposed with a validate-affirm (VA) activity, this traditional activity builds and bridges mainstream behavior.

Most Effective Uses: Taking a quiz or assessment; writing in a journal or completing a quick-write; reading silently; reflecting

Process

1. Everyone in the classroom, including the teacher, is completely silent for a moment to think and/or write.

2. This should be followed by a VA activity where students get to share their thinking with other students.

PICK-A-STICK

Validate and Affirm Cultural Behaviors: Spontaneity

Build and Bridge Behaviors: Turn-taking

Description: Pick-a-Stick is used for calling on students involuntarily and randomly after a social or collaborative activity.

Most Effective Uses: Randomly sampling students to assess prior knowledge or assess understanding; maintaining whole-group engagement during direct instruction

Process

1. The teacher writes each student's name on a craft stick and places the sticks in a container.

2. The teacher engages students in discussing an assignment or responding to a question.

3. After the discussion/collaboration, the teacher switches to individual responding for accountability by picking sticks with student names. (Example: Turn and Talk + Pick-a-Stick)

Variation: A teacher may use Pick-a-Stick as a fair and random way of calling on students to respond or participate if everyone wants to share.

POSITIVE BLAST

Validate and Affirm Cultural Behaviors: Communalism, Verbal Expressiveness, Immediacy

Build and Bridge Behaviors: Turn-taking

Description: This is an upbeat and uplifting way to celebrate classmates' thinking. Students energetically share a classmate's thinking or ideas because they think they are worthy of the whole class hearing. This spontaneous, voluntary protocol builds community, trust, and appreciation in the classroom.

Most Effective Uses: Processing or reviewing information in any content area

Process

1. Students work in pairs or small groups to complete a task, discuss a topic, or share ideas.

2. Students are asked if anyone wants to put a classmate on Positive Blast to celebrate their ideas. The student identifies their classmate with a great idea and then shares it.

3. As many Positive Blasts are shared as needed.

4. Affirmations are used upon completion of each blast.

RAISE A RIGHTEOUS HAND

Validate and Affirm Cultural Behaviors: Autonomous, Prompted, Individual Success

Description: This is a voluntary response protocol. When used with a variety of other response protocols, it is a good way to build and bridge. (Limit the use of voluntary protocols to 20 percent maximum.)

Most Effective Uses: Processing or reviewing information in any content area

Process

1. Before asking a question, the teacher names the protocol (e.g., "Raise a Righteous Hand" or "Hand Raising") and explicitly tells students this is a moment to practice traditional school culture. This ensures students understand how they should respond to the question.

2. The teacher asks a question, and students raise their hands to respond.

3. This can also be used after an involuntary response protocol to allow students who are eager to say something a chance to share.

4. Juxtapose this with involuntary response protocols such as Pick-a-Stick, Train/Pass It On, Roll 'Em, and so on to reinforce situational appropriateness and global dexterity, or the ability to culturally adapt to the context (Molinsky 2013). This allows students to practice Turn-taking.

ROLL 'EM

Validate and Affirm Cultural Behaviors: Spontaneity, Dynamic Attention Span, Communalism, Sociocentrism

Build and Bridge Behaviors: Turn-taking

Description: Group members work together to form a consensus, and then all are held individually accountable by a roll of the number cube.

Most Effective Uses: Randomly sampling students to assess prior knowledge or assess understanding; maintaining whole-group engagement during direct instruction

Process

1. The teacher places students in groups of four to six. The teacher gives each group a number, and students in the groups are numbered also.

2. The teacher asks a question, and students discuss their responses in their groups.

3. The teacher rolls number cubes. One cube represents the group number and the second represents the student's number. The teacher calls on the selected group and student to respond.

4. Answers should be the group's answers (focusing on communalism).

5. Rolling the cubes continues until ample answers are heard or all of the questions are answered.

SCATTERGORY SHARE OUT

Validate and Affirm Cultural Behaviors: Communalism, Spontaneity, Dynamic Attention Span

Build and Bridge Behaviors: Turn-taking

Description: Students produce a list of brainstormed ideas or answers and expand their lists with ideas from other groups. This protocol moves quickly and is a great way to share lots of ideas in a short period of time and hold groups accountable.

Most Effective Uses: Brainstorming ideas on a topic; generating a large number of responses to one or more questions

Process

1. The teacher asks a question with multiple responses, such as a brainstorming question.

2. Students work in groups to generate answers and record them on paper.

3. The teacher whips around to each group, having one person in the group share one of their ideas or answers. The groups share one idea at a time and cannot repeat ideas already shared.

4. The groups put a star by ideas on their list that other groups say, and add ideas to their list that they don't have.

5. The whip-around process continues until all ideas have been shared.

Scattergory Share Out pairs well with Round Robin Brainstorming.

SHOUT OUT

Validate and Affirm Cultural Behaviors: Spontaneity, Conversational Patterns/Verbal Overlap

Build and Bridge Behaviors: Turn-taking

Description: Students share one- or two-word responses to a question.

Most Effective Uses: Checking for understanding; brainstorming ideas; sharing responses/answers for review

Process

1. The teacher asks a question that can be answered in one or two words.

2. Students spontaneously shout out responses (Verbal Overlap).

Variation: Stadium Shout—This is a shout out that everyone does in unison. It can be louder. This works best for one-word answers. This VAs Spontaneity and Orality but not Verbal Overlap.

SOMEBODY WHO...

Validate and Affirm Cultural Behaviors: Spontaneity, Dynamic Attention Span, Immediacy*

Build and Bridge Behaviors: Turn-taking

Description: The teacher uses non-volunteerism to hold all students accountable for participation. This student-centered protocol is used after a discussion with classmates.

Most Effective Uses: Sampling students randomly to assess prior knowledge; selecting students randomly to assess understanding; maintaining whole-group engagement during direct instruction

Process

1. The teacher says, "Anyone who has more than four pets (or some other attribute, such as a birthday in May, a younger sister, and so on), please stand."
2. All students who fit the description stand.
3. The teacher asks a question related to the lesson.
4. The teacher then uses Whip Around or Train/Pass It On to move around the room and have the students who are standing explain their connection to the criteria and give their academic answers.

*This protocol can validate and affirm Immediacy if the prompt allows students to share something about their lives (e.g., somebody who saw a movie in the last week).

STAND AND DELIVER

Validate and Affirm Cultural Behaviors: Spontaneity, Dynamic Attention Span, Immediacy, Kinesthetic

Build and Bridge Behaviors: Turn-taking

Description: The teacher poses an open-ended question and asks students to stand, share an answer, and sit down. The goal is for the conversation to flow naturally as students talk to each other.

Most Effective Uses: Introducing or reviewing concepts and ideas for discussion

Process

1. The teacher asks an open-ended question.
2. A student who wants to respond stands and shares.
3. If more than one student stands at a time, they practice deference. Or, all students who want to share can stand and practice deference, sitting once they share. Students negotiate who speaks when, not the teacher.
4. Students are encouraged to talk to one another, not to the teacher, and to allow the conversation to ebb and flow.
5. Students may stand up again if they have something else to say or if they want to respond to a classmate's idea.

THUMBS UP, THUMBS DOWN

Validate and Affirm Cultural Behaviors: Spontaneity, Pragmatic Language Use, Subjectivity

Build and Bridge Behaviors: Prompted

Description: Students use nonverbal communication to indicate agreement or disagreement, respond to polls, or identify correct and incorrect answers.

Most Effective Uses: Responding to polls, votes, and questions requiring a yes, no, or unsure response

Process

1. The teacher asks a question or makes a statement and asks students to agree or disagree.

2. Students respond by putting their thumbs up for agreement or down for disagreement.

3. The teacher follows up by asking a few students to share why they responded the way they did.

Variation: The teacher prepares answers to questions (some correct, some incorrect) and asks students to use their thumbs to indicate whether they think an answer is right or wrong. The teacher follows up by asking a few students to explain their thinking.

TRAIN/PASS IT ON

Validate and Affirm Cultural Behaviors: Spontaneity, Dynamic Attention Span, Immediacy

Build and Bridge Behaviors: Turn-taking

Description: Students call on one another to answer a prompt or open-ended question. This student-centered protocol holds all students accountable for participation through non-volunteerism.

Most Effective Uses: Holding students accountable for and providing an opportunity for them to control participation; providing for improvisation and variety

Process

1. The teacher asks a question and starts the discussion by calling on a student.

2. The student answers and chooses the next student to respond, or they can pass on the question by calling on another student for help or to answer.

3. When the student answers or passes, they can toss a small soft object (a Koosh ball or beanbag) to the next student.

4. The train will eventually return to students who pass, so they need to be prepared to contribute the next time around.

WHEEL OF NAMES

Validate and Affirm Cultural Behaviors: Spontaneity

Build and Bridge Behaviors: Turn-taking

Description: The teacher uses the Wheel of Names to select students to respond to a question. The wheel can be used repeatedly to hear from different students. This protocol builds accountability and community.

Most Effective Uses: Randomly sampling students to respond and express ideas in any content area

Process

1. Before beginning a discussion, the teacher enters students' names in the Wheel of Names (wheelofnames.com).
2. The teacher tells students they will be called on using the Wheel of Names.
3. The teacher poses a question. To select a student to respond, the teacher spins the wheel.
4. Students respond when their name is called.

This protocol pairs nicely with Train/Pass It On.

WHIP AROUND

Validate and Affirm Cultural Behaviors: Spontaneity, Dynamic Attention Span, Immediacy, Realness

Build and Bridge Behaviors: Turn-taking

Description: The teacher quickly whips around to all students for a short answer to a question.

Most Effective Uses: Quickly checking whole-group understanding after direct instruction, a presentation, or reading a text

Process

1. The teacher asks an open-ended question that requires a short answer, such as, "What adjective describes the main character?" Questions should require answers that are no more than five words, and students should know that.
2. Beginning on one side of the room, each student takes a turn answering the question, moving quickly around the room in an orderly fashion until all students have responded. The teacher should not have to prompt the next student.

Use these scenarios and exercises to assist you in processing, practicing, and applying the concepts from the chapter.

Mr. Garcia

Mr. Garcia calls on the same students all the time—but for different reasons. He has unconsciously placed students into two categories. When he asks students to raise a hand to answer questions, he routinely calls on the students he expects to provide the answer he is looking for—despite whose hands are raised. During direct instruction, he routinely calls on another set of students and asks them questions when they appear to be displaying off-task behavior. When these students cannot answer the question posed, he then calls on one of the students he routinely expects to have the correct answer. This is Mr. Garcia's way of calling out a student who is not paying attention during direct instruction.

When asked, Mr. Garcia reveals that he is not aware of this pattern and wants suggestions about response protocols he could use to ensure more fair and equitable treatment of all of his students. Which protocols would you suggest Mr. Garcia try?

_____

_____

Possible Answer: To ensure his own bias is not influencing students' ability to participate in his lessons, Mr. Garcia can hold all students accountable for participation through the use of protocols that promote non-volunteerism. For example, he can use Shout Out to actively engage all students while checking for understanding when posing questions requiring short, one- to two-word answers during direct instruction. Or he can use Whip Around to assess whole-group understanding after direct instruction. Pick-a-Stick and Roll 'Em are response protocols Mr. Garcia can use to randomly select students to check for understanding.

Classroom Applications

Think about your own classroom and teaching practices. Use the following prompts to reflect on your past experiences and consider how you can effectively use response protocols to promote equitable participation in your classroom.

1. Reflect on how you currently choose students to answer questions or participate in discussions. Do you call on specific students with certain objectives in mind? How does this affect the students?

_____

_____

2. Select several different response protocols that you plan to use in your classroom. Describe the situations in which each protocol would be most appropriate.

_____

_____

Sample Lesson—Promoting Non-Volunteerism

While it is desirable to have students who frequently volunteer to participate, it is also important to ensure that *all* students are engaged in the lesson and comprehending the material. The following lesson demonstrates how to use two different response protocols (Thumbs Up, Thumbs Down; Train/Pass It On) to make sure all students are actively participating.

Procedure

1. After introducing the life cycle of a frog, tell the class, "We are going to use the Thumbs Up, Thumbs Down protocol so you can show me what you already understand about frogs' life cycles and what we still need to master. I am going to read a statement aloud. You need to think about whether you agree or disagree with the statement. I will wait a few seconds so everyone has time to think. Then I'll say, 'Show me your thumbs.' If you agree with the statement, show me thumbs up. If you disagree, show me thumbs down. If you're unsure, put your thumb sideways."

2. Read a list of prepared statements that assess students' understanding of the life cycle of a frog. For example, say, "Tadpoles hatch from frog eggs." Survey students' thumbs up/thumbs down responses and note whether they have a firm understanding of this part of the life cycle. Continue reading additional statements and recording areas that require further study.

3. Review any confusing content material using a combination of direct instruction and discussion. For instance, if students seem confused by the repetitive nature of a life cycle, provide a visual reference, such as a poster that shows how the frog life cycle continues in a circle, and explain the concept to the class. Then use a responding protocol, such as Train/Pass It On, to review the different stages of the life cycle and reassess the students' comprehension.

4. Once students have a more thorough understanding of the material, use a pre-taught Call and Response attention signal to indicate that they should refocus their attention on the teacher. For example, call out "Hocus pocus" and have the students respond "Everybody focus!" while directing their listening eyes and ears to you.

5. Say, "Now that we've had a chance to review the material, let's go over a few questions together. After I ask a question, I'm going to use Somebody Who… to choose who answers. For instance, if I say 'somebody who has a birthday in April,' everyone with April birthdays should stand up. I will select one or more of you to explain the concept or answer the question."

6. Ask a review question, such as "Where do frogs lay their eggs?" followed by a "Somebody who…" statement, such as "Somebody who is wearing turquoise." All students who are

wearing turquoise should stand up. Call on one or more of the students who stand up to answer the question or explain their thinking about the statement.

7. Continue asking review questions and using "Somebody who…" statements to determine participation.

Mr. Patel

Students were practicing evaluating expressions in Mr. Patel's math class. During the guided practice portion of the lesson, he provided the students with a numerical expression that they were expected to evaluate. After giving students time to evaluate the expression, he asked for volunteers to raise a hand to share their answers. Only a few students dared to raise their hands. Mr. Patel changed his response protocol and began to pull sticks to select students (Pick-a-Stick) to share their answers. He had to pull a few sticks before a student was able to provide the correct answer. This was repeated after each expression.

In this scenario, which response protocol might help Mr. Patel's students?

a. Train/Pass It On

b. Roll 'Em

c. Neither a nor b

Answer: c. Neither a nor b

Mr. Patel was on target when he switched to a non-volunteer-based response protocol after realizing his students were reluctant to volunteer their answers, but the students' responses indicated that more direct instruction was needed for them to be able to correctly evaluate numerical expressions.

Train/Pass It On would have allowed the chosen student to answer, or they could use Pick-a-Stick to choose another student to answer the question if they did not feel confident about their answer. But the fact that Mr. Patel had to pull several sticks after each expression was an indicator that many students did not feel confident about their answers. Roll 'Em would have given students time to collaborate with one another to figure out how to evaluate the expressions. It appears, however, that many students needed clarification before they would be able to effectively take part in this protocol.

Classroom Applications

Think about your own classroom and teaching practices. Use the following prompts to reflect on your past experiences and consider how you can effectively use response protocols to promote equitable participation in your classroom.

1. Think about students in your class who rarely participate. Why do you think they choose not to participate? What kind of response protocols would help these students?

   _____

   _____

2. Are there any social factors in your classroom, such as peer pressure or fear of embarrassment, that discourage students from getting involved even when they know the

correct answer or have ideas to contribute? Do you think that using response protocols would help reduce these social factors?

_____

_____

Sample Lesson—Response Protocols That Validate and Affirm Through Choice

Some response protocols are especially effective for ensuring that all students participate in a discussion or activity. Other protocols, however, are designed to give students some degree of control over their participation while still promoting non-volunteerism. The following lesson shows how to use the Train/Pass It On protocol to encourage participation while also affirming students' sense of control and validating different styles of discourse.

Procedure

1. Explain, "Today we are going to use the Train/Pass It On activity so that we can make sure everyone has a chance to participate. I will start by tossing this beanbag to someone in the class. Whoever has the beanbag shares their thoughts about the role of the steam engine during the Industrial Revolution. After sharing, the student calls someone else's name and tosses the beanbag to them. Then it is that person's chance to share."

2. Tell students that it is okay to say "pass" if they are not ready to contribute. In this case, the student says "pass" and tosses the beanbag to another student. However, remind students that if they pass, the beanbag will eventually return to them, so they need to be prepared to contribute the next time around.

3. Ask "How did the invention of the steam engine play a role in the Industrial Revolution?" and toss the beanbag to the first student. After the student responds, they toss the beanbag to another student. Encourage students to toss the beanbag to students in different areas of the classroom.

4. Continue having the students pass the beanbag to one another and respond to the question. Conclude by reviewing the content discussed and summarizing the main learning points mentioned by the students.

Mrs. Wong

Mrs. Wong was frustrated that the same students always seemed to raise their hands to answer questions in class. While reflecting on a lesson that did not go as smoothly as expected, she realized that she often asked, "Can I hear from students I haven't heard from?" In addition, she realized that some of the off-task behavior students engaged in during lessons occurred because the other students relied on those same students to answer all of the questions; therefore, they did not feel a need to become actively engaged in the lessons.

Upon reflection, she determined that adding the use of response protocols that promote non-volunteerism to lessons would hold more students accountable for lesson content, allowing a greater number of students to participate in instructional conversations.

She decided to begin with the Pick-a-Stick response protocol during her next lesson. Instead of assigning readings for students to complete silently, and then asking them to raise their hands to answer questions about the text, she planned to use this protocol to select students to read orally and to answer text-dependent questions.

She tried the protocol, but the lesson did not go as smoothly as planned. She used the protocol to select students to read chapters in the text aloud while the other students followed along. Some students read too quickly, while others read too slowly. Some students did not read fluently. Students who were not reading aloud would lose interest and go off task, often because they read the paragraphs more quickly than the student reading aloud. When non-fluent readers read aloud, Mrs. Wong would have the class chorally reread the paragraph before pulling sticks to have students answer questions about what was read. The lesson took much longer than expected; therefore she had to end the lesson before covering all of the content she had planned.

At the close of this lesson, Mrs. Wong was frustrated again. She felt like she wasted time trying something new—and was unable to cover all of the content she expected. She still wanted to engage more students in her lessons, but she decided she would not try that response protocol again.

What might have caused Mrs. Wong's lesson to fall short of the expected outcome?

   a. The protocol was utilized randomly and without intention.
   b. The students needed more time to practice effectively using the protocol.
   c. The teacher had not planned or prepared to effectively use this response protocol.
   d. She planned, but did not consider that using this protocol might not be the most appropriate one to use for the context of the lesson.

Answer: d. She planned, but did not consider that this protocol might not be the most appropriate one to use for the context of the lesson.

The purpose of the lesson was to assess students' comprehension of the text through the use of text-dependent questions.

Mrs. Wong was on the right track. She selected a response protocol that promotes non-volunteerism to be able to "hear from more students." However, this did not prove to be an effective oral reading strategy for her class. In this lesson, Pick-a-Stick was being used to randomly select students to read. Mrs. Wong could consider using another oral reading strategy first and using the response protocol when asking questions about the text that was read.

Classroom Applications

Think about your own classroom and teaching practices. Use the following prompts to reflect on your past experiences and consider how you can effectively use protocols to promote equitable participation in your classroom.

   1. Certain response protocols work better in some situations than in others. Have you ever used a response protocol that did not lead to the desired outcome? Describe a specific situation in your classroom where a particular response protocol would not be effective and why.

   _____

   _____

2. Think about the use of a response protocol for the oral reading activity in this scenario. What was the objective of the lesson? How could Mrs. Wong revise her lesson to make sure that her use of response protocols matches her teaching objectives?

_____

_____

Sample Lesson—Selecting When and How to Use Response Protocols

In this scenario, Mrs. Wong had two main objectives—to increase student participation in the lesson and to assess students' comprehension of the text. The following lesson illustrates one way that the teacher could accomplish these objectives by using a different reading strategy and response protocol (Roll 'Em).

Procedure

1. Before beginning the lesson, determine four to six groups based on reading levels. Divide an informational text into sections that are appropriate for each reading group. For example, you might give a group of fast or proficient readers a section of text that is four paragraphs long and assign groups that tend to read more slowly one paragraph of text.

2. Put students in their predetermined groups and give each student a copy of the group's text section.

3. Have each group read its assigned portion of the text aloud. Say, "Choose one person in your group to start reading. That student should read as long as they feel comfortable, then say 'popcorn' and name another student in the group to continue reading. Make sure that everyone in your group has a chance to read at least once." Provide time for students to read the text aloud in their groups.

4. When all groups have finished, assign each group a number. Ask students to count off within their groups so that each student has a number within the group.

5. Explain, "Now I would like each group to share the information it learned from the text with the rest of the class. I am going to roll two number cubes. The first cube I roll will indicate the group number. The number on the second cube will correspond to the student in that group. When I roll your number, I would like you to share at least one piece of information you learned from your portion of the text."

6. Roll the number cubes to select the first student. Have that student share one piece of information they learned from their text portion. Then give the number cubes to that student and have them roll to select the next student. Continue in this way until students have covered all important points from the text.

Ms. Brown

Ms. Brown was conducting a lesson designed to teach her students about signal words and phrases that can help readers identify the opinions being presented in a text. She started the lesson by asking the students to raise a hand (Raise a Righteous Hand) to share what they already knew about opinions. The students shared that they knew that opinions are different from facts.

Opinions allow people to express different ideas that others can decide to agree or disagree with, but a fact can be proven.

The teacher then shared a fact about content being studied in class and had the students participate in a Whip Around to state an opinion about the fact. Ms. Brown used this routine to have students share their opinions about different facts related to the content being studied.

After hearing the students share their opinions, Ms. Brown highlighted opinion signal words that the students used. She explained the function of the signal words and shared additional signal words students could use to express their opinions when speaking or writing. The students participated in one more Whip Around to express opinions about another fact, but this time, they were encouraged to use one of the new opinion signal words or phrases.

Ms. Brown followed this activity by displaying sentences one at a time. After giving students time to read and think about each sentence, she had them use the Shout Out protocol to share the opinion signal words they saw in the sentence.

To bring this lesson to a close, Ms. Brown listed a number of facts related to the content they were studying. The students were asked to use the Moment of Silence response protocol while they wrote opinion statements about each fact, and they were encouraged to use some of the opinion signal words discussed during the lesson.

In this scenario, the teacher used protocols that ranged from traditional to responsive to culturally responsive. Jot down examples of responsive practices and protocols Ms. Brown used.

Traditional:_____

Responsive:_____

Culturally Responsive:_____

Possible Answers:

Traditional: Raise a Righteous Hand, Moment of Silence

Responsive: Ms. Brown made the context of the lesson responsive to the students by validating and affirming what they knew about opinions, allowing them to share their opinions about facts being studied in class, and highlighting the opinion signal words she heard them using already as a bridge to help them acquire new opinion signal words.

Culturally Responsive: Whip Around, Shout Out

Classroom Applications

Think about your own classroom and teaching practices. Use the following prompts to reflect on your past experiences and consider how you can effectively use protocols to promote equitable participation in your classroom.

1. In this scenario, what other response protocols would have worked well in each part of Ms. Brown's lesson? Why?

    _____

    _____

2. What types of protocols do you typically use in the classroom—traditional, responsive, or culturally responsive? What types would you like to use more often? Why do you think these types of protocols would benefit your students?

_____

_____

Sample Lesson—Combining Protocols

The following lesson shows how to combine a discussion protocol designed to make sure all students participate (Put Your Two Cents In) with a movement protocol that allows for volunteerism (Graffiti Talk).

Procedure

1. Write a discussion question on the board, such as "What can humans do to reduce the amount of greenhouse gasses in the atmosphere?" Say, "I am going to place you in groups of four. I would like you to discuss the topic on the board in your groups. In order to make sure that everyone is able to participate equally during the discussion, we are going to use Put Your Two Cents In."

2. Give each student two tokens, such as two chips. Explain, "Each of you has two tokens. Everyone in the group will take turns sharing their thoughts about the discussion question. When it is your turn to share your thoughts and opinions about the topic, place one of your tokens in the middle of the group. After everyone has shared once, go around a second time and place another token in the middle as everyone takes a turn responding to the first round of comments. Remember that you should only share when it is your turn to put your token in the middle."

3. Put students into groups of four. Provide time for them to discuss the topic using the Put Your Two Cents In protocol. As they discuss, walk around the room, ensuring students are taking turns and using the tokens to facilitate the discussion.

4. Use sheets of chart paper to post concepts or questions related to the discussion topic around the classroom. For example, one topic could be "Things we can do at home to reduce greenhouse gasses." As a class, read the concepts and questions aloud.

5. Say, "Now that everyone in the group has had a chance to share their opinions and thoughts, I would like to discuss the following concepts and questions as a class. In a minute I will say 'go,' and those of you who would like to share your thoughts will move about the classroom and write comments on the chart papers. Make sure that the comments you write are relevant to the concept or question at the top of the chart paper."

6. Give the "go" signal and provide time for students to move around the classroom and record their thoughts and opinions on the chart papers.

7. After the designated amount of time, ask students to return to their seats. Read and discuss the ideas and opinions students expressed.

Post-Reading Assessment

Now it is your turn to start "swimming" with the use of protocols. Start today. As you are planning your next lesson, infuse response and discussion protocols however you can. Be intentional and strategic. Allow yourself the time and space to fail, to make mistakes, and to be uncomfortable. After a couple of weeks of implementing CLR, come back to this chapter and complete the survey (figure 2.3) about your use of protocols.

Figure 2.3 Effective Uses of Response and Discussion Protocols Survey: After Infusing the CLR Principles

0: *Never Emerging* 1: *Rarely Splashing* 2: *Sometimes Floating* 3: *Mostly Kicking* 4: *Always Freestyling*					
I use protocols for responding and discussing at least two to three times per instructional block.	0	1	2	3	4
I use protocols for responding and discussing with purpose (pre-planned).	0	1	2	3	4
I use protocols for responding and discussing that are specifically for validating and affirming.	0	1	2	3	4
I use protocols for responding and discussing that are specifically for building and bridging.	0	1	2	3	4
I use protocols for responding and discussing for other purposes: praising, shout-outs, check-ins.	0	1	2	3	4

STUDENT VOICE

Allowing Your Students to Be Engaged in Their Own Way, or "BeYou": Sociocentrism

BeYou is a call to action, reminding teachers to adjust instruction and classroom practices, ensuring that students can be themselves at school culturally and linguistically. Here we consider how students might express the importance of being validated and affirmed when being sociocentric at school.

How can sociocentrism be expressed and culturally misunderstood in the classroom? Learning by talking, or socializing, is very important to me. Sometimes, it's the most important part of what I do in school. When I can talk with my friends while I am learning, I am more engaged. The thing is, this can be seen as being too talkative and look like I might be off task. The truth is, I am actually doing my best learning when I can talk socially and learn at the same time.

How does it feel to be misunderstood? Sometimes in class, teachers avoid letting students talk because they can't make sure we are talking about what we are learning. Other times, when we do get to talk, we are told to stay on topic or "get back to work." For me, though, being able to talk socially is a huge part of staying engaged and can actually help me learn better. When we can dip in and out of school talk and social talk, talking in a way that lets us overlap and jump in, we connect with each other and what we are learning.

What do I need to be myself? I feel validated when I can talk with my friends while we are learning in class, and when teachers recognize that the act of socializing is sometimes more important to us than what is being taught at the moment. I am affirmed when you recognize sociocentrism as cultural and build in opportunities for us to talk socially while we are learning, letting us jump into it in the moment.

What CLR activities validate and affirm sociocentrism? Activities such as Campfire, Musical Shares, and Hot Seat are great, because they give students the opportunity to talk socially as part of the learning they do in class. Connecting with students one-on-one about things that are going on for them personally is another meaningful way to validate and affirm them.

Build CLR Community and Collaboration

What is my/our vision for CLR at our site? What benefits could it provide to our underserved students?

Think about the material presented in this chapter. Where are we strong as a site? Where do we need more work? How do the CLR topics in this chapter line up with the other initiatives we are working on at our site? *(Note: While the plans for infusing the protocols at a school site might evolve over time, it is good to give these questions some initial thought.)*

Reflection Question: How do we want to approach the reflective questions in this book? Do we want to share them with others? Do we have an electronic platform we could use for sharing?

CHAPTER 3

Get Up, Stand Up: Making Movement a Regular Part of Instruction

Understanding the Context

Of all the identified culturally and linguistically responsive instructional categories, the use of movement is, undoubtedly, the one category where we grow multiple trees out of one seed. The frequent use of movement in the classroom accomplishes several teaching goals. First, whenever students move in class, it is culturally responsive for most of them. Second, movement activities build upon the voluminous brain-based research (Schiller and Willis 2008; Duman 2010) on kinesthetic learning. The research is clear. When brain-body methods are utilized, long-term memory is increased (Tate 2025). Third, moving and interacting with classmates during a well-structured instructional activity is simply fun and engaging. Similar to many of the protocols discussed in the previous chapter, often teachers are already using movement activities without realizing their multiple benefits.

Most times, a movement activity should involve a structured conversation based on a prompt related to the content. Movement activities are paced quickly and typically take no longer than five minutes. Any classroom activity that employs movement increases the probability that students will have a positive response to the learning (Marzano 2007). According to Marcia Tate, movement strengthens memory and decreases behavior problems—but also makes teaching and learning fun (2025).

> For CLR, a movement activity is having students walk or dance around the room with a *specific instructional purpose* in mind.

According to the groundbreaking work of Barbara Shade, Cynthia Kelly, and Mary Oberg (1997), cultural behaviors are connected to how we think, as well as how we perceive and organize information. Therefore, the process for the student is twofold: perception and conceptualization. A CLR movement activity plays a role in the perception phase by tuning the student into the content being taught, and it plays a role in the conceptualization phase by helping the student organize the information. When used appropriately and strategically, movement activities can be scaffolds for rigorous content.

Considering the Research

Research supports the use of movement activities as a way to integrate CLR teaching techniques into the classroom to enhance engagement and create a culturally and linguistically responsive environment.

♦ Dancing improves attention to detail, assisting students with sequencing and thinking logically (Karten 2009). Further, dancing has been found to improve global cognition, memory, visuospatial function, and cognitive flexibility (Yuan, Li, and Liu 2022).

♦ Physical performance probably uses 100 percent of the brain (Jensen 2008).

♦ Instructional situations that involve the use of movement require more sensory input than activities that use only paper and pencil (Gregory and Parry 2006).

♦ Tasks learned through physical engagement remain in our memory for a very long time (Allen 2008).

♦ Some students, culturally speaking, learn best in a social context (Dembo 1988; Ladson-Billings 2021). CLR movement activities provide opportunities for students to interact.

Pre-Reading Assessment

Before reading this chapter, reflect on your current use of movement activities. Complete the survey (figure 3.1) and as you rate yourself, consider how to use movement activities effectively. There is a strong possibility that you use movement activities more regularly in your classrooms than you realize. The overall reflective question is: How effectively and how responsively are you using them?

Figure 3.1 Effective Uses of Movement Activities Survey: Before Infusing the CLR Principles

0: *Never Emerging* 1: *Rarely Splashing* 2: *Sometimes Floating* 3: *Mostly Kicking* 4: *Always Freestyling*					
I use movement activities at least two to three times per instructional block.	0	1	2	3	4
I use movement activities for the purpose of lifting energy and building community.	0	1	2	3	4
I use movement activities for the purpose of deepening understanding of content.	0	1	2	3	4
I use movement activities for the purpose of explicitly validating and affirming.	0	1	2	3	4

Beginning the Reflective Process

Learning happens when we reflect upon what we have experienced. Critical reflection generates, deepens, and documents learning (Ash and Clayton 2009). Are you ready to incorporate movement activities into your teaching practice?

Use the following checklist to gauge your readiness and ability to effectively integrate movement activities into your teaching. Each item represents an important aspect of understanding and using movement in a culturally responsive classroom. After completing the checklist, read the detailed descriptions of the items and reflect on how you plan to implement or increase your use of movement activities.

☑ **The Use of Movement Activities Reflection Checklist**

Item 3.1	Do I use movement activities with strategic purpose?	○ Yes ○ No
Item 3.2	Do I recognize that by using movement activities on a regular basis, I am being culturally responsive by default, and do I understand why?	○ Yes ○ No
Item 3.3	Do I juxtapose the movement activities with traditional activities when instructionally applicable?	○ Yes ○ No

Item 3.1 Do I use movement activities with strategic purpose?

Everything teachers do throughout the day should have an instructional purpose. This is especially the case for use of movement activities in CLR classrooms. Sometimes these activities are not taken seriously and are carried out in a haphazard or random fashion. Movement activities can yield high benefits, yet they take little effort to plan or implement. Having a strategic purpose when you use these activities will maximize the results for you and your students.

The prescription for movement activities is two to three times per hour for elementary students, one to two times per hour for secondary students, and once per hour for adult learners (Marzano 2007).

REFLECTIVE THOUGHT

> When planning, be sure to ask yourself what the strategic purpose of the movement activity is, and, going back to Marzano's (2007) framework, ask yourself what you will be accomplishing—lifting energy, building community, and/or deepening understanding around the content or your topic.

 ## Thought-Provokers: A Mindset for Moving Forward

1. I trust the prescription for movement activities.
2. I use one to two movement activities already but know I need to add additional activities. Every two weeks, I aim to intentionally add one to two new activities until I have enough to rotate consistently.

 ## Thought-Blockers: A Mindset for Staying Stagnant

1. I fear that I will lose control of my students.

   I often hear myself say, "Movement activities are a waste of instructional time" or "They are too distracting and do not provide enough learning."

Depending on the quality of your classroom management, you may have a rough start. However, do not be deterred or give up. Movement activities are investments. They are not meant to be high stakes in nature, although they can be when used skillfully. Look at these activities as scaffolds to the traditional activities to come later.

Item 3.2 Do I recognize that by using movement activities on a regular basis, I am being culturally responsive by default, and do I understand why?

A movement activity is validating and affirming on general principle. If structured appropriately, it involves the following cultural behaviors: kinesthetic (high levels of movement), sociocentrism, and communalism. Teachers often assume that movement activities are simply opportunities for students to move their bodies in the classroom. For example, a teacher who notices that students are having trouble concentrating might have them stand up and jog in place or stretch, before having them return to their seats and resuming the lesson. While this type of movement is not without merit, the intentional use of movement activities for culturally responsive purposes helps the class meet educational objectives while enhancing student engagement and comprehension. For instance, the Carousel Brainstorm activity allows students to interact socially while brainstorming about a topic. In this activity, the teacher posts four to six sheets of chart paper with topics or questions written atop each one. Students gather in small groups at each sheet of chart paper and work together to brainstorm about the topic. One student in each group acts as the recorder and writes notes on the chart paper. After a designated amount of time, the teacher turns on music and the groups move to the next chart paper and brainstorm about a different topic or question. The groups continue rotating until they return to their original sheet of chart paper. Through this activity, students combine movement and social interaction in a structured way that fosters learning and collaboration.

> By incorporating movement activities into your daily practice, you are being culturally responsive in your intention and strategy. A CLR movement activity is meant to be a stimulus for interaction, regardless of how elaborate or simple it is.

By incorporating movement activities into your daily practice, you are being culturally responsive in your intention and strategy. A CLR movement activity is meant to be a stimulus for interaction, regardless of how elaborate or simple it is. The key is to know how the movement activity is culturally responsive as compared to being responsive or traditional. For example, in a political science class I observed, students were reading scenarios in the newspaper and had to determine whether each one described a serious crime or no crime. The teacher had students stand at their desks. She called a level of crime (serious crime or no crime), and if students agreed with that level, then they had to sit down. This movement activity was very basic. The purpose was to lift the energy of the room, and culturally, it would be considered kinesthetic, or high level of movement.

Another example is a math class in which students did a version of Musical Shares. Each student started at a station, where they completed a math problem. When the music started, students shared their work with at least two classmates to compare answers. When the music stopped, they went back to their original stations and did the next problem. The process was repeated for three rounds. This example of a movement activity is much more complicated than the first. Therefore, it accomplishes more in relation to its strategic purpose. Not only does it lift energy in the room, it also deepens understanding and builds community. Culturally, it accomplishes the validation and affirmation of sociocentrism and communalism, because students are engaging in a social exchange and are supporting one another.

Even though movement activities are inherently culturally responsive, your familiarity and knowledge about applicable cultural behaviors will make a significant difference in your planning and preparation. Knowing exactly why you are doing a movement activity is necessary but not sufficient. Linking the validation and affirmation aspects completes the process. This chapter presents recommended movement activities and the accompanying cultural behaviors that are validated and affirmed when using the activity. In addition, you'll find directions for each activity, instructional purposes, and contexts for its most effective use.

Once you begin using movement activities on a consistent basis, you will witness the power of validation and affirmation with your students. Consciously validating and affirming students' cultural behaviors is liberating for both teachers and students.

REFLECTIVE THOUGHT

What are some movement activities you use regularly in your classroom? What purposes do these activities serve? Are you aware of the culturally responsive aspects of the movements? Which ones do the students react to most positively?

 ## Thought-Provokers: A Mindset for Moving Forward

1. Once I delve into movement activities on a consistent basis, I will witness the power of validation and affirmation with my students. Validating and affirming cultural behaviors is liberating.

2. I am explicit with my students about the varying movement activities and my strategic purpose for using them. I allow students to weigh in on what they think about the activity.

 ## Thought-Blockers: A Mindset for Staying Stagnant

1. I do not believe that there is value in validating and affirming the students culturally. As a result of this mindset, I may use movement activities superficially.

2. I ask myself, "How do I address the various cultures in my class with different movement activities?" I also ask, "What about the students who come from cultures that do not favor movement?"

   These questions are blocks and miss the point. Recall that movement activities are rooted in brain-based research, meaning they have less to do with culture and more to do with being responsive to how we learn. Second, you will probably have students who come from cultures that tend toward lower levels of movement. This is actually good news, because it will give them the opportunity to practice being cross-cultural or becoming comfortable with other cultures' norms.

Item 3.3 Do I juxtapose the movement activities with traditional activities when instructionally applicable?

In no way am I suggesting everything you do now in your room has to include a movement activity. When you understand CLR at its fullest, you know that there is more to it than validating and affirming activities. Validation and affirmation (VA) are the first parts of what you do. The other parts are building and bridging (BB). Many of the building and bridging activities fall in the traditional box and are in direct juxtaposition to the movement activities. There are going to be times when you have to lecture or have students work independently at their desks. In CLR, *traditional* activities are used to build and bridge students to the accepted behaviors of school culture.

> CLR juxtapositions occur when a VA strategy or activity is paired intentionally with a BB strategy or activity (Hollie 2018).

For example, you could do a Give One, Get One movement activity in one part of a lesson. Then later, while students are at their seats, call on them using a form of random urgency, such as Pick-a-Stick. Pairing these two activities is a CLR juxtaposition.

To be authentically culturally responsive, the use of building and bridging activities is necessary. The challenge is how to balance the use of the activities that are validating and affirming with activities that are building and bridging in a way that allows the students to practice situational appropriateness, or be linguistically or culturally appropriate.

REFLECTIVE THOUGHT

> What challenges do you encounter as you work to incorporate building and bridging activities into your instruction? What solutions have you attempted? To what extent are you aware of contexts in your classroom that involve "situational appropriateness" or "being linguistically or culturally appropriate depending on the situation"?

 ### Thought-Provokers: A Mindset for Moving Forward

1. I embrace incorporating movement activities into my classroom.
2. I realize that focusing on building and bridging activities sharpens my teaching.

   When teachers start validating and affirming, they unexpectedly become better at building and bridging.

 ### Thought-Blockers: A Mindset for Staying Stagnant

1. I see CLR challenging my pedagogy.

   The number one blocker to validation and affirmation is what was occurring in the classroom instructionally prior to implementing CLR practices. If you were struggling with building and bridging before you tried to validate and affirm, then that original struggle has to be addressed separately from CLR.

2. I prefer to keep using the traditional building and bridging activities I have relied on in the past.

   Cleaning out your closet of build and bridge activities can be a deal-breaker for becoming CLR. You might not like throwing an activity out, simply because you have been using it for so long. Use the process of planning for validating and affirming activities to reevaluate your traditional methodology.

Building Your Movement Activity Quantity

The next section of this chapter presents a comprehensive collection of movement activities. The section includes a description of each activity, the corresponding behavior, and directions for the activity. In addition to validating and affirming cultural behaviors, many protocols can be used to build and bridge. These movement activities can be easily infused into everyday teaching.

Movement Activities

ANSWER CHAIRS

Validate and Affirm Cultural Behaviors: Kinesthetic, Sociocentrism, Dynamic Attention Span, Immediacy, Collaboration

Description: Students review content while developing listening or thinking skills; this activity gamifies review sessions.

Most Effective Uses: Reviewing learning from reading, lecture, or other classroom content

Process

1. Desks or chairs are placed in one large circle or several small circles around the room.
2. Students line up behind the chairs.
3. At the teacher's signal, students begin walking around the chairs as in musical chairs.
4. As students are walking, the teacher asks a question from the lesson or reads a vocabulary word or lesson concept, and then states an answer or definition.
5. If the answer or definition the teacher reads is correct, students sit down. If the answer or definition the teacher reads is incorrect, students keep moving.
6. The students who sit down quickly review and provide evidence or an explanation of why they think the answer is correct. The teacher clarifies as needed.
7. Repeat the process with another question or definition.

Variation: Remove a chair from the circle each round just like musical chairs. The students who are "out" can form review partnerships or group stations.

CAROUSEL BRAINSTORM

Validate and Affirm Cultural Behaviors: Kinesthetic, Sociocentrism, Collaboration, Conversation Patterns, Dynamic Attention Span

Description: In small groups, students respond to questions or prompts in a short period of time.

Most Effective Uses: Reviewing learning; discussing or sharing ideas about literature, content texts, or other material; accessing prior knowledge; solving problems

Process

1. The teacher places sheets of chart paper around the room with predetermined topics, questions, or prompts.
2. The teacher places students in groups of three to six.
3. Each group is assigned a chart. The group members read the question and brainstorm responses. One student records the group's responses.
4. The teacher uses an attention signal when time is up, and students rotate to the next chart.
5. Students read the question and add onto what the group before them wrote.
6. The process continues until each group is back at their original chart.
7. The original group reads all of the responses, summarizes them in one to three sentences, and shares them with class.

CIRCLE THE SAGE

Validate and Affirm Cultural Behaviors: Kinesthetic, Sociocentrism, Collaboration, Communalism

Build and Bridge Behaviors: Individual Accountability

Description: Students use their expertise to teach and help each other learn content.

Most Effective Uses: Students who understand a problem explain to a small group; students share areas of expertise or specific knowledge

Process

1. All students begin working individually on a challenging problem.

2. The teacher identifies three to four students who understand the concept and can explain it to others. They assume the role of the sages or experts.

3. Each sage moves to a different area of the room.

4. The other students are put into groups by counting off, and move to their assigned sage.

5. The sage explains the concept while the other students listen, ask questions, and take notes. The goal is for the sage to prepare all students to be able to answer the question.

6. When students return to their desks, the teacher uses an involuntary response protocol to hear from students who were not sages.

CORNERS

Validate and Affirm Cultural Behaviors: Kinesthetic, Sociocentrism, Dynamic Attention Span, Subjectivity

Description: Students self-select groups based on what they most prefer and discuss/debate; they solidify and gain support for their opinions.

Most Effective Uses: Having students show where they stand on an issue; forming groups around common interests or specific skills

Process

1. In the corners of the room, the teacher posts sheets of chart paper, each with a prompt, choice, or answer.

2. The teacher asks a question that can be answered with one of the posted responses. For example, "What is the most significant effect of the Civil War?"

3. Students choose the chart paper with their answer (see examples below).

   a. The nation was reunited and the southern states were unable to secede.

   b. The South was placed under military rule and divided into military districts.

   c. The federal government established itself over the states.

   d. Slavery was ended.

4. Once in the corners, students discuss and explain their answers, while a scribe takes notes on the chart paper.

5. The teacher invites members of each group to debate ideas and opinions of other groups.

FIND SOMEONE WHO...

Validate and Affirm Cultural Behaviors: Kinesthetic, Spontaneity, Dynamic Attention Span, Communalism, Collaboration, Immediacy

Build and Bridge Behaviors: Individual Success, Autonomy (at first), Objectivity

Description: Students independently respond to prompts or questions about content. After a period of time, the work shifts into collaborative and social work.

Most Effective Uses: To frontload or review content from a lesson

Process

1. The teacher provides students with several questions or problems on an activity sheet.

2. Students work independently to answer as many questions as possible.

3. Upon the teacher's signal, students move around the room finding other students who can help answer questions they haven't answered or who can add more details to their answers or responses. Students write their initials next to the problem they help another student with and then move on to a different student for the next question.

4. Finally, the teacher can use an involuntary response protocol such as Pick-a-Stick or Somebody Who… to call on a few students to share answers.

GIVE ONE, GET ONE

Validate and Affirm Cultural Behaviors: Kinesthetic, Communalism, Spontaneity, Dynamic Attention Span, Immediacy, Subjectivity

Build and Bridge Behaviors: Turn-taking, Individual Accountability

Description: Students independently brainstorm, take notes, or answer questions, and then share, discuss, and exchange ideas with peers.

Most Effective Uses: Reviewing and clarifying information; accessing prior knowledge; reviewing learning and providing direct instruction

Process

1. After the teacher has finished direct instruction or content review and students have participated by taking notes and/or writing answers to questions or prompts, the teacher explains that they will review the main points of the lesson with Give One, Get One.

2. Students stand up and move around the room. They stop and talk to one classmate at a time, giving an idea and getting an idea to add to their papers. Then they move on and talk to another student. The teacher can establish a minimum number of exchanges, but students move at their own pace (it should move quickly).

3. At the conclusion, the teacher uses a response protocol to hear from a few students regarding what they "got" and who they got it from (individual accountability).

GRAFFITI TALK

Validate and Affirm Cultural Behaviors: Kinesthetic, Spontaneity, Sociocentrism, Immediacy, Dynamic Attention Span

Description: Students are given choice and spontaneity when reviewing content.

Most Effective Uses: Reviewing content from instruction or reading

Process

1. The teacher posts several questions or problems on chart paper around the room.

2. When students are given an attention signal, such as "When I say 'Time to,' you say 'Move,'" students go to a chart and write or draw their responses or solutions. They do this silently or in quiet conversation.

3. Students are encouraged to respond to several, but not all, questions. Students choose which ones they respond to and how long to spend on them.

4. When all questions have been responded to, students sit down, and the teacher leads the whole class in a review or discussion of the questions or answers.

Note: The difference between this and Carousel Brainstorm is that students choose when to move and how long to stay at each chart.

GUESS WHO

Validate and Affirm Cultural Behaviors: Kinesthetic, Spontaneity, Dynamic Attention Span, Communalism, Collaboration, Immediacy

Description: Students share and review content from a lesson or reading.

Most Effective Uses: Reviewing learning from reading, lecture, or other classroom content

Process

1. The teacher prepares two sets of index cards with questions and answers, such as vocabulary words and definitions, math problems and solutions, characters and character traits, and so on. The cards should be two colors—one color for questions and the other color for answers. There must be exactly enough cards for everyone in class.

2. The teacher shuffles the cards and spreads them out. When the teacher uses an attention signal (I say "Get a"/You Say "Card"), students get up and each choose a card.

3. Students move around the room, sharing and discussing, trying to find their match.

4. Once everyone has found their partner, the teacher uses a response protocol, such as Whip Around (to hear all of the questions/answers) or Pick-a-Stick (to hear some of them).

HUDDLE

Validate and Affirm Cultural Behaviors: Kinesthetic, Spontaneity, Communalism, Collaboration, Immediacy

Build and Bridge Behaviors: Individual Success, Autonomy (at first)

Description: Students use their skills and expertise to help and support one another.

Most Effective Uses: Practicing skills and concepts taught during direct instruction; during independent work

Process

1. Students begin working individually on a set of problems or an assignment.

2. The teacher pre-selects individual students as classroom experts for a particular task or for particular questions within a task.

3. If students are struggling or having challenges with an assignment, they call out "Huddle."

4. Student experts move to a designated place, and the students who want help huddle around them.

5. If multiple students call "Huddle," they can all meet as one group or split up and huddle according to need.

6. Students return to their seats once their questions are answered.

INNER-OUTER CIRCLE

Validate and Affirm Cultural Behaviors: Kinesthetic, Communalism, Spontaneity, Dynamic Attention Span, Collaboration, Immediacy

Description: Students ask and answer a variety of questions with many interactions in a short period of time.

Most Effective Uses: Reviewing for an assessment; practicing questioning or responding; checking for comprehension of a reading, a text, or other content

Process

1. The teacher prepares questions to help students review content or has students create questions themselves.

2. Students form two circles. One inner circle faces out toward the students making the outer circle, who face in.

3. Each student in the outer circle begins by asking a student in the inner circle a question. The student in the inner circle answers. Note: The teacher and students should make sure each student is asking a different question.

4. Once the inner circle has had an opportunity to answer (thirty seconds to a minute), one of the circles rotates clockwise and the process is repeated. Continue until a full rotation is made.

5. Repeat with the inner circle having the opportunity to ask questions as the outer circle responds.

MIX-PAIR-SHARE

Validate and Affirm Cultural Behaviors: Kinesthetic, Sociocentrism, Collaboration, Dynamic Attention Span, Immediacy

Build and Bridge Behaviors: Spontaneity, Individual Success, Autonomy (at first)

Description: Students review, share, or discuss several questions or problems with a variety of classmates.

Most Effective Uses: Reviewing learning; practicing problem solving; checking for comprehension; accessing prior knowledge; sharing open-ended responses to prompts

Process

1. The teacher prepares a list of questions or problems for students to answer or solve.
2. The teacher gives the students the attention signal "Mix/Move," and students walk around the room.
3. The teacher uses the attention signal "Pair/Share." Students then find partners and greet them with high fives, fist bumps, or other appropriate greetings.
4. The teacher then asks a question or displays a problem on the board. Students discuss it with their partners for thirty to ninety seconds.
5. The teacher uses the attention signal "Mix/Move," and students move again. Repeat the process until all questions or problems have been answered.

MOVE-STOP-GROUP

Validate and Affirm Cultural Behaviors: Kinesthetic, Spontaneity, Dynamic Attention Span, Sociocentrism, Collaboration, Immediacy

Build and Bridge Behaviors: Objectivity

Description: Students form groups based on how they would answer a question and work together to justify their answer.

Most Effective Uses: Reviewing learning; assessing understanding informally; solving problems

Process

1. Students stand. The teacher says, "Time to" and students respond, "Move!"
2. Students move around the room. When the teacher calls, "Time to," students say, "Stop!"
3. The students stop right where they are. The teacher then asks a multiple-choice question, such as "What word best describes the main character of the story?" The teacher provides several answer choices by number, e.g., 1 = generous, 2 = insecure, 3 = polite, 4 = assertive.
4. When the teacher gives the attention signal "Hold it/Up," the students hold up the number of fingers that correspond to their answers.
5. Students look around the room, find other students holding up the same number, and then forms groups according to their answers.
6. Students in each group work together to justify their answer.
7. The teacher reveals which group is correct and explains the problem or answers. Alternately, students can explain and provide support for the class.
8. The process repeats with other questions or problems.

MUSICAL SHARES

Validate and Affirm Cultural Behaviors: Kinesthetic, Sociocentrism, Dynamic Attention Span

Description: Students share, discuss, exchange ideas, or review material.

Most Effective Uses: Reviewing, summarizing, or clarifying information; sharing open-ended responses to prompts; sharing prior knowledge

Process

1. The teacher asks a question or provides a prompt for students. Students can respond in writing or simply think of their answer.

2. The teacher explains that students will be sharing their answers with several classmates.

3. The teacher turns on music. The students move or dance around the room. (Note: The music should be an upbeat style or a song that students like.)

4. When the music stops, students turn to the person closest to them to discuss their answers. The teacher gives students about thirty seconds and then resumes the music.

5. The process is repeated until students have had an opportunity to share with three or four different people.

ONE-THREE-SIX

Validate and Affirm Cultural Behaviors: Kinesthetic, Communalism, Collaboration, Immediacy, Subjectivity

Description: Students share, compare, validate, and record personal responses or opinions and build upon individual or small-group responses to clarify and strengthen their thinking.

Most Effective Uses: Expressing ideas, answers, and responses to questions

Process

1. Students write individual responses to a prompt or open-ended question.

2. Students move into groups of three to share their responses and create lists.

3. Groups combine, creating new groups of six students. Students share their responses and add to their lists of ideas.

4. The teacher uses an involuntary response protocol to select a student from each group of six to present their ideas to the class.

SILENT APPOINTMENT

Validate and Affirm Cultural Behaviors: Kinesthetic, Pragmatic Language Use, Sociocentrism

Description: Students create appointments with one another using nonverbal communication. They then move to verbal communication to respond to a prompt.

Most Effective Uses: Reviewing, summarizing, or clarifying information; sharing prior knowledge; sharing journal responses

Process

1. The teacher asks a question or provides a prompt.
2. Students take a moment to think or respond in writing.
3. When the teacher signals, students make a "silent appointment" with one another using nonverbal cues (eye contact, nodding, hand signals).
4. Students cross their arms over their chests to signal they have an appointment.
5. Students go to their appointments. They greet their partners nonverbally, and then share.
6. The teacher uses a response protocol such as Pick-a-Stick or Train/Pass It On to allow students to share what they discussed.

SNOWBALLS

Validate and Affirm Cultural Behaviors: Kinesthetic, Spontaneity, Dynamic Attention Span, Communalism, Immediacy

Description: Students review learning anonymously and assess what ideas need further discussion.

Most Effective Uses: Reviewing content as an informal assessment; practice and reinforcement of concepts

Process

1. The teacher poses an open-ended review question, problem, or prompt.
2. Students respond to the prompt on scratch paper without writing their names.
3. After a few minutes, students wad up their papers into "snowballs" and throw them to the front of the room.
4. When the teacher says "snowball," each student picks up a snowball that is not their own.
5. Students go back to their seats and review the answer on the snowball.
6. The teacher uses an involuntary response protocol to have students share the answers on their selected snowball. (Stand and Deliver works well here.) Answers are confirmed and explained.

STOP AND SCRIBBLE

Validate and Affirm Cultural Behaviors: Kinesthetic, Spontaneity, Dynamic Attention Span, Communalism, Subjectivity

Build and Bridge Behaviors: Objectivity

Description: Students move around to answer questions and share one another's thoughts and ideas. This allows for collective thought processing and communal task completion.

Most Effective Uses: Reviewing content as an informal assessment; practice and reinforcement of concepts

Process

1. Students each write a few review questions on a sheet of paper, or the teacher prepares an activity sheet with several questions or prompts and distributes them.

2. Students stand up, leave their papers on their desks, and take a writing tool with them.

3. The teacher turns on music, and students move or dance around the room. (Note: The music should be an upbeat style or a song that students like.)

4. When the music stops, students stop and sit in the seat closest to them. They read the question and write a response. Or, if there are multiple questions, they choose one question to answer.

5. The teacher turns the music on again, and the process is repeated until all the questions are answered.

6. When students get back to their own seats, they share and discuss the answers on their papers with their tablemates. The teacher can use an involuntary response protocol, such as Pick-a-Stick or Roll 'Em, to review the answers.

TEA PARTY OR MEET 'N' GREET

Validate and Affirm Cultural Behaviors: Kinesthetic, Spontaneity, Dynamic Attention Span, Communalism, Collaboration, Immediacy

Build and Bridge Behaviors: Individual Success, Autonomy (at first)

Description: Students share, discuss, and exchange ideas with three classmates, greeting one another in different ways to practice situational appropriateness.

Most Effective Uses: Accessing prior knowledge; reviewing learning; checking for comprehension; practicing explicit situational appropriateness

Process

1. The teacher poses an open-ended question or prompt. Students have time to think about their responses.

2. The teacher thinks of scenarios for which various appropriate greetings would be required, such as greeting the principal, greeting a potential employer at a job interview, greeting a friend at a soccer game, or greeting a friend who has moved away and is visiting.

3. The teacher shares one of the scenarios and instructs students that they will greet one another appropriately for that particular occasion.

4. Students then move around the room and greet one of their classmates appropriately. They then discuss the academic content.

5. The teacher uses a Call and Response attention signal, and students end their conversations. The teacher offers a new greeting scenario, and students move on to a new partner. Repeat until all scenarios have been enacted.

THINKING OR VOTING ON YOUR FEET

Validate and Affirm Cultural Behaviors: Kinesthetic, Subjectivity, Spontaneity, Dynamic Attention Span, Immediacy

Description: Students review and discuss concepts learned in class and/or think about and provide reasons and evidence for their choices. This activity helps students think critically and learn to be open-minded and accept different perspectives.

Most Effective Uses: Accessing prior knowledge; previewing material; reviewing learning; comprehending and analyzing ideas

Process

1. The teacher prepares a list of questions that have two potential answers or choices, such as "Which one was a more significant cause of the American Revolution—obligatory taxes or infringement of personal privacy?" or "Which is the best quality for a friend to have—loyalty or honesty?"

2. Students stand up, and the teacher asks one of the questions and provides the two answer choices. If students choose the first answer, they move to one side of the room. If they choose the second answer, they move to the opposite side of the room.

3. Once they have moved, each student shares with a partner standing near them one to two reasons for their choice.

4. The teacher selects two to three students from each side to share their thinking and reasoning with the whole class.

5. The process is repeated until all questions have been asked.

Variation: Students respond to or rebut briefly the reasoning of the opposing side.

WHO'S THE STRAY?

Validate and Affirm Cultural Behaviors: Kinesthetic, Communalism, Spontaneity, Dynamic Attention Span, Immediacy, Subjectivity

Description: Students share or discuss information and hear various perspectives and ideas.

Most Effective Uses: Discussing responses to prompts, open-ended questions, or questions with multiple responses; finding text evidence to support a response; solving challenging equations or word problems

Process

1. Students form groups of four. Each student is assigned a number from 1 to 4.

2. Students collaborate in their groups to respond to questions the teacher provides.

3. The teacher randomly calls a number from 1 to 4, and says, "Stray." The students who have that number get up from their group and move to another group to get information.

4. The teacher uses the call and response "Go/Home," and the strays go back to their original groups and share the information they received.

5. If time allows or more ideas are needed, the teacher repeats the process by calling another number.

CHAPTER EXERCISES

Use these scenarios and exercises to assist you in processing, practicing, and applying the concepts from the chapter.

Mrs. Grey

Mrs. Grey's students had a lot of energy, and she believed in allowing them to move around during class. She taught her students engaging yoga poses that they would practice during a lesson's stretch breaks. When transitioning into new lessons, she would play a song the class liked and allow them to take a dance break before moving on. Mrs. Grey would incorporate movement exercises into a lesson if it was taking longer than she planned, because she knew the students had been sitting too long. In addition, she taught her students meditation techniques that she encouraged them to use if they were having difficulties during the independent practice portion of a lesson.

Understanding that her students had a lot of energy, Mrs. Grey integrated the use of movement into her lessons to:

    a. lift the energy of the classroom.

    b. build community within the classroom.

    c. deepen students' understanding of a lesson's content or topic.

Answer: a. lift the energy of the classroom.

In this scenario, Mrs. Grey mainly used movement to lift, or manage, her students' energy during classroom lessons. While Mrs. Grey understands that her students need to be able to move because they have a lot of energy, she could also strategically integrate movement activities that allow her students to collaborate in order to practice or apply a concept learned during the direct instruction portion of her lessons. Including movement activities that have an instructional purpose in mind, in addition to those used to lift energy and build community, can help deepen students' understanding of the content of her lessons, and could decrease the amount of stretch breaks needed during a lesson.

Classroom Applications

Think about your own classroom and teaching practices. Use the following prompts to reflect on your past experiences and consider how you can effectively use movement activities in your classroom.

    1. Do you use movement activities to lift the energy in your classroom? If so, which activities do you find effective?

    _____

    _____

2. What are some ways that you can integrate movement activities into your teaching practices to help achieve instructional goals?

_____

_____

Sample Lesson—Introducing a Movement Activity

Teachers are often afraid that the use of movement activities in the classroom will lead to off-task behavior or create a chaotic classroom environment. The following lesson illustrates how to introduce a movement activity (Snowballs) in a structured way so that students have a clear understanding of the expectations associated with it.

Procedure

1. Create a review sheet containing several double-digit addition word problems and distribute one to each student.

2. Say, "Today we are going to be doing an activity called Snowballs that will help us review the different strategies we have learned to solve word problems involving double-digit addition. Each of you has a sheet with several review questions on it. I would like each of you to complete the questions on the review sheet independently. Please do not write your names on your sheets. When you finish, please take out your independent reading book from your desk and read silently until you hear me use the "It's time to/End" attention signal. When you hear me say 'It's time to,' put down your pencil or book, look at me, and respond with 'end.' After you respond to the attention signal, keep your eyes on me, your bodies quiet, and your ears listening, so I can explain the next step in the activity."

3. Give students several minutes to complete the review sheet independently.

4. Use the "It's time to/End" attention signal to get students' attention. Remind students again that they should not write their names on their review sheets. Say, "This activity is called Snowballs because you are going to make pretend snowballs out of your review sheets. When I say 'Go,' I would like you to crumple your review sheet into a ball and throw it to the front of the room. Please be careful not to rip the paper when you make your ball. Also, make sure you do not hit anybody else with your snowball. Ready? Go!"

5. Once everyone has thrown their snowballs to the front of the classroom, ask students to resume sitting in their seats. Explain that each student will now have a chance to come up and collect one snowball from the ground. Call students to the front of the class by groups, such as rows or tables. Once they each have a snowball, have them return to their seats, flatten out the paper, and review the responses.

6. Use the Pick-a-Stick response protocol to select students to share the strategies used to answer each question on the review sheets. Discuss the merits of each strategy as a class.

Mr. Price

While reading the first drafts of his students' essays, Mr. Price noticed his students using the same words over and over again in their writing. He made a list of the words that appeared repeatedly.

The next day he told students what he had noticed. Mr. Price facilitated an instructional conversation in which the class discussed how using vivid vocabulary words, or Tier Two vocabulary words as opposed to Tier One vocabulary words, would make their writing more engaging for readers. (See chapter 5 for more information.)

Mr. Price created a chart listing the words that frequently reoccurred in students' writing. He returned the drafts to students, and they highlighted any of the words on Mr. Price's list that appeared in their writing. The students used classroom resources to find synonyms for the words they highlighted.

Mr. Price then used the Give One, Get One movement activity to allow students to share the synonyms they found for the words they highlighted. Students were able to use the synonyms they collected from one another to revise their drafts and include more vivid Tier Two vocabulary terms in their writing to make it more engaging.

In this scenario, Mr. Price integrated the use of movement into his lesson to:

   a. lift the energy of the classroom.

   b. build community within the classroom.

   c. deepen students' understanding of a lesson's content or topic.

Answer: c. deepen students' understanding of a lesson's content or topic.

The use of the Give One, Get One movement activity gave his students the opportunity to walk around the classroom with a specific instructional purpose. In addition, talking to and collaborating with classmates as they revised the vocabulary they used in their writing responded to the sociocentric nature of Mr. Price's students—making the use of this movement activity culturally responsive.

Classroom Applications

Think about your own classroom and teaching practices. Use the following prompts to reflect on your past experiences and consider how you can effectively use movement activities in your classroom.

   1. Think about a concept that is challenging for your students. How could you use one or more movement activities to help them study the concept?

   _____

   _____

   2. What challenges do you foresee in using movement activities in your classroom? How can you structure the activities to eliminate or reduce these challenges?

   _____

   _____

Sample Lesson—Using Music to Increase Comprehension

The following lesson shows how to use Musical Shares to integrate music and movement in a way that helps students comprehend material while being social.

Procedure

1. Select an open-ended question relating to a current unit of study. For example, you might choose the question, "What were some of the most important inventions or discoveries made by the ancient civilizations of the Maya, Inca, and Aztec people?" Write the question on the board.

2. Provide each student with a graphic organizer for taking notes during the activity.

3. Say, "When I play the music, I want you to move around the classroom. You can walk or dance, whatever you prefer. When the music stops, take a seat in the desk closest to where you are standing. After everyone is seated, I want you to discuss the question on the board with a person sitting next to you. Take notes on the ideas you discuss on your graphic organizer. When you hear the music start to play again, stand up and move around the classroom until the music stops. Each time the music stops, find a seat and discuss the question with someone new. I will stop and start the music several times so that you have a chance to share your thoughts with multiple people."

4. Invite students to stand. Start the music and monitor the students as they move around the classroom. After a small amount of time, roughly thirty seconds, stop the music and wait until everyone has found a seat. Have students each turn to a student seated next to them and discuss the question on the board for about a minute. Encourage them to take notes on their graphic organizers as they discuss their ideas.

5. Turn the music back on and have students move around the classroom again. Repeat several times so that students have the opportunity to discuss the question with multiple people.

6. To conclude, display a copy of the graphic organizer. Use the Whip Around response protocol to have the students share their ideas about the discussion question. Record their responses on the displayed copy. Using these notes, review the different information students learned about the technological and cultural advances made by the ancient civilizations in the Americas.

Mr. King

Mr. King's class read a literary text. After reading the text, students compared and contrasted the story's two main characters, citing specific details from the text to explain how their words, motives, and actions impacted the story's main events. Mr. King's students created graphic organizers to compare and contrast the story's two main characters. They filled their graphic organizers with details from the text, providing evidence of how the main characters' words, motives, and actions impacted the story's main events.

Mr. King used the Give One, Get One movement activity throughout the duration of the lesson to encourage students to share their ideas with one another. As the lesson progressed, students lost interest in the movement activity and became less engaged in the conversations they were supposed to be having about the text. Despite student restlessness, Mr. King opted to continue using the Give One, Get One activity.

Mr. King's students lost interest with the movement activity because:

   a. the lesson's movement activity did not have a specific instructional purpose.

   b. the teacher needed to include different movement activities in the lesson instead of relying on the same one throughout it.

   c. the movement activity he used was not responsive to his students' cultural behaviors.

   d. All of the above

Answer: b. the teacher needed to include different movement activities in the lesson instead of relying on the same one throughout it.

CLR educators need to have a variety of movement activities in their toolboxes, adding one or two every couple of weeks. In addition, the use of this one movement activity lasted too long. Having a few more movement activities to choose from would have allowed Mr. King to rotate and strategically use another movement activity to keep the students engaged in the lesson.

Classroom Applications

Think about your own classroom and teaching practices. Use the following prompts to reflect on your past experiences and consider how you can effectively use movement activities in your classroom.

   1. Think about a time that you overused a certain activity or protocol. How did students react? What could you have done differently?

   _____

   _____

   2. Think about your daily schedule. How can you integrate movement activities into your schedule to help achieve instructional objectives?

   _____

   _____

Sample Lesson—Choosing Movement Activities

The scenario in Mr. King's classroom illustrates how the benefits of a movement activity can be diminished by overuse. The following sample lesson shows how to utilize a variety of different movement activities (Give One, Get One; Stop and Scribble) to avoid overusing any one activity.

Procedure

   1. Read *Frog and Toad Are Friends* by Arnold Lobel aloud to the class. Distribute a Venn diagram graphic organizer to each student. Display a copy of the organizer and model how to label one circle "Frog" and the other circle "Toad." Have students label their diagrams following your example.

2. Think aloud as you demonstrate how to write one similarity and one difference about the physical appearance of Frog and Toad in the appropriate areas of the diagram. For instance, you might write "tall" under Frog and "short" under Toad. In the area where the two circles overlap, you could write, "like to wear pants and jackets."

3. Say, "Now I want you to use the Give One, Get One strategy to record on your Venn diagrams two more similarities or differences about the physical appearances of these characters. When I ring the chime, please stand up and move around the classroom until you find someone with whom you can share information. You should tell your partner one thing Frog and Toad have in common or one of their differences. Then your partner should tell you one similarity or difference. Record the new information you learn on your graphic organizer. When I hit the chime again, move around the classroom again and find a different partner. Exchange information and record it on your activity sheet. When I hit the chime three times, return to your seats."

4. Use the chime to signal that the students should engage in the Give One, Get One activity. After they have each shared information with two different people, ring the chime three times and have them return to their seats.

5. Discuss the similarities and differences in the characters' physical appearances that the students learned through the activity. Use a response protocol, such as Whip Around or Pick-a-Stick, to ensure that everyone has a chance to share.

6. Say, "Now that we have identified several similarities and differences among the physical appearances of the characters, we are going to compare and contrast other aspects of these characters using an activity called Stop and Scribble. First, leave your Venn diagrams on your desks and locate pencils that you can take with you during the activity. When I turn on the music, I would like you to stand up and move around the classroom. When the music stops, sit down in the seat nearest to you. Think about Frog and Toad's personalities. How are they similar? How are they different? Write one similarity or difference on the Venn diagram at the desk where you are sitting. When the music starts playing again, leave the diagram on the desk and continue moving around until the music stops again. Each time the music stops, sit in an empty seat and add a new similarity or difference about Frog and Toad's personalities to the graphic organizer."

7. Play the music for a short interval while the students move around the classroom. Stop the music, wait for the students to find seats, and then provide time for them to each add a similarity or difference to the Venn diagram at that seat.

8. Repeat this process several times. Then have students return to their original seats and read the notes on their Venn diagrams. Review the similarities and differences between the main characters' personality traits as a class.

Mrs. Green

Students entered Mrs. Green's math class to find three charts, with one question posted on each, around the classroom. They each received three sticky notes as they entered and proceeded to their desks.

Mrs. Green informed her students that they had three sticky notes because they had three questions to answer, referring to the charts posted around the classroom.

Students were given time to answer each question with a number on each of their sticky notes. After a given amount of time, Mrs. Green played music, and her students walked to the charts to post their answers to the questions written on the charts. She told the class that their answers represented a data set for each question.

She placed the class into three groups and assigned each group a poster.

The first task she gave each group was to work together to rearrange the data represented on the charts by placing the values represented on the sticky notes in numerical order from least to greatest. This was a familiar classroom practice.

After having the students rearrange the numbers in their data sets, Mrs. Green introduced the terms *mode*, *median*, *range*, and *mean* one at a time. She introduced the terms in this order because they represented the easiest to the most difficult averages to compute.

Mrs. Green told the groups that they would begin analyzing the data represented on their posters by finding the mode of their data sets. After she introduced the term, she defined its purpose, explained the procedure students would have to use to find the answers, and asked the question, "What is the mode of your data set?" She would later ask questions about the data on each poster that helped students understand how to apply the analysis of the data to real life.

The class conducted similar activities to find the median, range, and mean of their data sets. Mrs. Green was pleased with her lesson and believed she was "Kicking."

When reflecting on her lesson, Mrs. Green considered herself to be "Kicking" while swimming with her use of movement activities in the CLR Pool because she:

   a. used movement activities at least two to three times during her lesson.

   b. used movement activities for the purpose of deepening understanding around the content.

   c. used movement activities for the purpose of explicitly validating and affirming.

   d. All of the above

Answer: d. All of the above

In this scenario, Mrs. Green used Musical Shares designed to validate and affirm her students culturally. She also used movement activities to build and bridge as she helped students analyze data sets to find different averages. Her use of movement activities allowed for collaboration, explicitly validating and affirming her students culturally. She also incorporated building and bridging activities to help her students understand the context.

Classroom Applications

Think about your own classroom and teaching practices. Use the following prompts to reflect on your past experiences and consider how you can effectively use movement activities in your classroom.

   1. What does it mean to use movement activities to build and bridge? How can you use building and bridging movement activities in your classroom?

   _____

   _____

2. Think about your students' cultural backgrounds and behaviors. What type of movement activities might be best suited to meet their needs?

_____

_____

Sample Lesson—Using Movement Activities to Assess

Movement activities not only affirm and validate students culturally, but they also benefit student learning and the classroom environment. In addition to using movement activities to teach, it is also possible to use these activities to assess students' comprehension both formally and informally. The following lesson provides an example of how to use a movement activity, Thinking on Your Feet, and a response protocol, Somebody Who…, to informally assess students' understanding of the events that led up to the beginning of World War II.

Procedure

1. Before beginning the lesson, prepare a clipboard with a list of all students' names, so you can record assessment information, and a series of review questions along with two potential answers for each question. For example, one question might be, "What was the main objective of the Treaty of Versailles with regards to Germany after World War I?" Two possible answers to the question might be "to make Germany accept the blame for World War I" and "to prevent Germany from having power."

2. On one side of the classroom, post a paper with the letter "A." Post a paper with the letter "B" on the other side.

3. Say, "I am going to read a review question along with two possible answers aloud. Think about the question and decide which answer you think is best. There is not necessarily a right and a wrong answer to each question, but you need to be able to explain why you chose the answer you did. After reading the question, I will pause for a moment to let you think. Then I will say 'Go,' and that is the signal for you to move to the side of the room that corresponds with the answer you choose. If you choose answer 'A,' move to this side of the room (point to the sign), and if you choose 'B,' move to this side of the room (point to other side)."

4. Explain, "After everyone has chosen a side, I will use a "Somebody who…" statement to pick several students to share their reasoning with the class. For example, if I say, 'Somebody who had an apple for lunch,' those students who had an apple at lunch will raise their hands, and I will call on several of them to explain why they chose the answer they did. Then I will read the next review question and use the 'Go' signal to indicate when you should move to the side of the room that represents your answer."

5. Read a review question aloud, pause to let the students think, then say "Go" and have students move to one side of the room or the other. Use a "Somebody who…" statement to identify several students to explain their reasoning. Use the class list on your clipboard to record information about the students' responses. For example, if a student is able to provide solid evidence and reasoning to support their answer, mark a "+" next to their name. If a student can provide some information about the answer, but does not show a thorough understanding, mark a "•" next to their name. If a student is not able to provide any

reasoning or evidence to support their answer, mark a "–" next to the name. At the bottom of your checklist, make notes about questions or subject areas that seem particularly difficult or confusing for students.

6. Repeat until you have covered all the questions. Use the assessment information from your notes and checklist to identify students who need further instruction and specific topics that are challenging for the class in general. Reteach and review the material as necessary.

Post-Reading Assessment

It is hard to make a case against using movement in your classroom. There are simple uses related to lifting energy in the room and having students move that are unrelated to instructional purposes. Then, there are more complex uses of movement activities that intentionally and strategically focus on being culturally responsive or validating and affirming. Use movement activities in this way—to push yourself to explicitly validate and affirm your students culturally. Lastly, remember that just validating and affirming is not enough. Building and bridging activities, which will be more traditional in nature, can accompany validation and affirmation when applicable.

Now it is your turn to start "swimming" with the use of movement activities. Start today. As you are planning your next lesson, infuse movement activities however you can. Be intentional and strategic. Allow yourself the time and space to fail, to make mistakes, and to be uncomfortable. After a couple of weeks of implementing CLR, come back to this chapter and complete the survey (figure 3.2) on your use of movement activities.

Figure 3.2 Effective Uses of Movement Activities Survey: After Infusing the CLR Principles

0: *Never Emerging* 1: *Rarely Splashing* 2: *Sometimes Floating* 3: *Mostly Kicking* 4: *Always Freestyling*					
I use movement activities at least two to three times per instructional block.	0	1	2	3	4
I use movement activities for the purpose of lifting energy and building community.	0	1	2	3	4
I use movement activities for the purpose of deepening understanding of content.	0	1	2	3	4
I use movement activities for the purpose of explicitly validating and affirming.	0	1	2	3	4

STUDENT VOICE

Allowing Your Students to Be Engaged in Their Own Way, or "BeYou": Field Dependence

BeYou is a call to action, reminding teachers to adjust instruction and classroom practices, ensuring that students can be themselves at school culturally and linguistically. In this section, we consider how students might express the importance of being validated and affirmed when being field dependent at school.

How can field dependence be culturally misunderstood in the classroom? Has a student ever asked you questions like this: "Why are we learning this?" "Why do I have to sit right here?" "Will this be on the test?" I am the student likely to ask these questions, because context and relevance help me learn. It may seem like I am questioning the teacher or I lack motivation, but I am basically telling you that I need that context and relevance to make meaning based on my own experiences.

How does it feel to be misunderstood? Imagine you're in a room with a lot of objects, like chairs, tables, and pictures on the walls. Field dependency is how much you rely on those objects to help you understand where you are or what you're doing. Culturally, it's bigger than that. It's about how much I need what's happening around me, the people, the stuff we're learning, to connect to my real life. If it doesn't relate, it's like trying to learn something without knowing why it matters to me. It's not that I don't want to learn, it's just harder when I can't see how it fits into my world.

What do I need to be myself? Learning experiences that connect to real-life situations and things I'm interested in can really help me understand how the information fits into other parts of life. When I see those connections, it's easier for me to learn and remember what is being taught. Also, chatting with friends and bouncing ideas off each other is super helpful for me. When we all learn from each other, it sticks better in my brain.

> **What CLR activities validate and affirm field dependence?** Activities like Whip Around and Save the Last Word for Me give students the opportunity to connect to the learning in ways that are relevant to them. However, most of what a teacher does to validate and affirm field dependent learners happens before the lesson, through planning how you will make the real-life connections and provide the context students need, and building in time for them to collaborate and learn with each other.

Build CLR Community and Collaboration

Complete the following Cultural Behaviors Continuum based on your own upbringing and culture.

- ◆ **Step 1:** Mark where you fall on the continuum for each behavior. (Think ethnic culture, how you were raised, heritage.)
- ◆ **Step 2:** Now, circle the traditional/historical school culture or school values for each behavior.
- ◆ **Step 3:** Reflect: Notice any distance between your markings and school markings. What is the implication of the distance?

◆ **Step 4:** Discuss how knowing your cultural behaviors assists you in collaborating with your colleagues and how knowing theirs allows you to validate and affirm them. How does the same process occur with your students?

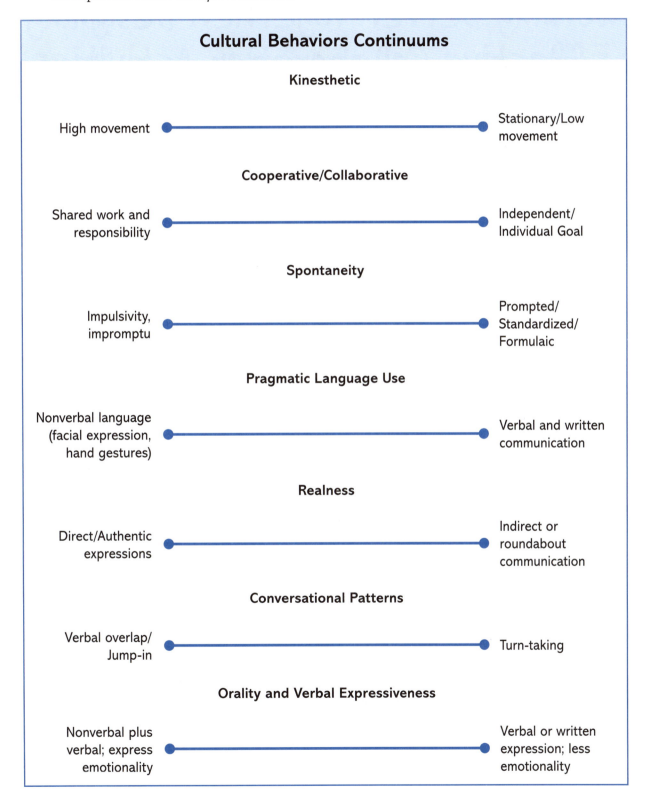

Cultural Behaviors Continuums

Kinesthetic

High movement ●————————————————● Stationary/Low movement

Cooperative/Collaborative

Shared work and responsibility ●————————————————● Independent/ Individual Goal

Spontaneity

Impulsivity, impromptu ●————————————————● Prompted/ Standardized/ Formulaic

Pragmatic Language Use

Nonverbal language (facial expression, hand gestures) ●————————————————● Verbal and written communication

Realness

Direct/Authentic expressions ●————————————————● Indirect or roundabout communication

Conversational Patterns

Verbal overlap/ Jump-in ●————————————————● Turn-taking

Orality and Verbal Expressiveness

Nonverbal plus verbal; express emotionality ●————————————————● Verbal or written expression; less emotionality

CHAPTER 4

Working Better Together: Designing Effective Collaboration Activities

Understanding the Context

Group work, as it was originally termed, has been around for a long time (Cohen, Brody, and Sapon-Shevin 2004; Johnson and Johnson 1987; Long 1977). In educational settings, it is commonly called cooperative or collaborative learning, and most teachers are expected to incorporate this type of learning in their teaching. Today, it is considered a key aspect for successful implementation of college and career readiness standards. The issue is that most teachers, outside of specialized professional development or teacher education experience, are not particularly skilled at implementing it. In attempting to apply collaborative learning, the unskilled practitioner wings it.

It is important to clarify the terminology associated with collaborative activities. Carol Cohen and colleagues (2004) define *collaborative learning* as students working together in a small group long enough that everyone can participate on a clearly assigned task. The key to this definition is that students are expected to complete the task without direct support from the teacher. "When teachers give students a group task and allow them to make mistakes and struggle on their own, they have delegated authority" (2). Delegating authority does not mean that the teacher loses control of the classroom. While students are free to accomplish the task how they choose, they are always accountable for the final product that will be evaluated by the teacher. Another key component of collaborative activities is that students need one another to complete the task. An effective collaborative activity requires interdependency. Students learn how to communicate in this form of collaboration through asking questions, making suggestions, thoughtfully criticizing, and joint decision-making. This type of interaction directly and positively impacts student engagement (Cohen, Brody, and Sapon-Shevin 2004).

> Collaborative learning involves students working together in a small group long enough that everyone can participate on a clearly assigned task (Cohen, Brody, and Sapon-Shevin 2004).

Designing culturally and linguistically responsive extended collaboration activities forces teachers to consider where they may need to shore up their collaborative learning skills. In some cases, CLR shows them how to do so concretely. What do I mean by *extended*? The discussion protocols covered in chapter 2 are meant to be brief and quick in nature, but they are considered collaborative. *Extended*, therefore, means going beyond a short time frame. That can mean a project of a few hours as well as a project that is worked on over several days or even a few weeks. *Extended* also means higher stakes are involved instructionally and the work is directly linked to learning outcomes. In contrast, the non-extended collaborative moments tend to be lower stakes instructionally and act more as scaffolds. Extended collaborative activities support students in learning socially and academically and are tied to specific outcomes.

School can be the ideal practice ground for learning social skills in addition to the necessary academic skills for mainstream and academic culture.

A high school AP English teacher in the Midwest, who readily admitted that the CLR engagement activities in general were more engaging for his students, asked me if using the engagement strategies was actually "better teaching." Meaning, is using engagement a more effective way of teaching? After giving this some deep thought, I responded with a resounding "yes." Extended collaborative activities best illustrate the added instructional value effect that the teacher inquired about. Cohen, Brody, and Sapon-Shevin (2004), Johnson, Johnson, and Stanne (2000), and Slavin (2010) report that when students can work long term in groups, they learn better and more. Cohen, Brody, and Sapon-Shevin (2004), in particular, contend that extended collaboration is more effective than lecturing, written exercises during classes, and large-group instruction. Group work can be more effective than traditional methods for gaining a proper understanding of abstract concepts, and hence the link to college and career readiness standards. However, there is a significant caveat to consider. Two conditions must be in place for the largest effect or result:

1. The learning task should require conceptual thinking rather than learning to apply a rule or memorization.

2. The group must have the resources to complete the assignment successfully. Resources include intellectual skills, vocabulary, relevant information, and prepared task instructions (Cohen, Brody, and Sapon-Shevin 2004).

A carefully crafted group assignment should call for academic rigor and critical thinking. Without question, use of extended collaborative activities goes beyond increased engagement. They are about increased learning and achievement.

> *Extended* means the extension of time, with higher stakes learning, including social learning, academic skills, and practice for real life.

Considering the Research

Research supports integrating culturally responsive teaching techniques and extended collaborative activities to enhance engagement, increase academic achievement, and create a culturally responsive classroom.

◆ Group interaction has a favorable effect on understanding of mathematical concepts (Fitzsimons and Fhloinn 2023; Cohen, Brody, and Sapon-Shevin 2004; Kane and Saclarides 2023; Koçak et al. 2009; Lovell and Elakovich 2018; Wickersham and Nachman 2023).

◆ Students who test low on cognitive development tasks show marked gains after working in groups on the post-test (Jensen and Lawson 2011; Rafique et al. 2021; Tudge 1990).

◆ Frequency of interaction is a predictor of individual as compared to group learning (Battistich, Solomon, and Delucchi 1993). Further, the outcomes for collaborative learning depend on the complex interplay of individual- and group-level factors (Haataja et al. 2022).

◆ For students in bilingual classrooms, talking and working together as the primary methodology led to higher gains on math word problems (Cohen, Brody, and Sapon-Shevin 2004; Lariviere, Agrawal, and Wang 2022).

◆ Experiencing frequent, positive, high-quality group interactions predicts improvements in classroom environment, perception of the school, student motivation, self-esteem, and concern for others (Battistich, Solomon, and Delucchi 1993; Rafique et al. 2021; Wickersham and Nachman 2023).

- ◆ When working in cooperative groups, English learners improve comprehension and production of the second language (Alghamdy 2019; Aslan Berzener and Deneme 2021).

Pre-Reading Assessment

Before reading this chapter, reflect on your current use of extended collaborative activities in your teaching by completing the survey in figure 4.1. As you rate yourself, think about the effectiveness and efficiency of the extended collaborative activities you use. As noted above, you are probably doing extended collaboration activities already. The extent that you have considered their connection to cultural responsiveness is the focus of this chapter.

Figure 4.1 Effective Extended Collaborative Activities Survey: Before Infusing the CLR Principles

0: *Never Emerging* 1: *Rarely Splashing* 2: *Sometimes Floating* 3: *Mostly Kicking* 4: *Always Freestyling*					
My students participate in extended collaboration at least 3–5 times per week.	0	1	2	3	4
I have a group project for each unit or grading period.	0	1	2	3	4
My students understand that our collaboration time is structured and that they are accountable with tasks and responsibilities.	0	1	2	3	4
I assess my students' ability to be social, communal, and cross-cultural.	0	1	2	3	4

Beginning the Reflective Process

Learning happens when we reflect on what we have experienced. Critical reflection generates, deepens, and documents learning (Ash and Clayton 2009). Are you ready to implement effective collaboration activities?

Use the following checklist to gauge your readiness and ability to effectively integrate collaborative activities into your teaching. Each item represents an important aspect of understanding and using extended collaborative activities in a culturally responsive classroom. After completing the checklist, read the detailed descriptions of the items and reflect on how you plan to implement or increase your use of collaborative activities in the classroom.

☑ The Use of Collaborative Activities Reflection Checklist

Item 4.1	Do I see myself more as a guide on the side (a facilitator of learning) than a sage on the stage (a conductor of learning)?	○ Yes ○ No
Item 4.2	Do I know how to structure group work with strategy and purpose?	○ Yes ○ No
Item 4.3	Do I know the cultural values I am affirming and validating when using extended collaborative activities?	○ Yes ○ No

Item 4.4 Do I avoid the pitfalls that can lead to ineffective collaborative learning? ◯ **Yes** ◯ **No**

Item 4.1 Do I see myself more as a guide on the side (a facilitator of learning) than a sage on the stage (a conductor of learning)?

The challenge for most teachers evolving to cultural responsiveness is the fear of losing control of the class and, perhaps more insidiously, the fear of not being seen as the authority figure in the room. In order to do extended collaborative learning effectively, a teacher must lose themself in a way that puts the spotlight on the students. Consider how much time is spent in front of students and what the cost/benefit is to their learning. Many teachers believe that the information or content is best when it comes directly from them and only them. I call this *Pinky and the Brain* teaching. If you know the cartoon, then you will understand the reference. The Brain is the very annoying know-it-all character, while Pinky is the supposedly not-so-smart sidekick. One immediate payoff with extended collaborative learning is that it puts the teacher in the role of facilitator and not the only source of knowledge in the room.

Schlomo Sharan (1976) found that when teachers delegate authority to students, there is a special socializing effect that gives students a greater sense of control of their own environment. This is in direct contradiction to the traditional methodology, where students play a more passive role.

REFLECTIVE THOUGHT

To what extent does the learning in your classroom center around you "standing and delivering" content? How can you empower students to construct the learning themselves with your guidance and facilitation?

Thought-Provokers: A Mindset for Moving Forward

1. I see the craft of my teaching as secondary to my students' learning.

   Ironically, taking the ego out of the learning leads to more connectivity with your students, because they trust that their learning comes first as opposed to your teaching.

2. Think of a context where you were the learner. Ask yourself: How did I learn best—through facilitation or direct instruction? Did I have a choice?

Thought-Blockers: A Mindset for Staying Stagnant

1. Facilitating learning requires a certain skill set on the part of the teacher. Ask yourself: Do I have the necessary skills to facilitate learning? Is my plan to wing it or plan for learning in advance?

2. Ask yourself: Am I afraid of failing? It is understandable if you are, especially if you are not accustomed to releasing control. Expect that initially working with groups through facilitation will be trial and error.

Item 4.2 Do I know how to structure group work with strategy and purpose?

There is a skill to structuring effective collaborative opportunities for students. The research is not lacking in describing those skills or providing recommendations. For example, Cohen, Brody, and Sapon-Shevin (2004) provide seven steps to ensure effective collaborative learning:

1. Prepare your students for collaboration. Do not assume that they come to "group work" ready.

2. Teach the norms and skills that they will need to be successful. The use of skill building exercises is strongly recommended. There are a variety of skills to learn. For example, discussing, listening, contributing, sharing, reflecting, and evaluating are all necessary for effective group work to ensue.

3. Provide opportunities for students to practice the skills and norms before high-stakes assignments.

4. When students are ready, create the task to be completed based on what you want the students to learn.

5. Provide clear and specific instructions with examples of what is expected at the end.

6. Strategically determine the size, composition, and physical spacing of the groups. Assign roles and tasks within the group.

7. Determine how the work will be evaluated.

The last item on the list highlights accountability. There must be individual and group accountability. Individuals should be responsible for some kind of individual product. The product can be related to participation in the group, contributions made to the group, an assessment related to the content, or a form of evaluation. Likewise, the group needs to be held accountable, with each person taking responsibility for some aspect of the product or the expected outcome. For example, literature circles have built-in accountabilities: Each member is given a role. The names for these parts can vary, but they usually correspond to the following roles: a director who is in charge of writing the questions used in the discussion, a word wizard who uses resources to clarify word meanings, a literary luminary who is responsible for identifying and examining important passages from the text, and a checker who helps to evaluate participation and makes sure that assignments are completed (ReadWriteThink 2006). In addition to these individual roles, the group is held accountable for a final product that is related directly to the content, such as a presentation, a physical model, an experiment, or a group report. Even though I do not recommend the use of competitive group rewards, they can be effective when used sparingly and purposefully.

Planning for effective collaborative groups takes time and requires adept preparation. Most teachers report that they do not have the time or the inclination to prepare in the way that effectiveness requires. In actuality, this type of planning is a matter of spending time to save time. And as we know, the effective teacher's work is done *before* the students arrive to class.

> REFLECTIVE THOUGHT
>
> To what extent do you use collaborative learning in your lessons? How do you plan for those activities? How have you prepared your students for collaborative work?

 ## Thought-Provokers: A Mindset for Moving Forward

1. I can take stock of what I already do well with my collaborative groups and use this opportunity to build upon that skill set.
2. I actively seek other sources to help me with my planning.

 ## Thought-Blockers: A Mindset for Staying Stagnant

1. I do not have the motivation to plan and prepare in advance. I rely on using the same lessons year in and year out.
2. My fear of losing control—management-wise and instructionally—cannot be overstated. This prevents me from focusing on more collaboration.

Item 4.3 Do I know the cultural values I am affirming and validating when using extended collaborative activities?

Similar to the protocols and movement activities, extended collaborative learning easily lends itself to being culturally responsive. They go hand in hand. Working in groups provides opportunities for students to express themselves through culture via sociocentrism, communalism, types of leadership, and cooperation, as well as through language via conversational patterns, tone of voice, and discourse styles. Instructionally, cultural responsiveness coupled with the extended collaborative learning opportunities is a win-win. All of these cultural and linguistic behaviors are being validated and affirmed when students are working collaboratively in groups.

In fact, extended collaborative learning allows for building and bridging as well. It enables teachers to create situations in which individuals can live in both worlds—home culture and school culture—"without guilt, anxiety, and isolation" (Shade, Kelly, and Oberg 1997, 57). These situations are the overarching goal of cultural and linguistic

> *Communalism* is a concept that says "we" is more important than "I," and my success as an individual is determined by the success of the group as a whole. *Sociocentrism* refers to the idea that social interaction is more important than the content being discussed; nonlinear discourse patterns are expected.

responsiveness. As Samuel Betances (1990) points out, the challenge is to educate students so they are empowered with skills for going into the workplace while maintaining their pride for their heritage, including their cultural norms.

REFLECTIVE THOUGHT

Your ability to validate and affirm students will not require any extra effort or thought when extended collaborative learning opportunities are infused throughout instruction. Not only are these opportunities validating and affirming, but they also build and bridge, achieving a balance of individualism and collectivism.

 ## Thought-Provokers: A Mindset for Moving Forward

1. I see being able to automatically validate and affirm students through collaboration as a relief, giving me one less element of my lesson plan to consider.

2. I acknowledge the academic benefit my students gain by participating in activities like this.

 ## Thought-Blockers: A Mindset for Staying Stagnant

1. My biased thinking about cultural behaviors, like communalism or contextual conversation patterns, prevents me from the validation and affirmation aspect of this work.

   To counteract this, check your filter, question your belief system, and listen to your deficit thinking.

2. I do not believe that there is an academic benefit to group work.

   If this is the case, then what I have suggested in the realm of cultural responsiveness will be meaningless. You must believe that your students will learn better this way.

Item 4.4 Do I avoid the pitfalls that can lead to ineffective collaborative learning?

Cohen, Brody, and Sapon-Shevin (2004) describe pitfalls to avoid in implementing collaborative learning; not doing so leads to ineffective collaborative learning. The importance of teaching the norms and procedures of collaborative group work to your students is essential. Not doing so is pitfall number one. Students need to know how to behave within the group. The second pitfall is a lack of structure and organization. Not having the adequate structure and organization leads to ineffective group work.

A third pitfall is failing to follow the "No Hovering" rule. Cohen, Brody, and Sapon-Shevin (2004) stresses the importance of allowing students to make decisions on their own and, most importantly, to make mistakes on their own. When groups are failing or not having success, you should avoid rushing to the rescue. However, there are times when it is appropriate to intervene, such as when the group is hopelessly off task, when the group seems to genuinely not understand enough to complete the task successfully, and/or when the group is not organized or group members are not cooperating with one another and are arguing, being petty, or trying to sabotage the work. A fourth and final pitfall is not recognizing the difference between healthy disagreements and more serious conflicts, and not managing those conflicts. In the latter instance, providing students alternate ways for resolving conflicts or being willing to change members within groups are ways to manage serious conflicts.

> We learn best by making mistakes in environments that teach us how to learn from our mistakes.

REFLECTIVE THOUGHT

> These four pitfalls are the most common ones, but that is not to say there are not others. The overall point is that you are going to make mistakes. Allow yourself time to fail and room to improve. Fortunately, you now have a heads-up on some mistakes to avoid as you move forward.

Thought-Provokers: A Mindset for Moving Forward

1. I consider what my experience with extended collaborative learning groups thus far has been: successful or unsuccessful, organized or unorganized, or a mixed bag. I see this as an opportunity to reevaluate my use of extended collaborative learning.
2. I proactively think of other possible pitfalls related to my specific situation, such as available resources, room space, furniture, and class size.

Thought-Blockers: A Mindset for Staying Stagnant

1. There are many excuses that prevent me from providing my students extended collaborative learning opportunities.
2. There are walls that I have to climb over or go around to incorporate extended collaborative teaching, so I am unwilling to change my teaching style.

Concluding Thoughts

Group work has come a long way since the 1950s and 1960s when the concepts of cooperative learning were initially developed. There is no reason why collaborative learning should not be a staple in every classroom. Additionally, there is no reason why the use of extended collaborative learning cannot be seen through the lens of cultural responsiveness. When students are working collaboratively, you are being culturally responsive. The two approaches are mutually supportive. This chapter gave you the reasons why they go together, demonstrated how through the research on collaborative learning, and provided reflective thoughts for your consideration in implementing the approach. There is a lot more to consider for a successful implementation of collaborative learning. I strongly suggest you continue to discover more tips and techniques about collaborative learning through other resources, such as the following:

- *50 Strategies for Cooperative Learning* by Sabrina Winkleman
- *Active Learning Across the Content Areas* by Wendy Conklin and Andi Stix
- *Kagan Cooperative Learning* by Spencer Kagan and Miguel Kagan
- *Cooperative Learning in the Classroom: Putting It into Practice* by Wendy Jolliffe

CHAPTER EXERCISES

Use these scenarios or exercises to assist you in processing, practicing, and applying the concepts from the chapter.

Mr. Gonzalez

The students in Mr. Gonzalez's health and fitness class were concluding their unit on stress. As a part of their culminating tasks, students worked in collaborative groups to create digital presentations to present to the class.

Students worked in groups of four to six. At some tables, all students in a group were taking turns presenting their individual slides to one another. At other tables, team members were either working together to conduct research or working on their individual slides. In each of these groups, students were using response protocols to provide constructive feedback about one another's work and the ideas that they were contributing to their team assignment. Mr. Gonzalez was moving between the groups, providing feedback and answering questions as needed.

Discussing it later, Mr. Gonzalez noted that this was a weeklong project in which students were given the entire class period to work on their projects. They worked on pieces in class and at home. When asked how he was able to facilitate this type of learning for his students, Mr. Gonzalez explained that when he assigned this project, he outlined the culminating requirements. Students were informed that their presentations should be designed to illustrate the impact that the types of stress studied in class can have on teens. They were also told to provide stress management tips that teens could use to cope with these types of stress. He explained that he had provided the students with criteria charts and rubrics outlining what was expected of each group's digital presentations, each student's individual slides within the group's presentation, and the oral presentations of their projects.

When asked how the teams were able to choose the material that they were going to include in their group presentations, Mr. Gonzalez explained that he placed students in groups and allowed the groups to identify team leaders. He said the team leaders used participation and discussion protocols to help their teams select the topics of their groups' presentations and then outlined the material their individual slides should contain to support the team's group presentation.

Was Mr. Gonzalez acting as a guide on the side (a facilitator of learning) or a sage on the stage (conductor of learning)? How?

Answer:

Mr. Gonzalez was acting as a guide on the side, facilitating learning for his students.

Evidence: "At some tables, all students in a group are taking turns presenting their individual slides to one another. At other tables, team members are either working together to conduct research or working on their individual slides. Mr. Gonzalez is moving between the groups providing feedback and answering questions as needed."

How does Mr. Gonzalez's culminating project represent an extended collaborative activity that provides opportunities for both individual and group accountability?

Provide evidence from the scenario that illustrates the following:

◆ Extended Learning
◆ Group Accountability
◆ Individual Accountability

Answer:

Extended Learning

◆ This was a weeklong project in which students were given the entire class period to work on their projects. They worked on pieces in class and at home.

Group Accountability

◆ Students worked in collaborative groups to create digital presentations to present to the class.
◆ Team members worked together to conduct research.
◆ Students used response protocols to provide one another with constructive feedback about the ideas that they contributed to their team assignment.
◆ Mr. Gonzalez provided students with criteria charts and rubrics outlining what was expected of each group's digital presentations and the oral presentation of their projects.

Individual Accountability

◆ Students in a group were taking turns presenting their individual slides to one another.
◆ Students were working on their individual slides.
◆ Mr. Gonzalez provided students with criteria charts and rubrics outlining what was expected of each student's individual slides (within their group's presentation) and the oral presentation of their projects.

What evidence does the scenario provide to support the following claim? "Mr. Gonzalez understood that an effective collaborative activity requires interdependency, and he prepared his students to be able to effectively communicate with one another in this form of collaboration."

Possible Answers:

Mr. Gonzalez's students knew how to use both response and discussion protocols to facilitate instructional conversations in the classroom.

◆ The students used both response and discussion protocols to provide one another with constructive feedback about one another's work.
◆ The students selected a team leader who was able to determine the response protocols necessary to effectively share their ideas with one another.
◆ The team leaders used participation and discussion protocols to help their teams select the topics of their group's presentations and then outlined the material their individual slides should contain to support the team's presentation.

Classroom Applications

Think about your own classroom and teaching practices. Use the following prompts to reflect on your past experiences and consider how you can effectively use extended collaborative learning experiences in your classroom.

1. Think about how you plan each unit of study. How can you integrate collaborative learning into your long-term plans?

_____

_____

2. Accountability is an important part of collaborative learning. When you think about doing an extended collaborative learning project in your classroom, how can you make sure that individual group members are accountable for their participation?

_____

_____

Sample Lesson—Using Book Clubs for Extended Collaborative Learning

Reading and comprehending text is an important part of learning in all content areas. Classroom book clubs are a tool for encouraging students to examine, discuss, and enjoy books in a social and collaborative setting. The following lesson plan (adapted from ReadWriteThink 2014) illustrates one way that a teacher can use book clubs to facilitate extended collaborative learning in the classroom.

Procedure

1. Before introducing the concept of classroom book clubs, it is important to first teach students the art of developing and asking questions based on the text. Tell students, "There are many different types of questions we can ask about books. For example, when I ask, 'When does the book *The Things They Carried* by Tim O'Brien take place?,' you can look in the text and find the answer. However, when I ask, 'Based on O'Brien's portrayal of war in *The Things They Carried*, how do you think he feels about war in general?,' I am asking you to think about how war is portrayed in the book and how that relates to the author's feelings based on your own experiences with conveying emotion through writing."

2. Using a sheet of chart paper, display the four different types of questions used in the Question-Answer Relationship (QAR) strategy:

   ◆ **Right There:** Questions whose answer can be found by reading the text.

   ◆ **Think and Search:** Questions that require the reader to gather information from different parts of the text and compile it in a meaningful way.

   ◆ **Author and You:** Questions that are based on the text but require the reader's interpretation based on their own experiences.

   ◆ **On My Own:** Questions that do not require the reader to have read the text but rather rely on prior knowledge or personal experience.

3. Provide each student with a copy of a short text selection. Read the passage aloud as the students follow along. Think aloud as you model how to develop four questions, one for each QAR category, based on the text.

4. Use the Pick-a-Stick response protocol to call on students to share other examples of questions that fit the four QAR categories based on the text. Record their questions on a separate sheet of chart paper under the appropriate QAR type of question. Display the chart paper in a visible area so that the students can refer to it.

5. Over the next several days, continue to have students practice using the QAR strategy to develop questions based on different types of text. Pay particular attention to their ability to develop "Think and Search" questions that are text based and require more than simple recall of information.

6. After students are comfortable with the QAR strategy, introduce book clubs. Say, "We are going to start using classroom book clubs to discuss books together. For the first book club, all groups are going to read the same text so that we can practice how to have a good discussion. In the future, each group will be asked to choose its own book."

7. Distribute copies of a text, such as Markus Zusak's *The Book Thief.* Explain that the students should read the text independently over the next week and be ready to discuss it by a certain date. Tell students to prepare a list of eight questions based on the text. Explain that they should have at least one question for each of the QAR categories.

8. On the designated date, place students into small heterogeneous groups. These groups should not be based on reading ability. As a class, discuss the expectations involved with participating in a discussion, such as listening when someone is speaking, referring back to the text for evidence to support your opinions, and providing positive feedback and constructive comments. Use a pre-taught discussion protocol, such as Put Your Two Cents In, to ensure that everyone in the group has a chance to participate. Say, "You can use the questions you wrote to start your discussion, but you do not have to rely only on these questions. Remember to refer to the text when answering a question or providing support for an argument whenever possible. Encourage the other members in your group to support their responses by asking questions, such as, 'Why do you think that?' or 'How do you know?'"

9. Give the students about thirty minutes to discuss the book in their groups. Walk around the class and monitor the discussions. Do not interrupt the discussions unless the students are off task or not following the discussion guidelines.

10. At the end of the discussion, have students return to their seats. Use the Whip Around response protocol to have every student share one thing they enjoyed or learned during the book club discussion. Also, have students reflect on what went well in their discussions and what they would like to change for future discussions.

11. Have students complete a Book Club Discussion Assessment. The assessment should include questions such as these:

    ◆ On a scale of 1–5, how much did I participate in the discussion? (1 = not at all, 5 = very much)

    ◆ On a scale of 1–5, how much did the other members in my group participate? (1 = not at all, 5 = very much)

    ◆ Was the discussion effective for helping you understand the book better? Why?

    ◆ What went well in the discussion? Why?

    ◆ What did not go well in the discussion? Why?

12. Use the assessment results to gauge students' participation and assess the effectiveness of the discussions in terms of meeting learning objectives. Continue to use book clubs throughout the year. In the future, have each group choose a book to read together rather than assigning the same book to the whole class. Once students become accustomed to participating in book club discussions, have them work together to integrate the information they discuss during group meetings into larger projects, such as visual displays, digital presentations, or analytical research papers.

Ms. Hall

Ms. Hall's students are practicing order of operations to evaluate numerical expressions. The students are seated in table groups and each student has an individual whiteboard. One at a time, Ms. Hall writes expressions such as $8 + (5 \times 42 + 6)$ on the board. As Ms. Hall writes an expression, the students copy it onto their whiteboards. After ensuring that all students have copied the expression down, Ms. Hall asks students to collaborate with their group members to draw an arrow pointing to the part of the expression they should calculate first. She reminds the students that if they calculate the numbers in the wrong order, they will get the wrong answer.

After one minute, Ms. Hall calls out "Show" and students show her their whiteboards. Ms. Hall draws an arrow on the board pointing to the correct part of the expression. The groups who identified the correct part of the expression cheer. The other students are told, "Don't sweat it, we learn from our mistakes!" Ms. Hall asks students to talk to one another about any mistakes they made.

Ms. Hall follows this same procedure to ask the students the following questions about the expression:

◆ What do the parentheses tell us about calculating this expression?

◆ How do we calculate exponents in expressions?

◆ Do we multiply or divide before we add or subtract?

Is Ms. Hall acting as a guide on the side (facilitator of learning) or a sage on the stage (conductor of learning)?

Answer: Ms. Hall is acting as a sage on the stage (conductor of learning).

Ms. Hall acts as a sage on the stage by providing the students with a maxim about an appropriate behavioral response and allowing the students to determine their own potential mistakes.

Classroom Applications

Think about your own classroom and teaching practices. Use the prompts on the next page to reflect on your past experiences and consider how you can effectively use extended collaborative learning experiences in your classroom.

1. What kinds of collaborative learning activities do you already use in your classroom? How could you modify these activities to make them more extensive?

_____

_____

_____

_____

_____

_____

_____

2. Good instruction involves a variety of different teaching and learning techniques. When you think about your classroom, what areas would benefit from more extended collaborative activities? What areas or topics are better suited for other teaching and learning techniques?

_____

_____

_____

_____

_____

_____

_____

Sample Template for Planning Extended Collaborative Learning

Use the following template to plan how to integrate collaborative learning experiences into your instructional practices.

Unit:_____

Standards, Objectives, and Learning Goals—List the standard, objective, and ultimate learning goal that students will achieve by the end of the unit.

Culminating Collaborative Project—Explain the final project that students will complete collaboratively at the end of the unit. The final project should allow students to demonstrate their mastery of the objectives you listed above.

Assessment for Culminating Collaborative Project—Describe an assessment for evaluating students' culminating collaborative projects. This assessment should be tied to the goal previously listed.

Lessons—Consider the skills and knowledge students need in order to be able to demonstrate mastery of the objectives through the culminating project. Briefly outline how you will teach these skills through a specific set of lessons. Below each lesson description, describe how you can integrate smaller opportunities for collaboration throughout the lesson.

- Lesson 1:_____

  Collaboration:_____

- Lesson 2:_____

  Collaboration:_____

- Lesson 3:_____

  Collaboration:_____

- Lesson 4:_____

  Collaboration:_____

- Lesson 5:_____

  Collaboration:_____

- Additional Lesson:_____

  Collaboration:_____

Collaboration Summary—Explain how the collaborative opportunities previously described help students meet academic objectives while also affirming and validating them culturally.

Notes:

Post-Reading Assessment

Now it is your turn to start "swimming" with extended collaborative learning opportunities. As you plan your next lesson, infuse a long-term group project. Be intentional and strategic. Allow yourself the time and space to fail, to make mistakes, and to be uncomfortable. After three weeks of implementing CLR, come back to this chapter and complete the survey (figure 4.2) on your use of extended collaborative learning opportunities.

Figure 4.2 Effective Extended Collaborative Activities Survey: After Infusing the CLR Principles

0: *Never Emerging* 1: *Rarely Splashing* 2: *Sometimes Floating* 3: *Mostly Kicking* 4: *Always Freestyling*					
My students participate in extended collaboration at least 3–5 times per week.	0	1	2	3	4
I have a group project for each unit or grading period.	0	1	2	3	4
My students understand that our collaboration time is structured and that they are accountable with tasks and responsibilities.	0	1	2	3	4
I assess my students' ability to be social, communal, and cross-cultural.	0	1	2	3	4

Allowing Your Students to Be Engaged in Their Own Way, or "BeYou": Orality and Verbal Expressiveness

BeYou is a call to action, reminding teachers to adjust instruction and classroom practices, ensuring that students can be themselves at school culturally and linguistically. Here we consider how students might express the importance of being validated and affirmed when demonstrating orality and verbal expressiveness at school.

How can orality and verbal expressiveness be culturally misunderstood in the classroom? Expression is not just about what you say but how you say it. When I'm really into something, my energy and emotions show not just in my words but in how I talk, my body language, and the vibe in my voice. Sometimes, I get so pumped that I jump in or my words overlap with others', because I'm just super excited. Other times my face and body say more than anything else, which is natural for me. In school, though, people might think I'm interrupting, being "extra," or doing too much, when really, I'm being myself.

How does it feel to be misunderstood? It's important for me to feel like I can be myself and express how I feel, whether it's with words or through my body language and tone of voice. When I'm really passionate about something, it all comes out—my facial expressions, gestures, and the way I speak. It's tough when the way I naturally express myself isn't understood or accepted, or I feel like I have to constantly monitor how I say things, especially when I'm super passionate about something. I get that there are times when I need to be mindful of how I come across, but it's exhausting when I feel like I have to do it all the time.

What do I need to be myself? I feel validated when I am free to express myself naturally, both verbally and nonverbally without judgment or retribution. My face, body, and voice are all part of how I show that something is important to me, and it means a lot when the ways I express myself are valued and seen as part of who I am.

> **What CLR activities validate and affirm orality and verbal expressiveness?**
>
> Activities like I Got This!, It Says...I Say...and So, and Radio Reading are great, because students can express themselves in so many different ways, both verbally and nonverbally, without having to monitor how they say things. Having opportunities to express themselves that aren't always part of a certain expectation makes the classroom much more fun, so finding ways to let students just talk to each other really helps.

Build CLR Community and Collaboration

Plan a CLR-infused lesson, invite a colleague to observe, and debrief the lesson with the colleague. The lesson can be related to an extended collaborative learning experience, or it can be part of another topic or unit of study. Your CLR-infused lesson should answer these three questions:

1. What cultural behavior(s) do you plan to validate and affirm and/or build and bridge? And why?
2. What CLR activities do you plan to use to accomplish #1?
3. What specific feedback do you want from the observing colleague?

Culturally and Linguistically Responsive Academic Vocabulary

Culturally and Linguistically Responsive Academic Vocabulary Overview

There are not many topics in education that find general agreement among educators. However, educators do agree on the importance of students increasing their academic vocabulary skills. Vocabulary development is a gatekeeper and must be part of culturally and linguistically responsive instruction. As educators—especially as practitioners—we bear a responsibility for how students learn to "own" words. It's our job to increase their reading, writing, and speaking skills and opportunities in school situations. Even though there is general agreement about the importance of vocabulary, I have discovered (albeit unscientifically) that the majority of teachers do not have a systematic way of teaching vocabulary. Those who do often resort to the traditional methodology of—you guessed it—"dictionary work."

The point is that before we can discuss how to make vocabulary teaching responsive, we have to ensure that vocabulary instruction is occurring. To an extent, some vocabulary teaching is better than nothing. Fortunately, college and career readiness standards require students to interpret words and phrases as they are used in a text, including how specific sentences, paragraphs, and larger portions of the text relate to each other and the whole. I strongly recommend that you have a baseline of vocabulary teaching in order to infuse CLR. In other words, if you are not teaching vocabulary on a regular basis, it may be difficult to practice cultural and linguistic responsiveness.

This section is about how to make your vocabulary instruction responsive in three ways.

1. Understand the overall validating and affirming aspect of the CLR approach, which is to honor the words that students bring from home and recognize that students are not blank slates when it comes to their word knowledge.

2. Equip students with the necessary skills for success, using research-based strategies students need to attack unfamiliar words.

3. Utilize developed tools for success—the personal thesaurus and personal dictionary—that help support validation, affirmation, and building and bridging.

To begin this section, we will look at how all words are not equal. We will then examine research-based strategies for expanding academic vocabulary (chapter 6) and learn about two essential tools: the personal thesaurus and the personal dictionary. The personal thesaurus is a tool to help students develop knowledge of synonyms and antonyms (Hollie 2018). The personal dictionary is based on the Frayer Model. After the teacher supplies a content-specific term and its definition, the student creates an illustration and makes a personal connection (Hollie 2018). These two tools are explained in chapter 7.

> **English Language Arts–Literacy Standards**
>
> Determine the meaning of domain-specific and general academic words or phrases in a text.
>
> Determine the appropriate figurative, connotative, and/or technical meaning of words and phrases as they are used in a text.
>
> Analyze the impact of word choice on meaning and tone.

CHAPTER 5

All Words Are Not Equal: Leveling Words and Increasing Ownership

Understanding the Context

Do not ask me why, but I recently read yet another dieting book hoping for the magic bullet to sustain weight loss. The author's claim was that all calories are not equal, and if I choose to eat foods with the right calories instead of the foods with the wrong calories, I can not only lose weight, but I can keep it off. Though I am still in the process of figuring out which are the right calories and which are the wrong calories, I realized that just as all calories are not equal, all words are not equal. However, unlike with calories, there is no such thing as right words versus wrong words. All words have value. It just depends on how they are used. Alternatively, a specific word may have more value in one context, such as an academic essay, compared to another context, such as a personal letter to a friend.

For students to understand the idea that all words have value and that the value can change depending on the situation fits squarely with cultural and linguistic responsiveness. The overall concept is that the vocabularies our students bring from home have value. But where is the value? In school, we have to teach students that all words are not equal and that some words will therefore have more value for Standard English (SE) or school language and academic language (AL). The research of Isabel Beck, Margaret McKeown, and Linda Kucan (2013) asserts that words in any language have different levels of utility, which leads to their notion of tiered words. Tier One words are the most basic words. Tier Two words are the high-frequency words for mature language users, and Tier Three words are those whose frequency of use is quite low and limited to a specific content domain.

- **Tier One:** Words that students already know, understand, and use.
- **Tier Two:** High-frequency words that are necessary for understanding the text or concept. Students generally have some conceptual knowledge of these words, but they may lack an academic label.
- **Tier Three:** Low-frequency, content-specific words that are only relevant for a particular text or area of study.

> While *tier* is the term used professionally, you may find the term *level* more digestible for students.

In CLR, we term the tiers as:

- **Tier One** ➔ Already know
- **Tier Two** ➔ Need to know
- **Tier Three** ➔ Should know

Teaching vocabulary in a culturally responsive way acknowledges that students have a comprehensive, conceptual knowledge base rooted in their culture, community, and life experiences that can be used to build academic vocabulary. Students have a multitude of thoughts, opinions, and concepts about the communities they live in and the world around them. They have given their own labels, names, and words to these concepts. Students have vast conceptual vocabularies upon which strategic vocabulary instruction can be built.

Keeping this in mind, responsive vocabulary instruction begins with knowing how to level words into the three tiers. Leveling words is directly connected to linguistic responsiveness because Tier One and Tier Two words can be used to validate and affirm the home language words of your students, while simultaneously teaching them research-based, lifelong methods of vocabulary acquisition.

> *Home language* refers to the language used by family members in the home and others in the community that is different enough from the parameters defined by language from Standard English.

Considering the Research

Research supports the teaching of academic vocabulary as a CLR teaching technique. The following studies represent a sample of relevant research supporting the instruction of academic vocabulary to create a culturally responsive classroom.

- Vocabulary knowledge in kindergarten and first grade is a significant predictor of reading comprehension in the middle and secondary grades (Cunningham and Stanovich 1998; Green 2021; Whorrall and Cabell 2016).

- Teaching vocabulary can improve reading comprehension for both native English speakers and English learners (Carlo et al. 2004; Green 2021; İlter 2019).

- Using the dictionary to define words is possible but difficult for elementary students and not 100 percent successful even for college students (Graves 2006). Still, the dictionary is a resource that many turn to for clarity of meanings and functions of words (Sadieda et al. 2019).

- Multilingual learners are especially likely to have underdeveloped English vocabularies (August et al. 2005; Heller, Lervåg, and Grøver 2019), even when from middle-income backgrounds (Umbel et al. 1992). It is important to note that underdeveloped vocabulary may be due to language disorder (LD), and, in other cases, it may be due to linguistic incongruence of the first and second language in multilingual speakers (Han and Brebner 2024).

- The words to be taught deeply should be words of high utility in nature and general-purpose academic words, such as *analyze*, *frequent*, and *abstract* (Beck, McKeown, and Kucan 2013; Graves 2000; Graves 2006; Stahl and Nagy 2006). Typically, the low-frequency and often relatively unimportant, if colorful and exotic, words, such as *refuge* and *burrowed*, are selected by teachers or targeted for instruction by textbooks (Hiebert 2005).

Pre-Reading Assessment

Before reading this chapter, reflect upon your current vocabulary instruction by completing the survey in figure 5.1. As you rate yourself, think about how effective and efficient your vocabulary instruction is. If you are not doing any vocabulary teaching, plan on starting immediately. Remember, your vocabulary teaching needs to be in place in order to make it responsive.

Figure 5.1 Leveling Words Survey: Before Infusing the CLR Principles

0: *Never Emerging* 1: *Rarely Splashing* 2: *Sometimes Floating* 3: *Mostly Kicking* 4: *Always Freestyling*					
I select my own vocabulary words to teach (versus those in the core reading text).	0	1	2	3	4
I divide vocabulary words into different levels with a focus on Tier Two words.	0	1	2	3	4
I explicitly validate and affirm the words my students bring from their home languages.	0	1	2	3	4

Beginning the Reflective Process

Learning happens when we reflect upon what we have experienced. Critical reflection generates, deepens, and documents learning (Clayton and Moses 2009). Are you ready to level words to increase ownership?

Use the following checklist to gauge your readiness and ability to effectively integrate academic vocabulary instruction into your teaching. Each item represents an important aspect of understanding and teaching academic vocabulary in a culturally responsive classroom. After completing the checklist, read the detailed descriptions of each item and reflect on how you plan to implement or increase your use of vocabulary instruction in the classroom.

☑ The Use of Leveled Words Reflection Checklist

Item 5.1   Do I have a method for selecting vocabulary words before leveling them?   ○ Yes   ○ No

Item 5.2   Do I have a plan for focusing on Tier Two words for robust vocabulary instruction?   ○ Yes   ○ No

Item 5.1 Do I have a method for selecting words before leveling them?

Believe it or not, this item is the biggest challenge for most teachers. How and from where to select the words present two hard questions. Typically, the words come from a core reading text or a content-area textbook. Either you use the words identified in the accompanying teacher's guide, or you select them on your own. In some cases, students are encouraged to select their own vocabulary words. I see this as an advanced step in the vocabulary acquisition process. If your choice is to use the words identified in the teacher's guide, then, in a sense, the hard work has been done for you. If the work has not been done for you, you have the freedom and latitude to choose. However, you have to be thoughtful in your selection, so let us explore how to make wise choices.

One factor to consider is word-use frequency. Tier Two words have the most frequency. In addition to considering frequency, Michael Graves (2006) offers four questions to ask yourself when determining what words to teach:

1. Is understanding the word important to understanding the selection in which it appears?

2. Are students able to use context or structural analysis skills to discover the word's meaning?

3. Can working with this word be useful in furthering students' contextual or structural analysis skills?

4. How useful is this word outside of the particular reading selection?

By looking at the frequency of a word's use or asking yourself these questions, you can now look toward focusing on Tier Two words—the words your students *need* to know. (See the Mr. Jackson exercise on page 156 for practice in the selection of words.)

Whether you select the words or use ones chosen for you, leveling the list to focus on Tier Two words is the most crucial aspect. Fortunately, Beck, McKeown, and Kucan's (2013) criteria for identifying Tier Two words are simple and straightforward. Here are their recommendations:

1. Eliminate the obvious Tier One words.

2. Eliminate the obvious Tier Three words, looking for content-specificity and likely low frequency across texts.

3. What should remain are words that are clearly Tier Two or that could go in either Tier Two or Tier Three.

4. A telltale sign of a Tier Two word is that the students already have a conceptual understanding of the word. What is missing is the academic label for it.

Understanding the fourth criterion is the foundation of the entire CLR approach, because this is where the validation and affirmation occurs for students. When you affirm that students already have a concept of a word, they gain confidence and motivation to want to learn the academic vocabulary.

REFLECTIVE THOUGHT

Having the words preselected for you is not necessarily a negative, because you will still need to level those words. On the other hand, when you select your own words, you get to play the role of textbook writer; you are in control. How do you select words? What advantages, if any, do you find with words preselected by textbook authors?

Thought-Provokers: A Mindset for Moving Forward

1. I am currently committed to teaching vocabulary.

2. I see the need to reexamine words already preselected in textbooks.

Thought-Blockers: A Mindset for Staying Stagnant

1. I am either not really teaching vocabulary or I am not purposefully teaching it. Yes, I go over words that students need to know. However, in terms of what the research calls for, I have not thought intentionally about the words and the rationale for teaching them.

2. I rely on dictionary work as the primary means of vocabulary instruction.

Item 5.2 Do I have a plan for focusing on Tier Two words for robust vocabulary instruction?

Once the words are selected, you can divide or level them into the three tiers Beck, McKeown, and Kucan (2013) prescribe. Tell yourself that each tier simply represents a way of approaching or teaching the words. Tier One words are presented in more of a survey fashion and are quickly covered, because the students already know them. Never forget that knowing the word conceptually, not just knowing the technical definition, is a core component of the approach. For Tier One words, students will typically have conceptual and technical knowledge of the word.

◆ **Examples of Tier One words are** *table*, *chair*, *sad*, *happy*, *nice*, *mean*, **and** *money*.

Tier Three words, on the other hand, are subject specific and more likely tied to a particular content area, such as mathematics, science, history, foreign language, physical education, music, or visual arts. Tier Three words are the easiest to categorize, because most students will not have a conceptual understanding of the word or a technical definition of it. A second signal for a Tier Three word is that its value is only for the current chapter or unit. Once you are finished with the chapter or unit, then a new set of Tier Three words will come along.

◆ **Examples of Tier Three words are** *isotope*, *lathe*, *peninsula*, *varicose*, *mitosis*, **and** *oligarchy*.

What remains are the Tier Two words, which will be your main focus for robust, intense vocabulary instruction. These words are the most important, because, according to Beck and colleagues, they have the most instructional potential and the most utility for students going forward.

◆ **Examples of Tier Two words are** *misfortune*, *exaggerate*, *compare*, *expectation*, *falter*, *vary*, *itemize*, **and** *relative*.

Beck, McKeown, and Kucan recommend teaching no more than five to seven Tier Two words per week to increase the likelihood of students internalizing the new words. Ownership of the word is your number one instructional goal. "The final decisions about which words to teach may not be as important as thoughtful consideration about why to teach certain words and not others" (Beck, McKeown, and Kucan, 37). Figure 5.2, "Identifying the Tier" (page 157 in the Chapter Exercises), will give you practice leveling words.

REFLECTIVE THOUGHT

Even though Tier Two words are your focus, this does not mean that you are abandoning the other two levels. In addition to adding the academic labels to students' existing conceptual knowledge, you are teaching them that words have different values depending on how and when we need them. How do you teach students to determine that words have different values depending on how and when they are used? How and when do you teach Tier One, Tier Two, and Tier Three words?

Thought-Provokers: A Mindset for Moving Forward

1. I buy into the idea that Tier Two words will be the stimulant for validating and affirming students. (Note: This topic is described in the next chapter.)

2. I subscribe to the notion that my vocabulary instruction will be more focused and organized.

 ### Thought-Blockers: A Mindset for Staying Stagnant

1. I am indecisive about what words go into what levels.

   Tip: Accept that you are not going to get it right every time, and keep going.

2. I am concerned that my plan to cover all of the vocabulary will be affected. As a result, I have decided that more words known superficially are better than fewer known in depth.

Concluding Thoughts

Being more intentional about how you select vocabulary words will pay off in multiple ways, not only because students are going to be owning more words, but because they are going to learn the importance of precise word knowledge versus general word knowledge. Whether you select the words yourself or from a preselected list in a textbook, responsive vocabulary instruction begins with selecting and then leveling the words. Based on the three levels of words, your aim is to choose Tier Two words, which leads to a very specific type of vocabulary instruction—instruction that is keenly focused on students building on what they already know conceptually.

Use these scenarios and exercises to assist you in processing, practicing, and applying the concepts from the chapter.

Mr. Jackson

Practice your selection of words by helping Mr. Jackson select the words he should focus on during vocabulary instruction.

Mr. Jackson's English class will be studying John Steinbeck's American classic *Of Mice and Men*. When considering which vocabulary words he should concentrate on during vocabulary instruction for Chapter 1, he finds a resource that provides him with the following list of words:

juncture	debris
brusque	contemplate
anguish	stake
elaborate	mimic
morose	recumbent

Circle five to seven words that Mr. Jackson should concentrate on during vocabulary instruction for chapter 1.

Answer: Tier Two words present in this list include *juncture*, *anguish*, *elaborate*, *debris*, *contemplate*, and *mimic*.

Tier Two words are the high-frequency words for mature language users. These represent the words that students need to know to be able to comprehend the increasingly complex texts they encounter across content areas.

Mrs. Joy

Mrs. Joy is planning a vocabulary lesson designed to introduce her first grade students to words they will encounter in the poem "Celebration" by Alonzo Lopez.

The vocabulary words Mrs. Joy selects for her vocabulary lesson include the following:

dusk	crawling
feasting	leaps
stomps	weave
laughter	among

Her vocabulary lists usually include up to seven words, but due to a holiday, this is a shortened week. She is worried that seven vocabulary words may be too many for her to teach and is trying to decide which words she can eliminate from this list. Circle the vocabulary words you think she should eliminate, and jot down notes you could use to support your decision.

_____

_____

Answer: Mrs. Joy could eliminate *crawling* and *stomps* from her vocabulary list, because they represent Tier One words.

Classroom Applications

Think about your own classroom and teaching practices. Use the following prompts to reflect on your past experiences and consider how you can effectively select appropriate vocabulary words for your students.

1. In the past, how have you selected which vocabulary words to teach?

    _____

    _____

2. What resources do you have access to that could help you improve your selection of appropriate vocabulary words?

    _____

    _____

Identifying the Tier

Identify the tier for the following vocabulary words. Write them in figure 5.2.

soft	deliberate
photosynthesis	pretty
swift	coefficient
quiet	rigid
intelligent	metamorphosis

Figure 5.2 Identifying the Tier

Tier One Words	
Tier Two Words	
Tier Three Words	

Answer:

- ◆ Tier One words: *pretty, soft, quiet*
- ◆ Tier Two words: *deliberate, swift, rigid, intelligent*
- ◆ Tier Three words: *photosynthesis, coefficient, metamorphosis*

Mr. Smith

Mr. Smith's class is reading the children's historical novel *Dragonwings* by Laurence Yep. Mr. Smith has reviewed chapters 5 to 8 and identified vocabulary words his students need to understand to comprehend the text in those chapters (figure 5.3). He wants to level these words to ensure that he is being strategic with his vocabulary instruction. He needs some help, as he is new to trying this strategy. Identify the tier for each of the following vocabulary words and provide a few notes to explain your choices. Use figure 5.4 to check your responses.

Figure 5.3 *Dragonwings* Vocabulary Preview

abacus	antiquated	benevolence	ironically
patronizing	schematics	tainted	vehemently

Tier One Words	Tier Two Words	Tier Three Words

Figure 5.4 *Dragonwings* Vocabulary Answers

Tier One Words	Tier Two Words	Tier Three Words
Tier One words are the most basic words. There are no Tier One words.	Tier Two words are high-frequency words for advanced language users. antiquated benevolence ironically patronizing tainted vehemently	Tier Three words are those whose frequency of use is quite low and are limited to a specific content domain. abacus schematics

Classroom Applications

Think about your own classroom and teaching practices. Use the following prompts to reflect on your past experiences and consider how you can effectively select appropriate vocabulary words.

1. Think about a specific lesson you taught recently. List three words from the lesson for each of the tiers.

   _____

   _____

2. Every classroom contains students with a range of abilities and knowledge. What vocabulary differences have you noticed among your students? How can you adjust your instruction to meet the needs of all students?

   _____

   _____

Identifying and Selecting Vocabulary Words

Read the following passage about ancient Mesopotamia (Stix and Hrbek 2013). Circle words that you think might be challenging for high school students. Sort the circled words into Tier One, Two, and Three by writing them in the columns.

The Ziggurat

The ziggurat first appeared on the flat Mesopotamian plain in Sumerian cities around 2000 BCE as the first major Sumerian structure. These large, solid pyramids had flat tops and sloping sides with wide steps. Often, the ziggurats were decorated with colorfully glazed, fired bricks. Sometimes, there were even trees and shrubs planted on its wide steps. There was at least one ziggurat built to stand as tall as 70 feet (21.3 meters). The ziggurats were testimonies to the Sumerian's skills as construction workers.

It remains a mystery as to why the ziggurats were built. The fact that the ziggurats were usually built in a temple complex implies a religious significance to the buildings. Excavation of sites has provided some insight into ziggurats. Uncovered sites have indicated that animal sacrifices took place there. This supports the idea that the ziggurats were religious temples.

Tier One Words	Tier Two Words	Tier Three Words

Template for Selecting Academic Vocabulary

Use the following template to select vocabulary words to teach in an upcoming lesson. Begin by identifying words in the text that are unfamiliar to your students. Then categorize the words using the three-tier system and select five to seven words to teach your students.

Text: _____

Identifying Words—Read the text. Record any words that you think might be unfamiliar or confusing to your students.

Categorizing Words—Sort the identified words into the three tiers.

Tier One	Tier Two	Tier Three

Selecting Words—Review the words for each tier. Select five to seven words from Tier Two to teach your students.

Post-Reading Assessment

Now it is your turn to start "swimming" and try leveling vocabulary words from upcoming lessons. As you plan your next lesson, sort your vocabulary list into three levels. Be intentional and strategic. As always, allow yourself the time and space to fail, to make mistakes, and to be uncomfortable. After two weeks of leveling words and implementing CLR, come back to this chapter and complete the survey (figure 5.5) on leveling words.

Figure 5.5 Leveling Words Survey: After Infusing the CLR Principles

0: *Never Emerging* 1: *Rarely Splashing* 2: *Sometimes Floating* 3: *Mostly Kicking* 4: *Always Freestyling*					
I select my own vocabulary words to teach (versus those in the core reading text).	0	1	2	3	4
I divide vocabulary words into different levels with a focus on Tier Two words.	0	1	2	3	4
I explicitly validate and affirm the words my students bring from their home languages.	0	1	2	3	4

STUDENT VOICE

Allowing Your Students to Be Engaged in Their Own Way, or "BeYou": Subjectivity

BeYou is a call to action, reminding teachers to adjust instruction and classroom practices, ensuring that students can be themselves at school culturally and linguistically. In this section, we consider how students might express the importance of being validated and affirmed when expressing subjectivity at school.

How can subjectivity be culturally misunderstood in the classroom? Sometimes there's only one right answer to a question, like $1 + 1 = 2$. But other times, there are lots of ways to look at something, like how you can see a glass as half full or half empty. When I think about things, I like to look at them in my own way and try to see all the different sides of it, based on who I am. I may say "I don't see it that way" or "There's another way to look at this." That's my subjectivity in action! I enjoy finding different ways to think about things, even if they might seem right or wrong, yes or no, to someone else. For me, not everything is clear or objective, and I learn best when things are open to interpretation. This can make it seem like I don't understand something or appreciate how others see things. That's not it at all. I find the many ways we can see things, or different ways to understand them based on our own perspectives, to be really interesting, and this makes learning more engaging for me.

How does it feel to be misunderstood? Sometimes, I don't see things the same way as everyone else, and that can be challenging, especially when people think there's only one correct answer or way to do something. Some might see me as defiant for questioning what seems like a straightforward task or answer, but that's not my intention. I'm not trying to be difficult—I'm a critical thinker. I like to approach

things from various angles, considering different perspectives, and adding my own interpretations to the mix.

What do I need to be myself? I thrive in situations where there is no right or wrong answer or just one way to do something, and the answer or solution can be many things. I feel validated when we do things in class that are open-ended and invite multiple perspectives. I feel affirmed when my way of looking at things is seen as adding value to the learning.

Build CLR Community and Collaboration

In a group of four or five of your colleagues, choose two of the cultural behaviors. Choose one that resonates with you and one that "annoys" or "triggers" you. Discuss with your colleagues what behaviors "work" for you and what behaviors "do not work" for you and why. For the one that triggers you the most, be intentional on validating and affirming that behavior only, at first. Then move on to other behaviors as they apply and as you progress throughout the year.

What CLR activities validate and affirm subjectivity? Activities like Put Your Two Cents In, Campfire, and Corners allow students to express their perspectives and show that there are multiple ways to answer a question or arrive at a solution.

CHAPTER 6

Learn Strategies, Not Words: Research-Based Strategies for Word Acquisition

Understanding the Context

Imagine having to cook a dish without all of the ingredients. Imagine trying to drive your car with flat tires. Imagine exiting your house only to discover that you have left your key inside. Now, imagine a student trying to figure out what a word means without adequate strategies. Increasing students' academic vocabulary is about giving them opportunities to learn more words by increasing their exposure to unfamiliar words and providing them with the strategic tools to figure out the word meanings.

Exposure to unfamiliar words comes best through wide reading (Graves 2006). Additionally, students need a repertoire of strategic tools to understand new words, such as how to use context clues, how to analyze root words, and how to make schematic connections with synonyms. Solely using traditional vocabulary instruction is like telling your students to cook a meal without all of the ingredients. Memorizing words as a primary means of instruction is ineffective (Kame'enui, Dixon, and Carnine 1987; Cooper 2000; Ford-Connors and Paratore 2014).

By focusing on evidence-based strategies, CLR uses "all of the ingredients" to create effective vocabulary instruction that teaches students meaningful word-acquisition strategies. In CLR, the use of the strategies—particularly synonym development—supports validation and affirmation. Many students' home language words are not only conceptually based but they are also synonyms of the academic Tier Two words that they need for school success. When a student makes a connection between their home language and the target vocabulary, not only does this validate and affirm the child's home language but it also builds and bridges to Standard English and academic language. Imagine a student moving from their word (or phrase) "talks a lot" to *talkative* to *loquacious*. This learning can be achieved through use of the personal thesaurus, a special CLR tool for building vocabulary. The process for this tool is further described in chapter 7.

The focus on word-acquisition strategies for Tier Two words is conducive to validating and affirming. However, building and bridging for Tier Three words requires a different strategy. Since Tier Three words are largely content specific and low in frequency, there is less of an expectation that students will own these words in the same way as the Tier Two words. Therefore, these words can be taught through a more traditional approach, or squarely from the "build and bridge" aspect. Meaning, the vocabulary instruction can be more focused around the technical definitions of the words as compared to the conceptual understandings made with Tier Two words. Both tiers, though, emphasize the students making personal connections. The personal dictionary, another special CLR tool, is used to help students acquire Tier Three words. This tool is also explained in chapter 7.

In responsive vocabulary teaching, Tier Two words are the focus for strategy instruction. As mentioned above, Tier Three words are taught differently. This distinction in vocabulary instruction is an important aspect of college and career readiness standards for English language arts and literacy, as shown in figure 6.1.

Figure 6.1 Sample English Language Arts Standards for Grade 4

Determine or clarify the meaning of unknown and multiple-meaning words and phrases based on grade 4 reading and content, choosing flexibly from a range of strategies.

- Use context (e.g., definitions, examples, or restatements in text) as a clue to the meaning of a word or phrase.
- Use common, grade-appropriate Greek and Latin affixes and roots as clues to the meaning of a word (e.g., *telegraph*, *photograph*, *autograph*).
- Consult reference materials (e.g., dictionaries, glossaries, thesauruses), both print and digital, to find the pronunciation and determine or clarify the precise meaning of key words and phrases.

Demonstrate understanding of figurative language, word relationships, and nuances in word meanings.

- Explain the meaning of simple similes and metaphors (e.g., *pretty as a picture*) in context.
- Recognize and explain the meaning of common idioms, adages, and proverbs.
- Demonstrate understanding of words by relating them to their opposites (antonyms) and to words with similar but not identical meanings (synonyms).
- Acquire and use accurately grade-appropriate general and academic and domain-specific words and phrases, including those that signal precise actions, emotions, or states of being (e.g., *wildlife*, *conservation*, and *endangered* when discussing animal preservation).

Considering the Research

Research supports teaching students how to use morphology and context clues to determine meanings of academic vocabulary words. The following studies represent a sample of relevant research supporting the instruction of vocabulary strategies in a CLR classroom.

- Children are competent in recognizing and using inflections well before entering school (Clark 1993), and their ability to use inflections increases rather quickly (Alamirew 2022). They are capable of acquiring any language if exposed early enough (Alamirew 2022).
- Children acquire about 600 root word meanings per year from infancy to the end of elementary school (Biemiller and Slonim 2001).
- Middle school students learn between 1,500 and 8,000 words from context (Nagy, Anderson, and Herman 1987).
- Researchers focused on vocabulary as a predictor of literacy outcomes have concentrated on estimating the number of words students know (Amorsen and Miller 2017; Green 2021; Konza 2016).
- Students at higher grade levels and higher reading ability are better able to use context clues (İlter 2019; Swanborn and de Glopper 1999).

- Context learning of word meaning increases substantially with additional occurrences of the word (Graves 2006) and is more likely when these words are taught in a way that "positively supports vocabulary growth and the comprehension of texts" (İlter 2019, 3).

- Strong word learners in fifth grade show more understanding of morphological generalization than average word learners in eighth grade (Nagy, Diakidoy, and Anderson 1993).

- While research has shown that having more vocabulary is a great indicator of how much one understands what one reads, (Green 2021; Ilter 2019), students' understanding of morphology is a better predictor of reading comprehension than their vocabulary level (Kieffer and Lesaux 2007).

- Limited vocabulary knowledge is a potential source of reading comprehension difficulties, and of negative attitudes toward reading (Ilter 2018), especially among older struggling readers, whether English language learners or native English speakers (Biancarosa and Snow 2006; Chall and Jacobs 2003; İlter 2018, 2019; National Institute of Child Health and Human Development 2000; Stahl and Nagy 2006).

- Since vocabulary is so closely tied to reading comprehension, this means that the role of having an extensive vocabulary significantly impacts students' overall school achievement (İlter 2017).

Pre-Reading Assessment

Before reading this chapter, reflect upon how you teach word-acquisition strategies—use of context clues, analysis of word parts, and synonym development—to your students by completing the survey in figure 6.2. Think about the effectiveness and efficiency of your word-acquisition strategy instruction. If you are not teaching any word-acquisition strategies, think about ways you can start.

Figure 6.2 Learning Strategies, Not Words Survey: Before Infusing CLR Principles

0: *Never Emerging* 1: *Rarely Splashing* 2: *Sometimes Floating* 3: *Mostly Kicking* 4: *Always Freestyling*					
My students participate in some form of free voluntary reading.	0	1	2	3	4
I teach the use of context clues at least once every two weeks.	0	1	2	3	4
I expose my students to word parts for analysis as applicable.	0	1	2	3	4
I explicitly teach synonyms with Tier Two words.	0	1	2	3	4
I am able to build and bridge my students' use of slang to academic vocabulary when appropriate.	0	1	2	3	4
I provide six exposures to vocabulary words.	0	1	2	3	4

Beginning the Reflective Process

Learning happens when we reflect upon what we have experienced. Critical reflection generates, deepens, and documents learning (Ash and Clayton 2009). Are you ready to implement strategies for word acquisition?

Use the following checklist to gauge your readiness and ability to effectively implement word-acquisition strategies into your teaching. Each item represents an important aspect of understanding and using word-acquisition strategies in a CLR classroom. After completing the checklist, read the detailed descriptions of each item and reflect on how you plan to implement or increase your use of word-acquisition strategies in the classroom.

☑ **The Use of Word-Acquisition Strategies Reflection Checklist**		
Item 6.1	Do I know how to teach the word-acquisition strategies?	○ Yes ○ No
Item 6.2	Do I see the necessary connection between Tier Two words and validation and affirmation?	○ Yes ○ No
Item 6.3	Do I recognize that my students' use of slang provides an instructional opportunity for building and bridging to academic language?	○ Yes ○ No
Item 6.4	Do I provide plenty of practice with new vocabulary?	○ Yes ○ No

Item 6.1 Do I know how to teach the word-acquisition strategies?

The majority of the teachers I work with do not have a systematic way of teaching vocabulary. Thus, the notion of teaching research-based strategies can, depending on the teacher, be either off-putting or a welcomed opportunity. A notable difference exists between teaching words individually or in isolation and teaching students how to use word-acquisition strategies. Fortunately, many resources are available for teaching word-acquisition strategies, such as the use of context clues, analysis of root words, and synonym development. The purpose here is to show you how to connect those strategies to culturally responsive teaching. Nonetheless, here are some tips for working with the strategies (Graves 2006):

1. The teacher provides an explicit description of the word-acquisition strategy and when and how it should be used.

2. The teacher and students (or both individually) model the use of the strategy in action.

3. The teacher provides opportunities for students to collaboratively use the strategy in action.

4. The teacher provides guided practice using the strategy with gradual release of responsibility to students.

5. Students use the strategy independently.

Taken together, these tips follow the Gradual Release of Responsibility model, where the teacher reduces the amount of guidance and support offered, enabling students to achieve independence.

I recommend these sources to further your vocabulary teaching development:

◆ *Edutopia*, an online educational magazine with many articles, resources, and blog posts useful for teaching vocabulary (edutopia.org)

◆ *Building Vocabulary with Greek and Latin Roots: A Professional Guide to Word Knowledge and Vocabulary Development* by Timothy Rasinski, Nancy Padak, Rick M. Newton, and Evangeline Newton (2020)

◆ *The Vocabulary Playbook: Learning Words That Matter, K–12* by Douglas Fisher and Nancy Frey (2023)

◆ *A Teacher's Guide to Vocabulary Development Across the Day* by Tanya S. Wright and Katie Wood Ray (2023)

◆ *Teaching Words and How They Work: Small Changes for Big Vocabulary Results* by Elfrieda H. Hiebert (2023)

Four exercises at the end of the chapter provide practice with the word-acquisition strategies.

REFLECTIVE THOUGHT

Recall that CLR inherently challenges your pedagogy. In this specific case, the challenge is to make your vocabulary teaching stronger, which in one context is unrelated to CLR. Embrace these three key vocabulary strategies—use of context clues, analysis of word parts, and synonym development—as part of this larger context, if for no other reason than you will be a better teacher for it. In what ways do the CLR methods challenge your vocabulary teaching? What kinds of word-acquisition strategies do you routinely use with your students? Which one(s) would you like to incorporate?

Thought-Provokers: A Mindset for Moving Forward

1. I started with a one word-acquisition strategy and then have added others as I became more confident. I allow the selected words to determine the appropriate strategy and when it is appropriate to teach it.

2. I make it a point to really praise students when they make those schematic connections between their home language and the academic language of school.

Thought-Blockers: A Mindset for Staying Stagnant

1. I realize I need to increase my knowledge around vocabulary instruction but I do not have time to research that.

2. I allow the pacing targets for covering content material to justify not giving students opportunities for using word-acquisition strategies.

Item 6.2 Do I see the necessary connection between Tier Two words and validation and affirmation?

Your responsive vocabulary teaching boils down to establishing the connection between the meaning of Tier Two words and what students know and understand conceptually about those words. Teaching students word-acquisition strategies will have a lasting influence on their academic learning in writing, reading, and speaking. This is the crux of validating and affirming students and the home language each brings to school. When students make connections between the Tier Two words, or academic words, and their home vocabulary, you will see the proverbial light bulb go on.

Validation and affirmation establish the foundation to build and bridge students to the vocabulary of school. Making a schematic connection between the concepts of the Tier Two words and the words they own legitimizes what students know from home. Figure 6.3 provides examples of students making validating and affirming connections between home language and Tier Two words.

Figure 6.3 Validating and Affirming Connections Between Words

Home Language Words	Tier Two (Academic) Words
show-off	pretentious
brief	succinct
important	vital
fall	collapse

Graves (2006) notes that one aspect of word knowledge is *polysemy*, which refers to the fact that many words have multiple meanings. Along with its Standard English meaning(s), a word or phrase may have additional meaning(s) based on a home language. For example, in African American Vernacular English (AAVE), a term like *bad* remains constant in usage with an increasing number of evolving meanings. In AAVE, *bad* has essentially three uses. There is the bad *bad*, meaning "not good." There is the good or awesome *bad*, as in "That is a bad car you have there!" Lastly, there is the phrase "my bad," which is an offer of contrition. Culturally responsive teaching recognizes this linguistic dynamic and uses it as an opportunity to validate and affirm the home language while building and bridging to academic language.

REFLECTIVE THOUGHT

Improving your vocabulary instruction with CLR is essential. Teaching through a responsive lens will give your students a greater opportunity to increase their academic vocabularies.

Thought-Provokers: A Mindset for Moving Forward

1. I understand that focusing on Tier Two words or words that students already have conceptual understandings of is automatically validating and affirming.

2. I know that I am not abandoning Tier Three words. I am just going to deal with them differently.

 ## Thought-Blockers: A Mindset for Staying Stagnant

1. I believe that students are blank slates or that their home vocabularies lack value, which limits their connection to academic learning.

2. I see Tier Three words as yielding the most mileage for students' learning.

Item 6.3 Do I recognize that my students' use of slang provides an instructional opportunity for building and bridging to academic language?

A powerful aspect of validation and affirmation is when you connect with your students' language at times or places they least expect. The use of slang terms is one of these times. While the use of profanity and racially charged words provide additional opportunities for academic vocabulary expansion, I will just focus on slang in this book. First of all, the use of slang has to be looked at through a cultural lens, as opposed to a deficit lens.

The use of slang is a vocabulary rite of passage for many teenagers regardless of their racial, ethnic, or economic background. This language separates teenagers and young adults from older adults. Indeed, youth culture relates more to the use of slang than racial or ethnic identities (Hollie 2012; Bucholtz 2000; Reyes 2005). Through a cultural lens, slang can then be seen in a few ways:

- linguistic capital—it shows capacity to learn vocabulary
- language of the youth—it is temporal, dynamic, and peer-driven
- leisure speak—it is fun, colorful, descriptive, and rich

How, then, do you build and bridge from the use of slang at school? Treat the slang terms as chances for synonym development. In no way is this a suggestion that slang is appropriate vocabulary for academic writing or speaking. The objective is to bridge the slang terms and their conceptual meanings to the academic words through a process I call *academization*. *Academization* means you learn students' slang terms and their conceptual meanings. Next, you supply the conceptual academic terms that match the slang words. Last, you validate and affirm the slang word through the use of the personal thesaurus (page 189). Figure 6.4 shows an example of how an academization process may look.

Figure 6.4 Examples of the Academization Process

Slang Phrase	Meaning	Academic Terms
standing on business	no nonsense, getting down to business	focused
bussin'	amazing, really good	astounding, remarkable
living rent free	dominating someone's thoughts	consume, engross
sus	suspect	shady, suspect, suspicious

The key is to be open to learning the slang terms students are currently using. Given how rapidly words fall out of favor and new meanings and words appear to take their place, staying current lends credibility and authenticity. And doing so leads to the teacher empowerment aspect of CLR. Anything that connects teachers to students culturally and linguistically is empowering and significant.

REFLECTIVE THOUGHT

Are you aware of all the slang terms your students use in their daily interpersonal communications, such as on the playground and with their peers? How do you learn about the new slang terminology that becomes part of your students' vernacular?

 ## Thought-Provokers: A Mindset for Moving Forward

1. I am open to surveying my students to compare slang terms from "my day" with slang terms they use.

   Think of general categories, such as money, food, or friends.

2. When in doubt about examples, I do some research.

   There are several popular websites for looking up the most recent slang terminology. One excellent source is Urban Dictionary (urbandictionary.com), but be aware that the site contains sexually explicit and profane language. The Online Slang Dictionary (onlineslangdictionary.com) offers a similar service, but with a slightly more delicate touch, applying asterisks in place of key letters in vulgar words on main pages and documenting the level of vulgarity associated with each term. The words do remain unaltered on their actual definition pages, however, so this site may not be considered work safe.

 ## Thought-Blockers: A Mindset for Staying Stagnant

1. I view the use of slang at school as inappropriate.

2. I feel like I am too old to learn slang or go to where the students are culturally and linguistically.

Item 6.4 Do I provide plenty of practice with new vocabulary?

Practicing new words through review activities and games is very important. Simply going over words once or twice will not cut it. Multiple exposures to words make a significant difference in terms of learning the words and actually owning them (Nagy and Scott 2000). Providing varied and prolific reading opportunities, contextualization of words, knowledge of word parts, and synonyms all help students learn new vocabulary.

REFLECTIVE THOUGHT

Vocabulary teaching does not stop after six exposures. Take the time to plan accordingly with practice exercises and games. You do not need tons, just some in your toolbox to have variety.

Thought-Provokers: A Mindset for Moving Forward

1. I acknowledge that practice, practice, and more practice is part of any effective learning and eventual academic success.

2. I am careful not to overwhelm my students.

   Too much practice without enough substance can be detrimental. Sometimes students need authentic opportunities to use the words they are beginning to own. Having students write op-eds to the local newspaper or fan letters to their favorite actors or musical artists are examples of such opportunities.

Thought-Blockers: A Mindset for Staying Stagnant

1. I am deterred from focusing on vocabulary strategies by the amount of content I must cover. I question whether increased vocabulary instruction will give me leverage.

2. Teaching vocabulary in this way may challenge my pedagogy and therefore seems too difficult for me.

Understanding Assessment

Assessment is the final piece, so be sure to test, quiz, or use the cloze procedure (provide a passage of text with missing words) to see what students know. Students' ability to use vocabulary words in their academic writing and speaking is the ultimate test. The following are some guidelines for effective assessment:

- Assessments gauge what students have gathered meaning from, connected to, and learned.
- Assessments should be administered to measure background knowledge of a new concept based on multiple exposures.
- Vocabulary assessments are opportunities to develop Standard English skills for taking standardized tests.

- Multiple-choice tests are appropriate for practice in using context clues or word parts to determine meaning.

- Multiple-choice assessments do not adequately assess a student's deeper level of word knowledge.

- Providing students with choices helps them discriminate between appropriate and inappropriate usages.

Focusing on word-acquisition strategies is the heavy lifting of the responsive vocabulary approach. The more you incorporate word-acquisition strategies into your regular teaching, the more likely you are to validate, affirm, build, and bridge your students' language development. The next section of this chapter presents a collection of vocabulary strategies. The section includes a description of the strategy, the corresponding cultural behaviors, and directions for using the strategy.

Vocabulary Strategies

A TO Z ASSOCIATIONS

Validate and Affirm Cultural Behaviors: Sociocentrism, Cooperation/Collaboration, Spontaneity, Subjectivity, Communalism, Realness

Build and Bridge Behaviors: Academic Vocabulary (Tier Two words)

Description: Students work socially and collaboratively using word associations, examples, synonyms and antonyms to "own" high-utility/Tier Two words.

Process

1. Choose a word that has already been taught or introduced. Challenge students to come up with related words for as many of the letters of the alphabet as possible. These could be synonyms, antonyms, examples, and more.

2. Use an involuntary response protocol like Whip Around to hear what students came up with. Or use Stop and Scribble, where the lists stay on the desks and students move around adding to one another's lists each time the music stops.

CAROUSEL VOCABULARY

Validate and Affirm Cultural Behaviors: Cooperation/Collaboration, Kinesthetic, Sociocentrism, Subjectivity

Build and Bridge Behaviors: Autonomous, Academic Vocabulary (Tier Two words)

Description: Students collaborate to use words in writing and build off one another.

Process

1. Select six to eight vocabulary words. You can use more if you have large class sizes.

2. Prepare vocabulary charts—one for each word. At the top or in the center of each sheet of chart paper, write the word. Hang the chart paper in various places around the room.

3. Small groups rotate to the posters. At each poster, students collaborate to use the word in different ways. Encourage students to draft sentences that use each word with common collocates. Students write one or two sentences, and the next group adds to what is already there.

   - Group 1—After the marathon, I *guzzled* so much water that I felt bloated. My throat had felt as dry as the Sahara Desert.

   - Group 2—Why did I not *guzzle* milk, you might ask? Well, have you ever run a marathon? A gallon of milk doesn't sit as well in your belly as a gallon of water.

   - Group 3—Some people like to *guzzle* juice and coffee, but those individuals are generally eating breakfast, not running around the world.

   - Group 4—If you choose to *guzzle* soda while running, that is your business, but I'd strongly advise against it.

   - Group 5—Next time you decide to eat or drink greedily, I'd suggest *guzzling* some pizza and Kool-Aid while lounging by the pool. This marathon running is for the birds.

   - Group 6—Now, let's get in my gas-*guzzling* car and go home.

CLOZE ACTIVITY

Validate and Affirm Cultural Behaviors: Cooperation/Collaboration, Communalism, Sociocentrism

Build and Bridge Behaviors: Autonomous, Academic Vocabulary (Tier Two words)

Description: Students make connections between their home languages and the target academic vocabulary using synonym development and context clues. Students work individually and then collaboratively to guess the words.

Process

1. Choose a text selection and identify four to six Tier Two vocabulary words. Replace the words with writing lines.

2. First, students work individually to fill in words they think fit the text.

3. Use a discussion or movement protocol (e.g., Merry-Go-Round, Numbered Heads Together, or Find Someone Who…) to have students share the words they used with one another.

4. Use a response protocol (e.g., Shout Out or Roll 'Em) to hear what students guessed.

5. Reveal the target words and validate the synonyms students thought of.

COLLABORATIVE SENTENCES

Validate and Affirm Cultural Behaviors: Cooperation/Collaboration, Sociocentrism, Communalism, Subjectivity

Build and Bridge Behaviors: Academic Vocabulary (Tier Two and Tier Three words)

Description: Students generate words related to a specific topic or concept and then collaborate to use the words.

Process

1. Give each student an index card. Have students work in groups of four.

2. Share a topic or concept that students are studying.

3. Have each student write down one word related to the topic. (Encourage them to use Tier Two or Tier Three vocabulary if appropriate.)

4. Each person shares their word with their group and explains why they chose it.

5. Have each team create a sentence using the words from students in their group. They should add as few additional words as possible to make it a coherent sentence.

6. Have one student in each group share the group's sentence with the class.

COLLABORATIVE WORD SORT

Validate and Affirm Cultural Behaviors: Sociocentrism, Cooperation/Collaboration, Spontaneity, Subjectivity, Communalism

Build and Bridge Behaviors: Academic Vocabulary (Tier Two and Tier Three words)

Description: Students share what they already know about a word or concept and build background knowledge.

Process

1. Create sets of vocabulary words/concepts by writing each word on its own index card. Prepare one set for each pair of students or for small groups.

2. The groups sort the words into the categories defined by you (closed word sort), or into categories students determine (open word sort).

3. Use a response protocol to have groups report on how they sorted their words as you list them on the board.

Variation: If you feel it is needed, add the protocol Who's the Stray? to allow one member of each group to move to and hear how another group is sorting the words. After a short amount of time, the strays report back to their groups.

DUMP AND CLUMP

Validate and Affirm Cultural Behaviors: Cooperation/Collaboration, Communalism, Subjectivity

Build and Bridge Behaviors: Academic Vocabulary (Tier Two and Tier Three words)

Description: Students generate and classify words related to a topic of study.

Process

1. Put students in pairs or trios.

2. Pose a topic. (It could be the same topic for the whole class, or each group could have a different topic.) Students brainstorm every word they can think of related to that topic. (This is the "dump.")

3. Have students work together to classify the words into categories. After grouping the words, students give each group a label that indicates how the words are related.

4. Students then write a descriptive summary sentence for each category.

5. Have the students share their word groupings with the whole class.

GRAFFITI WORD WALLS

Validate and Affirm Cultural Behaviors: Pragmatic Language Use, Dynamic Attention Span, Subjectivity

Build and Bridge Behaviors: Autonomous, Academic Vocabulary (Tier Two and Tier Three words)

Description: Students make personal connections by using their own words to define or describe vocabulary words and creating images to represent the vocabulary words. Since there is no "right way" to depict the words, this validates subjectivity and also validates students who like to represent their ideas in pictures. Adding a protocol where students observe and comment on each other's pictures validates communalism.

Process

1. Provide students with sheets of unlined paper.

2. Students write the vocabulary word in bubble letters. Students then explain what the vocabulary word means using their own words.

3. Have students draw pictures to represent the word. Tell them to fill up their papers completely, leaving no empty space.

4. Display the papers to create a class Word Wall.

5. Consider following this with a Gallery Walk. Students walk around the room looking at other students' posters, noting what they like or what pictures help them remember a word.

6. Use a response protocol to have students share.

HILARIOUS ILLUSTRATION TIME (H.I.T.)

Validate and Affirm Cultural Behaviors: Subjectivity, Sociocentrism, Cooperation/Collaboration, Dynamic Attention Span, Realness

Build and Bridge Behaviors: Academic Vocabulary (Tier Two words)

Description: Students discuss words and their associations, which validates their subjective opinions.

Process

1. Choose a Tier Two word to target through this activity.

2. Display four to six dramatic or funny pictures that represent the target word (pictures that represent the word's shades of meaning). Number the pictures.

3. Students work in groups. They discuss the pictures, and each group decides which one best represents the target word and why.

4. Use the Roll 'Em protocol to have groups share their answers.

5. Groups try to convince the other groups that their picture represents the word the best. Provide a speaking frame for sharing out: *Our group decided that picture number ____ represents the target word the best due to ____.*

Variation: Assign students to find pictures for various target words, participating in the creation of the H.I.T.s.

INTERVIEW A WORD

Validate and Affirm Cultural Behaviors: Sociocentrism, Cooperation/Collaboration, Spontaneity, Subjectivity

Build and Bridge Behaviors: Academic Vocabulary (Tier Two and Tier Three words)

Description: Students develop a deeper understanding of a word by "becoming" the word.

Process

1. Select key words important to understanding a concept or unit and create a list of interview questions (e.g., *Where can you be found? What makes you stand out? What do you like? What do you dislike?*).

2. Place the class in teams of two to four students.

3. Give each team a word and the list of interview questions.

4. Have students "become" the word and write answers to questions.

5. Act as an interviewer and ask the questions (or have a student do so). Team members read their written answers. After the interview, the class guesses the word.

ODD WORD OUT

Validate and Affirm Cultural Behaviors: Cooperation/Collaboration, Communalism, Sociocentrism, Subjectivity

Build and Bridge Behaviors: Academic Vocabulary (Tier Two or Tier Three words)

Description: Students discuss similarities and differences between word meanings to determine which word doesn't belong in the group.

Process

1. Create sets of words on a slideshow or on a group of cards. Each card set or slide has four words that all have some connection, but one word doesn't belong. This could be because of the meaning, the part of speech, content connections, and so on.

2. Have students work collaboratively in groups, discussing similarities and differences they see in the words and trying to identify the word that doesn't belong in each set. Students may come up with a word other than the one you planned and may have a good reason for their choice (subjectivity).

3. Use a response protocol such as Shout Out or Roll 'Em to hear what the groups decided and why.

Use these scenarios and exercises to assist you in processing, practicing, and applying the concepts from the chapter.

Using Context Clues to Define Vocabulary Terms

Choose a few Tier Two vocabulary words. Teach students to identify two types of context clues to use in determining the meaning of an unknown vocabulary word. See figure 6.5 for an example.

Figure 6.5 Example of Using Context Clues with Tier Two Vocabulary Words

Type of Context Clue	Sentence Example	Description
Definitions	When he referred to the foliage in the painting, he meant the cluster of dark green leaves along the bottom portion of the scene.	The author provides a direct definition of an unfamiliar word right in the sentence. **Signal words:** is, are, means, refers to
Synonym	She found him in a deep state of repose. He looked like he was asleep, and his face held a tranquil, dreamy expression.	The author uses another word or phrase that is similar in meaning to or can be compared to an unfamiliar word. **Signal words:** also, as, identical, like, likewise, resembling, similarly, too

Follow these guidelines for teaching the use of context clues.

1. Teach students the meanings of two types of helpful context clues.
2. Teach students how to identify the signal words that can accompany these types of context clues.
3. Have students decipher the meanings of targeted vocabulary words using the context clues provided.
4. Have students construct sentences (oral and written) that demonstrate their understanding of the targeted vocabulary terms.
5. Have students work together throughout this process using discussion protocols (see chapter 2).

Classroom Applications

Think about your own classroom and teaching practices. Use the following prompts to reflect on how you have used word-acquisition strategies in the past and the types of changes you would like to make in your classroom.

1. In the past, what did your students do when they encountered an unfamiliar word? Were these strategies effective for helping them gain a conceptual understanding of the word?

_____

_____

2. Think about how you can teach your students to use context clues to determine word meaning. Aside from traditional textbooks, what other types of texts might be good resources for practicing this word-acquisition strategy?

_____

_____

Sample Lesson—Using Context Clues to Determine Word Meaning

The following lesson provides an example of how to teach students to use context clues to determine the meanings of unfamiliar words.

Procedure

1. Tell the class, "Sometimes the text itself provides clues to the meaning of a word right there. This is called a context clue. We can use context clues to help us determine the definitions of unfamiliar words when we are reading."

2. Write the word "definition" on the board and below it, write an example of a sentence that provides the definition of a word within it, such as "When we recycle, we use an item again."

3. Read the sentence aloud. Ask, "What does the word *recycle* mean? How do you know?" Underline the portion of the sentence that contains the definition of the word *recycle* and discuss how you can use this context clue to determine the meaning of the word.

4. Write the word "synonym" on the board and say, "A synonym is a word that means the same thing as another word. *Joyful* is a synonym for happy, and *wealthy* is a synonym for rich." Underneath the word "synonym," write a sentence that uses a synonym to help the reader understand the meaning of a word, such as "He was overcome by a feeling of remorse, or shame, when recalling his actions." Read the sentence aloud to the class. Discuss how the sentence uses a synonym, shame, to define the word *remorse*.

5. Write several examples of sentences that use definition or synonym context clues on sentence strips. Distribute them to students using the Pick-a-Stick response protocol. One at a time, have these students come to the front of the room, place their sentence strips under either the "definition" or "synonym" heading, and explain their reasoning about the type of context clue.

6. Read each sentence aloud and discuss the context clue used in the sentence.

7. Provide each student with a copy of an activity sheet containing twelve context clue sentences. Each sentence should have a bolded vocabulary word. Put students into small groups. Use the Think-Pair-Share discussion protocol to have the students work together to classify each sentence as containing either a definition or synonym context clue. Then have students provide a definition for the bolded word based on the context clue. Have students analyze the first four sentences together in their small groups, then assign each student a partner and have the pairs work to complete the next four sentences. Finally, have students complete the last four sentences independently.

8. Discuss the answers as a class and review the importance of using context clues to determine word meaning.

Using Movement and Discussion Activities for Vocabulary Review

After introducing vocabulary terms, incorporate an activity designed to help students practice. Musical Shares works well here. Use a non-explicit or instrumental version of a song that resonates with students. Students use context clues to determine the meaning of an unknown word. They use the discussion protocol in three ways: to share what they think the word means, to explain the context clues they used to determine this meaning, and to share any other synonyms for the targeted vocabulary word.

Classroom Applications

Think about your own classroom and teaching practices. Use the following prompts to reflect on how you have used word-acquisition strategies in the past and the types of changes you would like to make in your classroom.

1. What discussion protocols work well with your students? How could you use these protocols to practice and review vocabulary?

    _____

    _____

2. Think about your daily schedule. If you do not already do so, how can you incorporate vocabulary practice and review into your instruction on a frequent basis?

    _____

    _____

Sample Lesson—Using Movement and Discussion in Vocabulary Instruction

The following lesson describes how to use the Musical Shares activity to facilitate discussion and review previously taught vocabulary words.

Procedure

1. Before beginning the lesson, write a series of sentences that use context clues to provide meaning for the target vocabulary words. Put the vocabulary words in bold so they are easily identifiable. You will display these on the board, one at a time, for the class.

2. Review with students how to use context clues to determine word meaning. Write two examples on the board and discuss how it is possible to use the context clue in each one to understand the meaning of the vocabulary word. For example:

    ◆ The rain poured down. The steady stream of rain made it hard to see the house across the street.

    ◆ Let's split, or evenly divide, the sandwich.

3. Say, "Now we are going to use the Musical Shares activity to practice using context clues to determine the meaning of our new vocabulary words. I am going to turn music on, and I would like you to move around the classroom until you hear the music stop. When you hear

the music stop, find a partner by turning to the person closest to you and look to the front of the classroom. I am going to display a sentence that contains one of our vocabulary words. Read the sentence aloud with your partner and then discuss three things: the definition of the word in bold, the context clue you used to determine the meaning of this word, and other words, or synonyms, that mean the same thing as the bold word. When you hear the music start to play again, resume moving around the classroom."

4. Display an example sentence and think aloud as you demonstrate how to talk about it, for instance: "We saw many different types of birds in the *aviary*, or bird enclosure, at the park." Say, "The first thing I would discuss with my partner would be the meaning of the word *aviary*. After talking about how an aviary is a place that contains birds, we would discuss how this sentence contains an example of a context clue that provides the definition of the word directly in the sentence. Finally, I would work with my partner to think of other words that mean the same thing as aviary, such as 'a large bird cage.'"

5. Turn on the music for about thirty seconds and monitor students as they move around the classroom. Pause the music and display one of the sentences on the board. Give students one to two minutes to discuss the sentence before starting the music again. Repeat this process until students have discussed all of the vocabulary words.

6. As a class, review the meaning of each vocabulary word and summarize the ways in which the students were able to use context clues to help determine the meanings of these words.

Incorporating Games into Word Part Review

A game is an engaging way for students to practice and review word parts. As students learn to use word parts to determine the meanings of unfamiliar words, they can use games to practice applying this new strategy. While the traditional Jeopardy game is played individually, you can have students play as individuals or in groups. To play this game, the teacher provides clues for words that fall into one of the categories (prefix, suffix, or root) and the students try to guess the vocabulary word that uses the targeted word part. Figure 6.6 offers several examples of word clues and the following sample lesson illustrates how to incorporate this type of game into a lesson plan.

Figure 6.6 Jeopardy Sample

Prefix *pre–* (before)	Root Word *geo–* (earth)	Suffix *–able* (capable of)
A word that means to see something before someone else (*preview*)	A word meaning the study of Earth's physical features (*geography*)	A word for something that cannot be moved (*immovable*)
A word that means to say that something is going to happen before it does (*predict*)	A word for the mathematical study of lines, points, places, and figures (*geometry*)	A word for something you can throw away or get rid of (*disposable*)
A word that means to give permission in advance (*preapprove*)	A word describing the study of Earth's composition, including rocks and soil (*geology*)	A word describing a performance or behavior that is flawless and without fault (*impeccable*)

Classroom Applications

Think about your own classroom and teaching practices. Use the following prompts to reflect on how you have used word-acquisition strategies in the past and the types of changes you would like to make in your classroom.

1. Think about the specific students in your class. Are there examples of prefixes, suffixes and/or root words from their home languages that you could use to help them relate to the concept of etymology?

   _____

   _____

2. In addition to Jeopardy, what other games or game show formats could you use to practice and review vocabulary with your students?

   _____

   _____

Sample Lesson—Jeopardy Word Part Review

The following lesson describes how to use the Jeopardy game show format to help students practice identifying and using words parts to determine the meaning of unfamiliar vocabulary words.

Procedure

1. Before beginning the lesson, prepare a set of word clues based on prefixes, suffixes, and root words in the target vocabulary words.

2. Arrange a table or row of desks with four to six chairs facing the rest of the class. This will be the game show "stage."

3. Decide on a strategy for choosing which students will come up to the front. You can use a response strategy, such as Pick-a-Stick, or go in alphabetical order. Everyone will have a chance to participate.

4. Call the first four to six students, or contestants, to the front of the room and have them sit on the stage facing the rest of the class. Say, "I am going to read a clue for one of our vocabulary words. As soon as you think you know the answer, raise your hand. I will call on you in the order that you raise your hands. If you get the answer wrong, I will call on the next person. After someone guesses the correct answer, we'll discuss it as a class and then I will call the next four to six students to the front of the room."

5. Read the first word clue aloud, such as "a word whose roots mean 'across' and 'to send.'" Call on the first student who raises their hand. When a student guesses the correct answer (*transmit*), write the word on the board and discuss how the Latin root *trans* means "across" and the Latin root *mit* means "to send," so together they mean "to send across." Ask students to use the word *transmit* in a sentence and discuss how the definition "to send across" works in the sentence.

6. Have the first group of students return to their seats and call up the next set. Continue playing the game until all students have had a chance to play at least one round and you have reviewed all of the vocabulary words.

Synonym Review: Shades of Meaning

Any given word usually has a variety of synonyms, and while synonyms have the same general definitions, they almost always have subtle differences in meaning. In this activity, students work collaboratively to identify synonyms for target vocabulary words and then explore the nuances between the words by arranging the synonyms according to their shades of meaning. For example, by putting the words *afraid*, *scared*, and *terrified* in that order, the students demonstrate an understanding of the intensity implied by each word. By studying synonyms and the nuances of their meanings, students gain a more exact understanding of the vocabulary words while also making connections to words with similar meanings.

Classroom Applications

Think about your own classroom and teaching practices. Use the following prompts to reflect on how you have used word-acquisition strategies in the past and the types of changes you would like to make in your classroom.

1. How do your students already use synonyms in their daily speech? What examples can you draw from their home languages to illustrate shades of meaning?

   _____

   _____

2. What type of discussion protocols might be useful in this exercise? How does this activity allow you to build and bridge?

   _____

   _____

Sample Lesson—Synonyms and Shades of Meaning

The following lesson describes how to incorporate the study of synonyms and shades of meaning into vocabulary instruction.

Procedure

1. Select one word from your vocabulary list, write it on the board, and then list two to three synonyms for that word below it. Read the words aloud. For example, if the Tier Two vocabulary word is *imperative*, you could list the synonyms *necessary*, *vital*, *important*, and *crucial*.

2. Ask a student volunteer to explain how the synonyms relate to the target vocabulary word.

3. Have students work with desk partners to arrange the synonyms in order according to their shades of meaning. As a class, review how the words *necessary* and *important* are less intense

and signify less urgency than the words *imperative*, *crucial*, and *vital*. Have several pairs of students share how they arranged the words. Discuss how there can be variations to the order because some words, like *imperative* and *crucial*, convey a similar intensity of meaning.

4. Place the students into four to six groups (one group for each remaining vocabulary word). Give each group a sheet of chart paper with the vocabulary word written at the top.

5. Discuss resources the students can use to identify synonyms for their assigned words, such as using word walls, thesauruses (digital or print), or any other classroom resources that could help them locate synonyms.

6. Say, "You'll have five minutes to work together to find synonyms for the vocabulary word and write them at the top of your chart paper. Choose one person from your group to be the recorder. When I use the Call and Response signal 'Bring it back now,' you respond, 'I'll show you how.' That is the signal for you to stop looking for synonyms and start discussing the shades of meaning for the words listed on the chart paper. Then, I will use the signal again to let you know that it is time for you to start working with your group to put the synonyms in order. Once you agree on an order, have the recorder write it at the bottom of the chart paper."

7. After the allotted time, use the Call and Response signal to get the students' attention and have them return to their seats. Display the chart papers at the front of the room.

8. One at a time, have the groups come to the front of the room and explain their work. Assign each student in the group a number 1–6, then use the Roll 'Em response protocol to select different students to read the synonyms, explain the shades of meaning, and describe how they ordered the words. After each group is finished presenting, ask the rest of the class if they can think of any other synonyms for the target vocabulary words. Add these words to the chart papers.

9. If possible, keep the chart papers on display throughout the unit of study so students can continue to familiarize themselves with the vocabulary words and their synonyms.

Using Synonyms

Often a single word can be used in a variety of contexts. To help students bridge and begin to use more precise words (when appropriate or desired), conduct discussion activities where students do the following:

◆ Match a word to a context.

◆ Generate Tier Two synonyms to express the concepts in more academic or descriptive ways.

Classroom Applications

Think about your own classroom and teaching practices. Use the following prompts to reflect on how you have used word-acquisition strategies in the past and the types of changes you would like to make in your classroom.

1. Think about times when your students use terms from their home languages in the classroom. How can you use synonyms for those terms as "teachable moments" to help students bridge between home and academic language?

_____

_____

2. Brainstorm scenarios where it is important for students to be able to use academic vocabulary in their speech and writing. Describe different ways to integrate these scenarios into your instruction to help students understand contexts that require the use of academic language, such as a job interview.

_____

_____

Sample Lesson—Matching Words to Contexts

The following lesson provides an example of how to teach students to use the nuances in word meaning to select the appropriate context for specific words.

Procedure

1. Before beginning the lesson, create an activity sheet with cloze sentences based on three of the target vocabulary words. Write sentences for each word as well as for several synonyms for each word. For example, if the target word is *quandary*, and the synonyms are *predicament*, *plight*, and *situation*, you could use the following sentences:

   ◆ It was a confusing _____; he didn't know which direction to turn. (situation)
   ◆ The conservation group spoke about the _____ of the endangered owls. (plight)
   ◆ The president found himself in quite a _____ after he unknowingly insulted the visiting prime minister. (predicament)
   ◆ I have a moral _____; I know it is right to tell the truth, but I will get in trouble with my boss if I do. (quandary)

2. Review the meanings of the vocabulary words and synonyms with the class. Discuss the subtle differences in meaning for each synonym.

3. Distribute a copy of the activity sheet to each student. Say, "We are going to use the Think-Pair-Share discussion protocol to complete this activity sheet on using context to match words."

4. Allow students time to complete the activity sheet independently. Remind them to use the context clues in each sentence to try to determine which synonym works best in that specific context.

5. Tell students, "When you hear me say 'Macaroni and cheese,' you respond, 'Everybody freeze' and give me your full attention with eyes on me, quiet mouths, still bodies, and listening ears. When I have everyone's attention, we will partner up. You can work with your partner to discuss your answers and reasoning. After five minutes, I will use the 'Macaroni and cheese' attention signal again. Stop working and give me your full attention."

6. Explain to students that for the last stage of the activity, they will be assigned to a larger group. Say, "Discuss the sentences on the activity sheet in your larger groups until you agree on which words to use in which sentences. At the end, I will ask one representative from each group to share their answers with the rest of the class."

7. Allow students to work independently for several minutes to use the context clues to match each synonym with the correct sentence. Use the attention signal to get students' attention and have them turn to their table partners and discuss their work. Then use the attention signal again. Assign each pair of students to a larger group and have the groups discuss their answers until they reach agreement.

8. Ask each group to designate one person to represent the group to the class. Have each representative present their group's answers for one set of synonyms. Ask the other groups if they agree with the answers. Discuss any disagreements or inconsistencies.

9. Review how the context of each sentence determined which word was the best fit based on subtle differences of meaning between the various synonyms.

Post-Reading Assessment

Now it is your turn to start "swimming" with word-acquisition strategies. Start today. As you plan your next lesson, think about how you will incorporate the strategies. Be intentional and strategic. As always, allow yourself the time and space to fail, to make mistakes, and to be uncomfortable. After two weeks of using word-acquisition strategies and implementing CLR, come back to this chapter and complete the survey (figure 6.7).

Figure 6.7 Learning Strategies, Not Words Survey: After Infusing the CLR Principles

0: *Never Emerging* 1: *Rarely Splashing* 2: *Sometimes Floating* 3: *Mostly Kicking* 4: *Always Freestyling*					
My students participate in some form of free voluntary reading.	0	1	2	3	4
I teach the use of context clues at least once every two weeks.	0	1	2	3	4
I expose my students to word parts for analysis as applicable.	0	1	2	3	4
I explicitly teach synonyms with Tier Two words.	0	1	2	3	4
I am able to build and bridge my students' use of slang to academic vocabulary when appropriate.	0	1	2	3	4
I provide six exposures to vocabulary words.	0	1	2	3	4

Strategies for Culturally and Linguistically Responsive Teaching and Learning—152468

STUDENT VOICE

Allowing Your Students to Be Engaged in Their Own Way, or "BeYou": Cooperation/Collaboration

BeYou is a call to action, reminding teachers to adjust instruction and classroom practices, ensuring that students can be themselves at school culturally and linguistically. In this section, we consider how students might express the importance of being given opportunities for collaboration at school.

How can collaboration be culturally misunderstood in the classroom? My favorite classes are the ones where my teachers understand what collaboration is and what it's not. Collaboration is all about working together with others to solve a problem or complete a task. Collaboration helps us and gives us lots of opportunities to work together. In school, we are asked or expected to work alone a lot, or sometimes even competitively. I enjoy a good competition, don't get me wrong! I also know there are times I have to get my work done alone. It's just that sometimes my preference to work with others on things we do in school can be seen as not knowing what I'm doing, or not wanting to work. It's the opposite. It's not that I can't or don't want to do it on my own. I just know I am going to be at my best when I can work with others.

How does it feel to be misunderstood? In some classrooms, working independently is seen as more valuable or more important because there is this belief that I have to do it alone to prove I know something or am capable of finishing my work. I know that is important sometimes, but collaboration teaches us important skills like communication, teamwork, and problem-solving. These are skills we'll use not just in school but also in our future. Collaborating in class isn't just about getting work done—it's about shared responsibility and learning to work together as a team.

What do I need to be myself? Collaborating in class is so important to me because it helps me learn. It's like having a support system where we can bounce ideas off each other, help each other out, and share the workload. I am validated when I can work together with classmates and get to hear different ideas and perspectives, which can help me understand the topic better. I am affirmed when collaboration is seen as a valid cultural behavior and we are given chances to share our own thoughts and contribute to something bigger than just what we know individually.

What CLR activities validate and affirm collaboration? Turn and Talk and Silent Appointment are great activities to use to get students talking to each other. Post Your Thoughts and Team-Pair-Solo not only get them talking but also give them time to gather their thoughts and bring them to the group. This means they work both independently and collaboratively. To level students up, mix in writing and movement with Carousel Brainstorm. These activities make learning more fun and engaging.

Build CLR Community and Collaboration

For this community check-in with your colleagues, divide up into pairs. Take turns answering the following questions:

1. How are you generally feeling about your CLR-ness?
2. What do you most appreciate about validating and affirming your students?
3. What is your biggest struggle in CLR right now?
4. How can our group be more supportive?

CHAPTER 7

Tools for Success: Accurate Use of the Personal Thesaurus and Personal Dictionary

This chapter provides a step-by-step guide to using two resources for the CLR vocabulary approach—the personal thesaurus and the personal dictionary. These resources are basic graphic organizers used for very specific purposes: to validate and affirm and to build and bridge. Background information, key steps, and the graphic organizer for each will be presented.

Personal Thesaurus Background

The personal thesaurus concept is rooted in Dr. Mary Montle Bacon's work during the 1990s. Dr. Bacon reminded educators that students do not come to us as blank slates. This graphic organizer was first used in the Academic English Mastery Program at Los Angeles Unified School District, and it was fully developed at the Culture and Language Academy of Success to help students build knowledge of synonyms and antonyms.

Students connect words they own conceptually as a result of their experiences at home and in the community to the concept of the target vocabulary word. Through this process, the student develops a host of synonyms for the target word and builds schematic connections. This enables the teacher to validate and affirm, and build and bridge. The personal thesaurus is a powerful and popular tool for not only reading but for writing and speaking in academic situations. It is meant to be used for Tier Two words, slang terminology, and other like terms.

Key Steps

Students create the personal thesaurus after you have selected Tier Two words (chapter 5) and taught word-acquisition strategies such as using context clues or analyzing word parts (chapter 6). Students develop a list of their own words to enter into the personal thesaurus. The steps for creating the personal thesaurus are as follows:

1. Students brainstorm synonyms for the target word, using words they own from their own vocabulary bank, indicating that they understand a concept. (The words do not have to have the exact meaning.) For example, for *normal*, the synonyms might be *usual*, *standard*, and *ordinary*.
2. Students make a list of synonyms for the target word.
3. Students place and highlight one of their owned words (from the synonyms generated in step 2) at the top of the chart. For example, *usual*.
4. Students write the target word on the line beneath the owned word.
5. Students add other academic (Tier Two) synonyms on the following lines.

6. An antonym (academic, owned, or both) goes in the last box, below the dashed line.

7. Students use their personal thesaurus during writing and speaking activities.

Figure 7.1 shows three example entries of a completed personal thesaurus.

Figure 7.1 Example of a Personal Thesaurus

usual	accept	important
normal standard ordinary	condone allow disregard	significant momentous compelling
abnormal	forbid	trivial

Developing a personal thesaurus occurs over time as students engage in a range of instructional activities. Figure 7.2 shows a week's lessons centered on developing vocabulary using the personal thesaurus.

Figure 7.2 Sample Lesson Plan for the Personal Thesaurus

Day 1	1. Conduct an interactive read-aloud of the selected text, *Stellaluna* by Janell Cannon. During the read, stop periodically to ask students questions about how the characters felt and acted in the story. 2. Engage students in instructional conversations to draw conclusions and create a list of adjectives pertaining to the main characters. For example, ask students to suggest words to describe the feelings and actions of Stellaluna, Mother Bat, Pip, Flitter, and Flap. 3. Record the words on the board and invite students to note the adjectives generated in their discussions on their own graphic organizers. 4. Collect students' graphic organizers and create a word bank of the Tier One adjectives that frequently reoccur.
Day 2	1. Display the word bank of the adjectives students used to describe the characters' feelings and actions on Day 1. 2. Ask students to think about the specific evidence in the text that helped them understand the characters in the story. Read the text again, stopping to discuss the sections that describe the characters' feelings and actions. 3. As the students discuss the text, guide them to notice specific Tier Two words that help them understand the characters. For example, the use of the word "trembling" (Tier Two) to describe Stellaluna at the beginning of the story shows that she felt scared (Tier One). Other Tier Two words from the text that you might choose to use include *anxious, startled,* and *peculiar.* Draw connections between these words and the adjectives students listed on Day 1. 4. Have students use the personal thesaurus to generate additional academic vocabulary words to describe the characters. 5. Thinking aloud, demonstrate how to choose a Tier Two synonym for a word in the Day 1 word bank.

Day 3	1. Encourage students to share their Tier Two vocabulary words.
	2. Have students use their Tier Two vocabulary words to engage in instructional conversations about the story's main characters.
	3. Have students begin writing about the main characters, using their new vocabulary words if possible.
Day 4	1. Provide time for students to move through the stages of the writing process (drafting, revising, and editing).
	2. During the revision step, review students' use of Tier Two vocabulary words in their writing. Check to make sure that they are using the words appropriately and encourage them to add additional vocabulary words wherever possible.
	3. Students can use discussion protocols (chapter 2) to share their work in small groups— giving and receiving constructive feedback based on classroom-generated rubrics.
Day 5	Have students publish their writing and share it with the whole group or in small groups.

Personal Dictionary Background

The personal dictionary is intended for use in content areas such as mathematics, science, and social studies. Vocabulary instruction in these subjects focuses on Tier Three words, which students rarely encounter in speech or print and for which they would have difficulty generating synonyms. The personal dictionary is a tool based on the Frayer Model. The Frayer Model is a strategy that helps students visualize vocabulary using a graphic organizer (Frayer, Frederick, and Klausmeier 1969).

Blachowicz and Fisher (2015) identify seven possibilities for using the Frayer Model to develop students' understanding of technical vocabulary. The model can be used to:

1. define a new concept, discriminating the relevant attributes
2. discriminate the relevant from the irrelevant
3. provide an example
4. provide a non-example
5. relate the concept to a subordinate concept
6. relate the concept to a superordinate concept
7. relate the concept to a coordinate term

The model in its purest form can be very complex and elaborate. In CLR, teachers have simplified it to a four-square, six-square, or eight-square graphic. The teacher selects the categories, changing them as needed for the subject area. Remember that the personal dictionary is for Tier Three words only. Recall that Tier Three words are mainly content specific with low frequency. Students will probably not have their own concepts for these words. Instead (unlike for the personal thesaurus), a technical definition is supplied. The personal dictionary is meant to be cumulative and is recommended for each subject area.

Key Steps

Students use a personal dictionary after building concept knowledge through direct instruction. The following are directions for using the personal dictionary.

1. In the first square, students record the Tier Three vocabulary term and the technical definition, as provided by the teacher or a (text) source.

2. Students describe their personal connection(s) in another square. Teachers can supply students with personal connection starters, such as *It is a thing that...*; *It was a time when...*; *It is a place where....*

3. Students add a personal illustration of the term in another square. (These illustrations can be either associated with their personal connection or a literal illustration of the term itself.)

4. Students add, revise, and edit their personal definitions as they continue to build their knowledge of the term.

Samples of personal dictionaries for English language arts, math, science, and history/social studies follow in figures 7.3, 7.4, 7.5, and 7.6, respectively. The organizers include four parts: an academic term and its technical definition, a personal illustration of the term, a statement of personal connection to the term, and a personal definition of the term. Some teachers have students use index cards, color-coded by subject. Other teachers have students make slides using presentation software, or have students use spreadsheet software.

Figure 7.3 Personal Dictionary English Language Arts Example

Academic Term: erudite	My Personal Illustration:
Erudite means having or showing great knowledge or learning.	
My Personal Connection:	My Personal Definition:
My erudite math teacher was able to answer every question I asked. It's like he's a college professor.	Erudite means someone who knows a lot of things because they study a lot. They are really smart.

Figure 7.4 Personal Dictionary Math Example

Academic Term: Congruent	My Personal Illustration:
Congruent is a word that describes figures or angles that have the same size and same shape.	
My Personal Connection:	My Personal Definition:
I had to use measurement tools to make sure that I drew congruent triangles.	Congruent means two shapes that are exactly the same size and shape. They match perfectly if you put one on top of the other, like two puzzle pieces that fit together just right.

Figure 7.5 Personal Dictionary Science Example

Academic Term: Metamorphosis	My Personal Illustration:
Metamorphosis means the physical changes some animals undergo as they transform from an immature stage to an adult stage.	
My Personal Connection:	**My Personal Definition:**
In science class, we watched a video that showed a frog develop from an egg, to a tadpole, and then to an adult through metamorphosis.	Metamorphosis is when something changes into something completely different.

Figure 7.6 Personal Dictionary History/Social Studies Example

Academic Term: Federal	My Personal Illustration:
Federal means national.	
My Personal Connection:	**My Personal Definition:**
The federal government of the United States of America is run from Washington, DC.	Federal means the part of the government that is in charge of the whole country.

Classroom Applications

Think about your own classroom and teaching practices. Use the following prompts to reflect on how you can incorporate word-acquisition strategies into your classroom instruction.

1. Reflect on your past methods for teaching academic vocabulary to your students. How do these CLR methods differ from your past practices? How are they the same?

   _____

   _____

2. Think about the resources available to your students. What will be the most practical way for them to create and maintain personal thesauruses and personal dictionaries?

   _____

   _____

3. Consider your long-term and immediate (weekly and daily) instructional planning processes. How can you include the use of personal thesauruses and personal dictionaries in your planning and instruction?

   _____

   _____

4. Remember that personal thesauruses are for Tier Two words and personal dictionaries are for Tier Three words. What resources do you plan to use to identify and select these two different types of words for your instruction?

_____

_____

5. Once you have implemented the use of personal thesauruses and personal dictionaries in your classroom for learning new academic vocabulary words, how can you integrate these tools into other aspects of your instruction?

_____

_____

Concluding Thoughts

The personal thesaurus and the personal dictionary are tools. They do not replace instruction but are meant to complement it. Maintaining the thesaurus and dictionary can become an issue for students over time, which is why I highly recommend using technology if it is readily available for all students (i.e., 1:1 classrooms). Students tend to lose paper versions, or they become tattered after frequent use. Lastly, remember that the personal thesaurus is for Tier Two words and the personal dictionary is for Tier Three words.

STUDENT VOICE

Allowing Your Students to Be Engaged in Their Own Way, or "BeYou": Immediacy

BeYou is a call to action, reminding teachers to adjust instruction and classroom practices, ensuring that students can be themselves at school culturally and linguistically. Here we consider how students might express the importance of being validated and affirmed when demonstrating a preference for immediacy.

How can immediacy be culturally misunderstood in the classroom? Have you ever had a student who asks to hang out in your room during their free times, or who regularly seeks your attention during class, needing a response immediately? That's me. To learn at my best, I need to feel a connection with my teachers, and I seek that out. I need regular, in-the-moment interactions with you, like when you stand by me, give me a smile, or ask about things in my life outside of school. It's not just about feeling good—it actually helps me learn better. It makes me feel like I'm important to you, and it can also help me feel less anxious or stressed, which sometimes gets in the way of my learning. I also ask questions about why we are learning something and how it connects to me. These interactions help me feel connected to you and to the class. It can feel like I am being demanding, but really, I'm just trying to feel that positive connection with you that helps me learn and feel supported.

How does it feel to be misunderstood? I know teachers have a lot of students, and sometimes my need to connect *right now* can be challenging because you have so much going on. The thing is, I am not doing it just to get attention and I don't want to intentionally take too much of your time. I actually need that interaction. It's very important to me. Even things like a quick check-in before class or a nod and smile mean so much to me. My sense of urgency is about that feeling of warmth and connection, and sometimes waiting creates stress for me. I can practice waiting because that nod or check-in reminds me that you are there for me.

What do I need to be myself? I feel validated when my sense of urgency and need for connection are recognized as valid cultural behavior. I am affirmed when I can sense a positive connection, both in tangible and intangible ways. In order to be engaged in my own unique way, I may need a response in the moment sometimes, but I promise I am practicing waiting, especially when I know you get it, and we can work on it together. I also thrive when we can check in, even with just a look or being closer in proximity. A nonverbal signal that you see me and will get to me when you can means so much to me!

> **What CLR activities validate and affirm immediacy?** Circle the Sage, Yesterday's Headlines, and Snowballs all validate students' sense of immediacy. They encourage conversation and connection and help students learn in relational ways. Other ways to validate and affirm immediacy include greeting students at the door, walking around the room and interacting with them, laughing with them, getting to know them personally, and creating a positive environment that feels warm and inviting.

Build CLR Community and Collaboration

Create personal dictionary cards for three cultural behaviors. Share your cards with your colleagues. Then share them with your students. Have your students do their own.

Academic Term:	My Personal Illustration:
My Personal Connection:	My Personal Definition:

Academic Term:	My Personal Illustration:
My Personal Connection:	My Personal Definition:

Academic Term:	My Personal Illustration:
My Personal Connection:	My Personal Definition:

Culturally and Linguistically Responsive Literacy

Culturally and Linguistically Responsive Literacy Overview

An essential determinant of a student's academic success is the ability to read and write proficiently in English and academic language. Having strong literacy skills—reading, writing, listening, and speaking—is *the* gatekeeper to success in almost all content areas. Students who are proficient and advanced in reading and writing also tend to be in the accelerated mathematics courses. But we know that is not the case for all students. The discouraging statistics around reading achievement that we have become accustomed to in our schools tell the other half of the story. Not only are many underserved students doing poorly in reading, but teachers also know that they are doing just as badly in mathematics and other subject areas.

Consider the National Assessment of Education Progress (NAEP), "the nation's report card," which showed that not even half (43 percent) of fourth graders in the U.S. scored at or above a proficient level in reading. And for marginalized students, the numbers are much worse: just 17 percent of Black students, 21 percent of Latino students, 11 percent of students with disabilities, and 10 percent of multilingual learners can read proficiently by fourth grade (U.S. Department of Education 2022).

Being academically literate makes all the difference. Even so, the main challenge is getting all educators to accept that it is everyone's responsibility—including mine and yours!—to develop students' strong academic literacy skills. We understand that texts are important in students' daily lives for reading and writing and for developing the skills to comprehend authorial intent. But it is equally crucial to understand how texts function as social practices that show identities, values, beliefs, and social networks. What is the overall point? We have every reason to be focused on all students' increased academic literacy.

As you know by now, the question is: How do you make your instructional focus on academic literacy culturally responsive? Part 3 of this book lays out three ways to do so. Chapter 8 outlines how to supplement your instruction with culturally responsive texts. Chapter 9 shows the importance of engaging read-alouds as a form of responsiveness because of the storytelling aspect and the emphasis on oral language. Lastly, Chapter 10 provides a collection of literacy activities that are culturally responsive.

Today's standards ask students to read stories and literature, as well as more complex texts that provide facts and background knowledge in such areas as science and social studies. Students are challenged and asked questions that push them to refer back to what they've read. This stresses critical-thinking, problem-solving, and analytical skills that are required for success in college, career, and life.

CHAPTER 8

Texts as Mirrors: Expanding Culturally Relevant Texts to Culturally Authentic Texts

This chapter is more of a "how-to" than a "why-do" and helps you understand how to select culturally responsive texts that will validate and affirm students. Culturally responsive texts are those in which students can find themselves, their families, and their communities reflected and valued. To enhance your knowledge, criteria for evaluating the authenticity of texts are presented.

There are two challenges to overcome in order to take advantage of infusing culturally responsive texts into academic literacy instruction.

> By using culturally responsive texts that accurately reflect students' cultural and linguistic selves, teachers provide the critical link between prior knowledge and texts, connecting texts directly to students' own lives and the lives of their peers.
>
> —Carrie Eicher (2023)

Challenge One: Slim Pickins

Educators who practice cultural responsiveness frequently encounter difficulty in finding appropriate instructional resources. This challenge is threefold.

- After decades of a dismal sparsity of culturally specific and authentic children's books, the number of such books has been steadily increasing over the past several years (Dickinson 2024). However, availability and use of these resources in school districts varies widely across the United States (O'Kane 2022; Woo et al. 2023).

- Furthermore, the likelihood of finding authentic pieces of culturally responsive text in mandated curricula, commercial literacy programs, or content-area textbooks varies as well. According to a recent meta-analysis, when it comes to educational materials, "There is disparity in representation of characters from different racial, ethnic, and gender groups. When portrayals of these groups are present, they tend to be affirming. However, stereotypes, limited roles, and inaccurate information are still present" (Armstrong 2022, para. 2).

- Finally, the question of availability must consider whether texts are culturally, and not just racially, based. If books are cultural, are they specific and authentic? Not all culturally responsive texts present cultural and linguistic backgrounds, historical information, images, and cultural traditions and behaviors with the same level of authenticity.

Challenge Two: Culturally Authentic or Bust

There are three types of culturally responsive texts:

- *culturally authentic*
- *culturally generic*
- *culturally neutral*

The CLR educator should aim to infuse as many *culturally authentic texts* as possible into instruction. *Culturally authentic texts* illuminate the authentic, nuanced (deep), and accurate cultural and linguistic experiences of particular cultural groups or Rings of Culture (religion, socioeconomic status, gender, ethnicity, nationality, orientation, or age), using language, situations, and images that depict culture and language in a genuine, native manner. Race is not one of the rings.

> *Culturally authentic texts* illuminate the experience of a group culturally and not racially. The text realistically taps into the norms, mores, traditions, customs, and beliefs of the culture in focus. There may be a stress on the history of racial discrimination and strife, the struggle for freedom, or an emphasis on racial or cultural pride.

Culturally Authentic (CA) Texts	*Culturally authentic texts* illuminate the authentic, nuanced (deep), and accurate cultural and linguistic experiences of particular cultural groups or Rings of Culture (religion, socioeconomic status, gender, ethnicity, nationality, orientation, or age), using language, situations, and images that depict culture and language in a genuine, native manner.
Culturally Generic (CG) Texts	*Culturally generic texts* feature characters of various racial identities, but unlike culturally authentic texts, contain only superficial cultural details to define the characters or storylines in a responsive manner.
Culturally Neutral (CN) Texts	*Culturally neutral literature* features characters and topics of "diversity" but includes content that is drenched with traditional or mainstream themes, plots, characterizations, and/or generalizations. *Culturally neutral informational texts* are devoid of culture or may include tokenistic portrayals of race or culture and avoid addressing authentic issues.

Figure 8.1 Questions to Determine If a Text Is Culturally Authentic or Generic

1. Do the majority, if not all, of the characters in the story represent various underserved racial identities?

   • If the answer is yes, the text could be either culturally authentic or culturally generic.

   • If the answer is no, this text is probably culturally generic.

2. Does the text include specific details about the characters' culture, such as culturally specific traditions, lifestyles, challenges, and language throughout the book?

   • If the answer is yes, the text is probably culturally authentic.

   • If the answer is no, the text is probably culturally neutral.

3. Could you replace the characters of color in this book with mainstream characters with little or no effect?

   • If the answer is yes, the text is probably culturally generic.

   • If the answer is no, the text is culturally authentic.

The second type of text is culturally generic. Culturally generic texts feature characters of various racial identities, but, unlike culturally authentic texts, they contain only superficial cultural details to define the characters or storylines in a responsive manner. Some publishers and media simply change the color of the characters—a practice I call "dipping"—with the expectation that these materials will be accepted as examples of racial diversity as opposed to cultural diversity.

Culturally generic texts feature characters who are members of racial minority groups. However, they contain few, if any, details that define characters culturally. In effect, the text could be about anybody from the national culture, regardless of race. The characters, plots, and themes focus on mainstream cultural values without revealing the cultural diversity found in culturally authentic texts.

For example, the book *Corduroy* by Don Freeman prominently features characters of color, but the substance of the book does not include culturally relevant information.

Figure 8.2 Questions to Determine If a Text Is Culturally Neutral or Culturally Generic

1. Does the text include some main characters who represent underserved groups?

   • If the answer is yes, the text could be either culturally neutral or culturally generic.

   • If the answer is no, this text is probably culturally neutral.

2. Does the text include some information about the characters' culture, such as generic references to superficial cultural preferences like food or clothing?

   • If the answer is yes, the text is probably culturally generic.

   • If the answer is no, the text is probably culturally neutral.

3. Imagine substituting the characters of color in the text with dominant culture characters. Would that change affect the story? Would you have to rewrite any of the text?

   • If the answer is yes, the text is probably culturally generic.

   • If the answer is no, the text is culturally neutral.

The final type to choose from is culturally neutral. Culturally neutral literature features characters and topics of "diversity" but includes content that is drenched with traditional or mainstream themes, plots, characterizations, and/or generalizations. Culturally neutral informational texts are devoid of culture or may include tokenistic portrayals of race or culture and avoid addressing authentic issues.

For example, in the popular Katie Kazoo, Switcheroo series by Nancy E. Krulik, the main character, Katie, is white, while her best friend, Suzanne, is African American. However, the reader only knows that Suzanne represents an underserved population by looking at the limited number of illustrations in the chapter book; the text itself does not contain any reference, authentic or otherwise, to culture or race. Any racial group could be substituted for Suzanne's character, and it would not change the story. Culturally neutral texts are the least preferred texts and should be avoided when possible by the culturally responsive educator. (Note that there are always exceptions, as there are many quality texts that build literacy but are culturally neutral.) What we need to avoid is using a culturally neutral text thinking that it is culturally authentic. The teacher's understanding of the type of text selected is crucial.

> *Culturally neutral texts* are the least culturally responsive. These feature characters of color and themes that seem to be about people of color but fundamentally are about something else. This type includes informational books that show people from diverse backgrounds engaged in activities from commonly told stories. Other notable examples include alternate versions of traditional fairy and folk tales. For example, *Mary Had a Little Lamb* becomes *Monique Had a Little Lamb*, where the female main character is literally blackfaced, with nothing being different about her other than her skin color.

Figure 8.3 provides some guidelines for avoiding the pitfalls of selecting culturally neutral texts (LeMoine 1999).

Figure 8.3 Tips for Avoiding the Pitfalls of Selecting Culturally Neutral Texts

- Choose well-known authors, illustrators, publishers, and sellers who have already developed solid reputations for producing culturally appropriate materials.
- Critically analyze how the characters are portrayed in the story, how the facts are presented, and in what context they are presented.
- Evaluate factual information for accuracy.
- When applicable, analyze the author's use of nonstandard language for authenticity and thoroughness.
- Carefully examine the illustrations for appeal, ethnic sensitivity, and authenticity.

Thus, it's essential to take the time to find good, culturally authentic books. Brooke Jaffe writes: "Think of a child going into a library and looking through the books, and not seeing anyone who looks like them. All of the covers have animals or little white girls and boys. It is the same phenomenon—their experiences aren't being acknowledged. Growing up with that concept, developing a self-image with that concept, trying to navigate a world that constantly sends you the message that you are not worth portraying in any story—that's not okay" (2013, para. 6).

REFLECTIVE THOUGHT

Test your knowledge of selecting culturally authentic texts. Out of the titles listed, which one is culturally authentic? What evidence did you use to make your choice?

a. The Rainbow Magic series by Daisy Meadows

b. *The House on Mango Street* by Sandra Cisneros

c. *The Snowy Day* by Ezra Jack Keats

Answer: b, *The House on Mango Street* by Sandra Cisneros. This book tells the story of a young Mexican-American girl, Esperanza, on the cusp of adolescence. Through a series of vignettes, Cisneros provides a bounty of authentic cultural information through the eyes of a young girl growing up in Chicago.

The Snowy Day by Ezra Jack Keats is a culturally generic text. This book chronicles the adventures of a young boy as he explores the outside world after a big snowstorm. *The Snowy Day* is often thought to be a culturally authentic text, because it features an African American child as the main character, but in reality, the story does not contain very much cultural context or information. In 1962, *The Snowy Day* was the first popular children's book to include a main character of color, and the book eventually won the Caldecott Medal in 1963 for Keats's stunning use of collage to illustrate the story. Despite its historical importance at the time it was published, this story is not culturally authentic. If you substituted a mainstream character for the little boy, the story would not change significantly. As a result, *The Snowy Day* is considered to be a culturally *generic* text.

That leaves the very popular Rainbow Magic series as the culturally neutral texts. These beginning chapter books follow two mainstream girls, Kirsty Tate and Rachel Walker, as they help different types of fairies resolve a series of predicaments created by the evil Jack Frost and his mischievous goblins. Most of the plot takes place in the land of the fairies and the stories contain very little, if any, authentic cultural information.

Solutions to Sustaining Responsive Literacy

You might already have a few authentic texts that your students enjoy. But how can you build your library? These are three solutions educators can use to address the challenges of sustaining culturally responsive literacy:

1. Know that you have to analyze texts to determine whether they are culturally authentic. Your district, state, or publisher will not do this for you. Keep in mind that most selections will be culturally generic, based on the fact that the number of books about people of color (as opposed to culture) is relatively low. Even so, avoid culturally neutral texts being used as culturally authentic or culturally generic.

2. Think broadly about making connections between your core curricular texts and your culturally authentic texts. A multitude of opportunities exist to plug in culturally responsive

texts regardless of the content area or grade level. Consider instructional themes, college and career readiness standards, district pacing plans, unit topics, and so on. For example, *March On! The Day My Brother Martin Changed the World* by Christine King Farris and *As Good as Anybody: Martin Luther King, Jr., and Abraham Joshua Heschel's Amazing March Toward Freedom* by Richard Michelson provide excellent opportunities to integrate culturally responsive texts into lessons about history while also engaging students in analyzing how two different texts address similar themes.

3. Think in terms of all the cultures. Do not just lock into race. Remember the Rings of Culture (figure P.2, page 14). Collectively, the rings increase chances of selecting culturally authentic texts. Look beyond black or white ethnicity, as well. Consider these factors:

   ◆ age
   ◆ orientation
   ◆ socioeconomic status
   ◆ gender
   ◆ geographical location
   ◆ religion
   ◆ nationality

Figure 8.4 Decision Tree for Determining If a Text Is Culturally Neutral, Generic, or Authentic

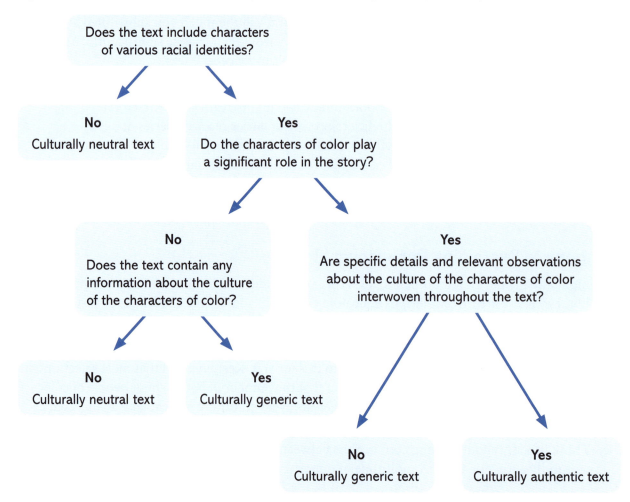

Concluding Thoughts

The website culturallyresponsive.org contains a list of culturally authentic texts; the site is updated periodically. Those resources are useful starting points.

You must be committed to being on the lookout for culturally authentic texts in your everyday life when reading periodicals, online materials, and books. The goal is to always search for culturally authentic texts, falling back on culturally generic texts when needed.

Use these scenarios and exercises to assist you in processing, practicing, and applying the concepts from the chapter.

Expanding to Culturally Authentic Texts

Text complexity includes variables specific to readers (reader and task), encouraging educators to consider student-centered variables such as motivation, knowledge, and experiences when selecting texts. Notably, college and career readiness standards expect educators to use professional judgment when matching texts to particular students and tasks. In this respect, the reader and task considerations support using culturally responsive texts for literacy instruction. The exercises that follow provide opportunities for you to practice identifying the three text types—culturally authentic, culturally generic, and culturally neutral.

Understanding Definitions of Text Types

Match the text type with its definition in figure 8.5.

Figure 8.5 Distinguishing Text Types

Text Type	Definition of Text
1. culturally authentic texts 2. culturally generic texts 3. culturally neutral texts	_____ a. These texts feature characters of various racial identities but contain superficial details to define the characters or storylines in a responsive cultural manner. _____ b. These texts feature characters of color but the stories are drenched with a traditional or mainstream theme, plot, and/or characterization. Any racial group could be substituted and it would not change the story. _____ c. These pieces of fiction or nonfiction text illuminate the authentic cultural experiences of a specific cultural group.

Answers: 1. culturally authentic texts = c; 2. culturally generic texts = a; 3. culturally neutral texts = b.

Selecting Culturally Responsive Texts

Selecting any text requires the culturally responsive educator to distinguish among three types of text: culturally neutral, culturally generic, and culturally authentic. Evaluate three different texts in your classroom library. Record reasons to support your evaluation.

My Text Type Preferences

Text 1:_____

Text Type:_____

Why?_____

Text 2:_____

Text Type:_____

Why?_____

Text 3:_____

Text Type:_____

Why?_____

Culturally Generic or Culturally Neutral

Mrs. Troy wants to conduct literacy activities with a culturally authentic text. She refers to a list of text exemplars for grades 2 and 3, and she finds *The Stories Julian Tells* by Ann Cameron.

Mrs. Troy is excited about finding *The Stories Julian Tells* on the list because it has an African American boy as the main character. After conducting a little research on the internet, she concludes that the book is not culturally authentic.

- The cover of the book includes a photograph of a real-life African American boy.
- The main character, Julian, is described in the publisher's description as a quick fibber and wishful thinker, capable of telling great stories to his younger brother—who actually believes the stories Julian tells.
- Julian apparently tells outlandish stories that can cause havoc but lend to interesting stories for kids to read.
- Some of his stories lead to trouble. This is where Julian and his younger brother end up.
- The book comes from a series that describes Julian's different adventures.
- The description of the book explains that this is a tale of little brothers, and it is about growing up.
- Julian's warm and loving family provides the perfect place for growing up.
- On one website, Mrs. Troy could see inside the book, and she saw a scene in which Julian and his younger brother make lemon pudding with their father.

Mrs. Troy is having a hard time placing the book in one of the remaining two categories. Using the information provided here about *The Stories Julian Tells*, determine whether it is culturally generic or culturally neutral. Record the text type and provide some of the evidence found in the text to support your opinion. See below for the answers.

I think this book is_____

Evidence from the text that supports this conclusion:

_____

_____

_____

_____

_____

_____

_____

_____

_____

_____

Answers

This book is an example of a *culturally generic* text.

Evidence from the text that supports this conclusion:

The cover of the book includes a photograph of a real-life African American boy and describes an African American family in culturally specific ways.

- Julian, the main character, is capable of telling great stories. His ability to tell great stories speaks to the oral tradition of African Americans.

- The description of the book explains that this is a tale of little brothers. It is all part of growing up. The theme of growing up is generic.

- The great family adventures described apply to all families, including African American families.

Culturally Authentic vs. Culturally Generic Poetry

The internet is a great source to find poetry of all kinds, including culturally responsive poetry. Sites such as Family Friend Poems (familyfriendpoems.com), Poetry Out Loud (poetryoutloud.org), the Poetry Foundation (poetryfoundation.org), and Poets.org serve as clearinghouses for poems. Using one of these sites (or another resource), select a culturally authentic poem. (See figures 8.1, 8.2, and 8.4 for examples of how to go through the decision-making process.)

Next, provide evidence to support your claim that the poem you selected is culturally authentic and illuminates the authentic cultural experiences of a specific cultural group.

Think about how the indicators outlined in this chapter and the relevant Rings of Culture apply to the poem. Culturally authentic texts do not need to contain information about all possible superficial cultural details, such as food and traditions. But each culturally authentic text will include some specific details about various aspects of the culture and racial identity. Record your thinking. Then see below for a sample answer.

Figure 8.6 Text Evaluation Template

Culturally Authentic Text Selected:_____

<table>
<tr><td colspan="2" align="center">**Evidence to Support My Conclusion**</td></tr>
<tr><td colspan="2">**Superficial Cultural Details:**</td></tr>
<tr><td colspan="2">**Food:**_____</td></tr>
<tr><td colspan="2">**Traditions:**_____</td></tr>
<tr><td colspan="2">**Rings of Culture:**</td></tr>
<tr><td colspan="2">**Age:**_____</td></tr>
<tr><td colspan="2">**Socioeconomic Status:**_____</td></tr>
<tr><td colspan="2">**Gender:**_____</td></tr>
<tr><td colspan="2">**Geographical Location:**_____</td></tr>
<tr><td colspan="2">**Orientation:**_____</td></tr>
<tr><td colspan="2">**Religion:**_____</td></tr>
<tr><td colspan="2">**Nationality:**_____</td></tr>
</table>

Figure 8.7 Sample Text Evaluation

Culturally Authentic Text Selected: "Knoxville, Tennessee" by Nikki Giovanni

Evidence to Support My Conclusion

Superficial Cultural Details:

Food: Fresh corn, okra, greens, cabbage from Daddy's garden, homemade ice cream, and buttermilk are specific to African American culture.

Rings of Culture:

Age: It is culturally responsive for students who have close ties with their families or elders or grandmothers.

Socioeconomic Status: The poem references being able to go barefoot all the time, not only when you go to bed.

Geographical Location: The poem references going to the mountains.

Religion: The poem references gospel music as well as going to the church picnic and homecoming.

Nationality: Knoxville, Tennessee, is a city in the American South. The poem is culturally responsive to those students who either live in the South or visit family members in the South.

Classroom Applications

Think about your own classroom and teaching practices. Use the following prompts to reflect on how you have selected texts in the past and the types of changes you would like to make in the future.

1. In the past, how did you select the texts you used with your students?

    _____

    _____

    _____

2. What resources can you use to find culturally authentic texts for your classroom?

    _____

    _____

    _____

3. What different cultures are represented in your classroom? Do you foresee any challenges in finding authentic texts that represent these cultures?

_____

_____

_____

4. Consider the books you currently have in your classroom. Are most of them culturally neutral, culturally generic, or culturally authentic? How do you know?

_____

_____

_____

5. What are the next steps you plan to take to ensure that you supply your students with more culturally authentic texts?

_____

_____

_____

STUDENT VOICE

Allowing Your Students to Be Engaged in Their Own Way, or "BeYou": Communalism

BeYou is a call to action, reminding teachers to adjust instruction and classroom practices, ensuring that students can be themselves at school culturally and linguistically. In this section, we consider how students might express the importance of being validated and affirmed when demonstrating communalism at school.

How can communalism be culturally misunderstood in the classroom? In my community, we all look out for each other. We always think about others and put the whole group's needs above our own. It's not always easy, but as my mom says, "we before I." We've got each other's backs and sometimes that means giving up some of my own success. I'm alright with it though, because when one of us wins, we all win. I've always been told that it's important to focus on making sure everybody is successful, not just me. In the classroom it's not always like that and thinking like that can, believe it or not, get me in trouble sometimes.

How does it feel to be misunderstood? Most of how we learn in school is individual or about whether I am able to be successful on my own, like grades and tests and stuff. That's not really how I see things or what I think is best. I look out for others because *we is greater than me*. It is confusing for me, because sometimes teachers think I'm cheating or giving help when it's not needed, but I've always been told it's about everybody's success, not just mine. I think it's important to offer help if someone is confused or doesn't understand something. It's all about the greater good for me.

What do I need to be myself? It is important for me to be able to support the other people in class. I feel validated when I am able to work on projects and assignments where it's about our shared success, and when I can check in with others and help out if needed. I am affirmed when my teachers recognize communalism for what it is—having each other's backs.

> **What CLR activities validate and affirm communalism?** Stop and Scribble, I Got This!, and Numbered Heads Together are all about working together **and** making sure everyone has got it and is successful. They give students the chance to contribute to the overall success of the class and everyone in it.

Build CLR Community and Collaboration

Pair up with a colleague and discuss the following three questions:

1. What cultural behaviors do you feel the most confident validating and affirming?
2. Conversely, what cultural behaviors do you struggle with validating and affirming?
3. For the second question, how can you be supported?

After the discussion, what is your first next step?

CHAPTER 9

Back to Storytelling: Engaging Uses of Read-Alouds

Understanding the Context

In 1982, Jim Trelease published the first edition of *The Read-Aloud Handbook* in which he describes the benefits of reading aloud to students and provides an invaluable resource for teachers and parents. Trelease notes that the pleasure of being read to contributes to children becoming lifelong readers. The value and popularity of Trelease's work is evidenced by the publication of the eighth edition of *The Read-Aloud Handbook* in 2019.

Karen Kindle (2012), in *Issues and Trends in Literacy Education*, supports the academic benefit of reading aloud when she writes, "The read-aloud context has proven to [be] an effective vehicle for vocabulary instruction, but teachers need to recognize the practices that optimize word learning and determine the most effective manner for adding elaborations and explanations during the story reading without detracting from the pleasure of reading itself" (101). We haven't even mentioned the term *cultural responsiveness*, yet we have already identified two benefits of reading aloud: improving literacy skills and finding pleasure in reading. The dual benefits of reading aloud cannot be underestimated. Using read-alouds strategically can have a meaningful impact on the skill levels of the students for vocabulary, fluency, and comprehension. Joseph Torgesen and Roxanne Hudson (2006) advise that the most productive and research-based approach to the prosody-comprehension connection is for teachers to model prosody regularly when reading aloud to students and to always expect students to read with prosody. *Prosody* refers to stress, intonation, and pauses (known as reading with expression or feeling) (Hollie 2018, 231).

> An engaging read-aloud is one that involves students by having them participate as active listeners or as the readers themselves.

In CLR, all of these factors also serve to support the build and bridge aspect of the strategy. But there is an even more important benefit related to the validation and affirmation of students: storytelling.

When using engaging read-alouds, the culturally responsive teacher is also validating and affirming by simulating the oral tradition of storytelling. When you read aloud to your students, no matter what their grade, you are responding to the cultures in your classroom that have oral language and storytelling as important norms and traditions. "Many people within certain cultures, namely Native American, consider storytelling an art form because it combines the talents of the speakers, who use their hands, bodies, and voices to express emotion, spirit, and style. Storytelling produces strong responses in both the teller and the listeners. It can be used to entertain or to educate" (Torgesen and Hudson 2006, 126).

In addition to the benefits of enjoying hearing stories read aloud, interactive read-alouds create opportunities to discuss the process of comprehending text while sharing aesthetic and personal reactions with the group (Ivey 2003; Wiseman 2011). "With read-alouds, there is space for students and teachers to co-construct knowledge because culturally and historically responsive read-alouds provide all participants a seat at the table to listen to stories from multiple perspectives" (Vlach, Lentz, and Muhammad 2023, 129).

In summary, the evidence is overwhelmingly in favor of using engaging read-alouds. Some say that reading is a silent activity and that when we focus too much on reading aloud, we could be doing students a disservice (Garan and DeVoogd 2008; Reutzel, Fawson, and Smith 2008). Let us say that this assertion is true, but this point does not outweigh the clear advantages of using engaging read-alouds as part of CLR. Rarely does research look at cultural aspects. However, studies that do include cultural aspects find that reading aloud has a positive effect on cultural competence (May, Bingham, and Pendergast 2014).

Considering the Research

Read-alouds help students develop fluency and improve their comprehension skills. The following studies represent a sample of research supporting the use of read-alouds in a culturally responsive classroom.

- Reading aloud to children provides a powerful context for word learning (Bravo, Hiebert, and Pearson 2007). It also challenges students to practice a new language, and to engage in deeper processing and understanding of that new language and the ideas connected to it (Giroir et al. 2015).

- ASCD's Scientific Advisory Committee advises teachers to give read-alouds a central role: "Through read-alouds and text-based discussion, young students can engage with more complex ideas and vocabulary than what they can yet read themselves, building the knowledge they need to engage with more sophisticated texts in the future" (2023).

- Books chosen for read-alouds are typically engaging, thus increasing both students' motivation and their attention (Fisher et al. 2004; Young, Ricks, and MacKay 2023).

- Oral reading is one of the best ways to help students develop fluency, expression, and correct phrasing (Rasinski and Young 2024; Reutzel, Hollingsworth, and Eldredge 1994). It also contributes to students' literary skills, including vocabulary (Baker et al. 2020; Walpole et al. 2017), comprehension (Conradi Smith et al. 2022), and listening and speaking (Adams and Kaczmarczyk 2021; Hollie 2018; Montag 2019; Young, Ricks, and MacKay 2023).

- For Standard English learners and English language learners, oral reading provides four important factors: low-anxiety learning environment, repeated practice, comprehensible input, and drama (McCauley and McCauley 1992). Further, using translanguaging read-alouds enhances ELLs' academic success and promotes empathy (Moody and Matthews 2020).

- Read-alouds can sometimes be for simple enjoyment (Scholes 2021; Young, Ricks, and MacKay 2023). By centering and celebrating the diverse lived experiences of students, read-alouds can be windows for activating joy (Vlach, Lentz, and Muhammad 2023).

Pre-Reading Assessment

Before reading this chapter, reflect on your current use of engaging read-alouds by completing the survey in figure 9.1. As you rate yourself, think about how frequently and effectively you use read-alouds. If you are not doing any reading aloud, think about how you can start doing so by the end of the chapter.

Figure 9.1 Engaging Uses of Read-Alouds: Survey Before Infusing CLR Principles

0: *Never Emerging* 1: *Rarely Splashing* 2: *Sometimes Floating* 3: *Mostly Kicking* 4: *Always Freestyling*					
I read aloud to my students at least twice a week.	0	1	2	3	4
I use a variety of materials for read-alouds.	0	1	2	3	4
I encourage my students to engage in the activity of reading aloud as much as possible.	0	1	2	3	4

Beginning the Reflective Process

Learning happens when we reflect upon what we have experienced. Critical reflection generates, deepens, and documents learning (Ash and Clayton 2009). Are you ready to implement strategies for reading aloud?

Use the following checklist to gauge your readiness and ability to incorporate read-aloud strategies into your teaching. Each item represents an important aspect of understanding and using these strategies in a culturally responsive classroom. After completing the checklist, read the detailed descriptions of each item and reflect on how you plan to implement or amend your use of read-aloud strategies in the classroom.

☑ The Use of Read-Aloud Strategies Reflection Checklist

Item 9.1	Do I have a list of engaging read-alouds ready to use strategically?	○ Yes ○ No
Item 9.2	Is there enough variety in the texts I am reading to my class to warrant using read-alouds?	○ Yes ○ No

Item 9.1 Do I have a list of engaging read-alouds ready to use strategically?

Like all aspects of effective teaching, thoughtful lesson planning is the key to successful culturally responsive teaching. Plan for engaging read-alouds by having texts in your toolbox ready for use and then using them strategically. Following is a collection of culturally responsive read-aloud activities.

BUDDY READING (PAIRED READING)

Validate and Affirm Cultural Behaviors: Cooperation/Collaboration, Sociocentrism, Immediacy

Description: Students read a text together. This can be done with peers, by pairing proficient readers with less-proficient readers, or by pairing upper-grade students with lower-grade students.

Process: The teacher assigns students as buddies who will read the text together. Students share the reading of the text, even if it is one student reading and the other listening.

Pros: The students are motivated to work with peers; engaging; low affective filter; student-centered

Cons: The teacher must actively check up on pairs to ensure that students are reading; frustration can occur for proficient readers when the non-proficient reader reads

CHORAL READING

Validate and Affirm Cultural Behaviors: Cooperation/Collaboration, Communalism, Orality and Verbal Expressiveness

Description: The teacher and students read aloud together.

Process: Just as a choir sings in unison, the teacher leads the students to read together in one voice. The teacher points out where to start in the passage and cues students to read. All students are expected to join in and read together in unison.

Pros: Low affective filter; sense of cooperation

Cons: Some students may not be engaged; some may not participate

ECHO READING

Validate and Affirm Cultural Behaviors: Communalism, Cooperation/Collaboration, Orality and Verbal Expressiveness

Description: The teacher reads and students echo. Echo Reading is often used with struggling readers, because students are not put on the spot but instead are only required to echo what they hear.

Process: The teacher reads one sentence, paragraph, or section and then stops. Students echo the teacher by reading the same piece of text in the same way.

Pros: Low affective filter; modeling prosody

Cons: Some students may not participate

Strategies for Culturally and Linguistically Responsive Teaching and Learning—152468 © Shell Education

FADE IN/FADE OUT

Validate and Affirm Cultural Behaviors: Conversational Patterns, Orality and Verbal Expressiveness, Communalism

Description: The teacher uses nonverbal cues to choose students to read. Students must be able to read and listen for another reader's cues.

Process: The teacher walks around the room and touches the shoulder of a student who starts to read with a whisper and gradually increases the volume to a normal reading voice. After the first student has read a paragraph or so, the teacher touches another student's shoulder. That student starts reading at a whisper and gets louder. The student who is reading then fades out, going from a normal volume to a whisper.

Pros: Models one aspect of fluency by focusing on tonality

Cons: High affective filter; lack of student choice; struggling readers will not want to read

FILL-IN-THE-BLANK READING

Validate and Affirm Cultural Behaviors: Communalism, Orality and Verbal Expressiveness, Dynamic Attention Span

Description: Teacher reads aloud and periodically stops to ask students to "fill in the blank" with a word or sentence in the text.

Process: The teacher previews the text and identifies where students will "fill in the blank" with key words and phrases. The teacher then reads aloud. When the teacher stops, students chime in with the missing text. Then the teacher reads again, pausing for students to fill in the next "blank." Words can also be displayed on the board for students to fill in.

Pros: High engagement; builds community

Cons: Students may not all participate

JUMP-IN READING

Validate and Affirm Cultural Behaviors: Spontaneity, Conversational Patterns, Orality and Verbal Expressiveness

Description: Students have the autonomy to choose when they would like to participate and read aloud by "jumping in."

Process: A student reads, and another student can jump in at a sentence or a paragraph break. Students must read at least one sentence, or they can read for as long as they want or until someone jumps in. A student can stop reading and allow for a brief time of silence. Having moments of silence allows students to think and reflect about what was just read. If two or more jump in at the same time, one student defers to the other.

Pros: Highly engaging; low affective filter; student-centered

Cons: Lack of equitable participation

RADIO READING

Validate and Affirm Cultural Behaviors: Orality and Verbal Expressiveness, Dynamic Attention Span, Spontaneity

Description: Proficient readers are chosen to read a text with different voices. They can choose an emotion to relay, such as happy, sad, or sleepy. Alternatively, they can choose a voice type, such as an elderly person or a baby.

Process: Beforehand, the teacher chooses proficient readers who read expressively. The teacher can also ask for volunteers. After practicing their voice of choice, the students read to the whole class. Options include individuals or groups of students reading parts of the text or the whole class chorally reading.

Pros: High engagement; allows students to add dramatic interpretation; shows that reading can be fun

Cons: Limited to proficient readers; readers may focus on their role and lose track of the storyline

TAG READING

Validate and Affirm Cultural Behaviors: Communalism, Cooperation/Collaboration, Orality and Verbal Expressiveness, Spontaneity, Kinesthetic

Description: Students take turns reading while walking, then tagging the next person to read.

Process: The teacher chooses the first student to read. The student stands up and reads while walking around the classroom. After reading at least three sentences, the student tags another student to read. That student then stands up, reads, and walks. They then tag another student, and so on.

Pros: High engagement

Cons: May make struggling readers uncomfortable; students tend to pick friends or students not paying attention; can be distracting to some students

TEACHER READ-ALOUD

Validate and Affirm Cultural Behaviors: Simulates the oral tradition of storytelling

Description: The teacher reads an engaging text aloud while students listen.

Process: The teacher selects an engaging text and reads it aloud, modeling the prosodic features of the language. Students listen and follow along in their books while the teacher reads.

Pros: All readers benefit from hearing a proficient reader; low affective filter

Cons: Students may want to participate but are required to listen

TRAIN READING

Validate and Affirm Cultural Behaviors: Communalism, Cooperation/Collaboration, Orality and Verbal Expressiveness

Description: Just as a train has an engine, cars, and a caboose, the teacher is the engine as the first reader and chooses the proficient readers to be the cars and caboose.

Process: Prior to reading, the teacher chooses three to five proficient readers and either assigns them a section by number or gives them an indication of how much they should read (e.g., a few sentences, a paragraph). The teacher begins, the next student follows, and so on.

Pros: Prosodic reading is modeled

Cons: Lack of equitable participation

REFLECTIVE THOUGHT

In what ways and for what purposes do you use read-aloud activities? In your experience, what factors have limited your use of read-alouds? Which activities described above are new to you and which do you want to try with your students?

Thought-Provokers: A Mindset for Moving Forward

1. When I think back to my school experiences with reading aloud, were they fun? Were they boring? What can I do to make the experience better for students?

2. What are my cultural norms or traditions for reading aloud or storytelling? What are my childhood memories of tradition being passed down orally?

Thought-Blockers: A Mindset for Staying Stagnant

1. My hesitancy comes from being placed outside of my comfort zone rather than a resistance to the actual idea of reading aloud.

2. To what extent do I value the overall benefits of modeling reading aloud in terms of fluency, comprehension, and vocabulary?

Item 9.2 Is there enough variety in the texts I am reading to my class to warrant using read-alouds?

This is a call to do more oral reading with your students. As students advance through the grades, less reading is done in class, whether it be oral, silent, independent, or whole group, and to a certain degree that is to be expected. As students move from the elementary level to the secondary level, the emphasis on oral reading diminishes. This shift is a recognition of the changing instructional demands at the higher grade levels. However, reading aloud should not be completely excluded from secondary classrooms. Reading texts in class builds students up or builds and bridges them to more independent reading, especially in the early secondary grades. Reading aloud provides an excellent model for struggling readers as they listen to a proficient reader. Any and all texts can be read aloud, including textbooks, newspaper articles, blogs, journals, fiction, technical manuals, poetry, and comic books.

> *Fluency* is the ability to read text with speed (appropriate rate), accuracy, and proper expression (National Reading Panel 2013). "*Rate* is the speed at which a person reads. *Accuracy* describes the students' ability to recognize words and read them instantly" (Hollie 2018, 227).

REFLECTIVE THOUGHT

> How do you use read-alouds with struggling readers? What are your instructional purposes? What advice would you give a content-area teacher who maintains that there is not enough time to read aloud to students?

Thought-Provokers: A Mindset for Moving Forward

1. I approach the search for a read-aloud text as fun.
2. I am the best possible model for a proficient reader.

Thought-Blockers: A Mindset for Staying Stagnant

1. I rarely read for pleasure, which makes it more difficult to find good reads outside of my classroom.
2. I think improving my students' reading levels is not my responsibility.

Read-Alouds That Work

Now that you have reviewed several read-aloud strategies, stop to think about what makes a read-aloud effective. Fisher and his colleagues observed seven common practices among expert practitioners of interactive read-alouds (2004):

- Books should be specifically chosen for students. Important elements include students' interests, their academic needs, quality models of writing, and meaningful representations of diverse groups.
- Teachers should preview and practice before the read-aloud. Preparing for the read-aloud ensures that teachers will smoothly tackle unexpected sentence structures or unusual words. It also allows teachers to plan for meaningful modeling and prompting.
- Teachers should establish a purpose. The purpose may be tied to comprehension or vocabulary work or may be connected to content-area learning.
- Teachers should read fluently. This is made possible by previewing and practicing before the read-aloud. Teachers can model sophisticated nuances of intonation and pacing in response to the text.
- Teachers should be animated. Students become more thoroughly engaged when teachers actively use their voices, gestures, and facial expressions to bring text to life.

◆ Teachers should stop to prompt students. In addition to modeling comprehension strategies and personal responses to the text, the teacher prompts students to do the same. In a truly interactive model, students are empowered to interrupt the reading as well.

To support students in reading aloud, the teacher must consider the type of text to be read, the strategy that works best with the students and/or text, and the skills or literary elements on which the students should focus. For example, a short story that consists mostly of dialogue might be best suited for Radio Reading, while a poem that contains examples of poetic devices such as rhyme and alliteration might be better suited for Echo Reading. Here are some last tips for implementing engaging, effective oral reading:

◆ During oral reading, concentrate on the three components of fluency—accuracy, rate, and prosody.

◆ Students need daily opportunities to read and consistent practice with different types of reading, such as oral, silent, independent, and whole group.

◆ Never put new English learners or non-proficient readers on the spot for oral reading.

◆ English learners and non-proficient readers need plenty of time to experience receptive language (listening) in order to be more confident in speaking and reading aloud.

◆ Use the activities to create an atmosphere that is affirming and conducive to academic learning and cultivates the pleasure of reading.

Concluding Thoughts

Engaging read-alouds have a number of benefits for students. They improve reading skills, cultivate the pleasure of reading, and build the social interaction of oral language. Importantly, engaging read-alouds provide opportunities for you to be culturally responsive. You validate and affirm because of the simulation of storytelling and the focus on oral language traditions. In order to put engaging read-alouds into practice, you must fill your toolbox with actual read-aloud strategies and increase the frequency of oral reading in class.

Use these scenarios and exercises to assist you in processing, practicing, and applying the concepts from the chapter.

Mrs. Navarro

Mrs. Navarro teaches a seventh grade language arts class, and although her students are "older," she makes sure to incorporate regular read-alouds into her instruction. Today, Mrs. Navarro has selected *Walk Two Moons* by Sharon Creech to read aloud. This book tells the story of thirteen-year-old Salamanca (Sal) Tree Hiddle's search, both literal and metaphorical, for her missing mother. As Sal embarks on a six-day car trip with her grandparents to retrace her mother's route, she relies on her inner strength and Native American ancestry to help her cope with the emotional turmoil of hope, loss, and acceptance. Mrs. Navarro believes that her students will identify with the storyline and characters in the book because of their shared culture and familiarity with situations regarding absent parents.

After selecting the text, Mrs. Navarro carefully rereads the story, noting particular areas that might be more or less demanding for readers. She also gauges how long she thinks it will take to read the text aloud and plans time each day during the coming week for the read-aloud.

After introducing the book to her students, Mrs. Navarro tells them that they will use the Fade In/Fade Out read-aloud strategy. The students are familiar with this activity and have practiced it before. Mrs. Navarro selects a student to begin and then walks around the room and quietly taps the next student to fade in after a designated amount of time. Mrs. Navarro uses her notes about the difficulty of the text to decide which students to select for different sections. The students quickly become engaged with the story and follow along so that they can participate if they are chosen to read aloud. When Mrs. Navarro tells them they have to stop because the bell is about to ring, they protest and make her promise that they can continue reading the story again tomorrow.

What are some of the ways that this type of read-aloud will benefit Mrs. Navarro's students?

   a. Engaging read-alouds can improve literacy skills for all learners.
   b. Engaging read-alouds can help students find pleasure in reading.
   c. Engaging read-alouds simulate the oral tradition of storytelling from many different cultures by emphasizing the reliance on oral language.
   d. All of the above

Answer: d. All of the above

Mrs. Navarro's students clearly enjoy this read-aloud. While listening to the text, they are hearing examples of prosody and acquiring new words. The Fade In/Fade Out protocol helps keep all students engaged in the reading and allows Mrs. Navarro to control who reads which sections of text based on her knowledge of the text's difficulty and her students' reading ability.

Classroom Applications

Think about your own classroom and teaching practices. Use the following prompts to reflect on how you have used read-alouds in the past and the types of changes you would like to make in the future.

1. What type of planning did Mrs. Navarro do to ensure that the read-aloud activity was successful?

   _____

   _____

2. Have you used read-alouds in the past? If so, did you feel that they were successful? If not, what obstacles prevented you from doing so?

   _____

   _____

Mr. Martin

Mr. Martin likes to do a read-aloud with his class at the beginning of the day. Depending on the book, Mr. Martin uses different read-aloud strategies. Today, Mr. Martin is reading *Lin Yi's Lantern: A Moon Festival Tale* by Brenda Williams. He is reading the story aloud because the level of text is higher than his first graders' instructional or independent reading levels. In this story, the main character, Lin Yi, goes to the market to buy several food items for his mother. Lin Yi desperately wants to buy a red rabbit lantern for the Moon Festival, but his mother has no extra money for it. However, she tells him that if he bargains well at the market, he may be able to save enough to buy a lantern. Throughout the story, Lin Yi frequently repeats a list of food items that he needs to buy from the market for his mother. As he reads the story aloud, Mr. Martin pauses as Lin Yi is about to recite the list and encourages the students to "read" the list with him. Together, Mr. Martin and the students recite the list. Mr. Martin continues this practice throughout the story.

After reading the book, Mr. Martin discusses the story with the class. Most of the students already know the concept of bargaining from their own experiences, such as bargaining for an extra dessert or later bedtime, but they do not know the term *bargain*. Over the next several weeks, Mr. Martin overhears his students using the word *bargain* repeatedly when they are working together in the classroom or talking on the playground. They use the term correctly and clearly understand the concept and technical meaning.

Review the research at the beginning of this chapter (page 214). What research was supported by Mr. Martin's observations of his students in the weeks after the read-aloud?

a. Oral reading can be used as a window for independent reading practices.

b. Reading aloud provides a context for word acquisition.

c. Oral reading helps develop fluency and expression.

d. Reading aloud increases attention.

Answer: b. Reading aloud provides a context for word acquisition.

In this example, Mr. Martin's students learned the word *bargain* and were able to apply it to their prior knowledge and ideas about the concept.

Research-Based Instructional Practices

Refer to the research section at the start of this chapter regarding the benefits of using read-alouds in the classroom. For each bullet point, provide an example of an instructional activity you could use to support this research evidence. List your examples below.

Revisiting the Research

◆ Reading aloud to children provides a powerful context for word learning (Bravo, Hiebert, and Pearson 2007). It also challenges students to practice a new language, and to engage in deeper processing and understanding of that new language and the ideas connected to it (Giroir et al. 2015).

_____

_____

◆ Books chosen for read-alouds are typically engaging, thus increasing both students' motivation and their attention (Fisher et al. 2004; Young, Ricks, and MacKay 2023).

_____

_____

◆ Oral reading is one of the best ways to help students develop fluency, expression, and correct phrasing (Rasinski and Young 2024; Reutzel, Hollingsworth, and Eldredge 1994).

_____

_____

◆ For Standard English learners and English language learners, oral reading provides four important factors: low-anxiety learning environment, repeated practice, comprehensible input, and drama (McCauley and McCauley 1992).

_____

_____

Possible Answers:

◆ Use the read-aloud to select, highlight, and practice new Tier Two vocabulary words.
◆ Use an engaging read-aloud at the beginning of a science or social studies unit to increase students' motivation to learn more about the topic.

- Use read-alouds as part of small-group instruction to increase fluency while also teaching literary concepts, such as text structure, theme, and word meaning.
- Read, study, and perform an episode of reader's theater as a way to engage English language learners.

Mrs. Gonzalez

It is the end of the day, and Mrs. Gonzalez's students have just returned from recess. After playing outside, they are hot, sweaty, and tired. Mrs. Gonzalez decides to read aloud as a way to help students focus and relax before concluding the school day. She grabs a book from the shelf and tells the class that they are going to use the Tag Reading activity to read aloud from the story. The students are familiar with this activity because they have used it in the past. Mrs. Gonzalez hands the book to a nearby student and asks him to start walking around the class while he reads aloud. The selected student starts to read aloud, but even though he is a strong reader, he struggles to read the first several sentences because he is unfamiliar with the narrative's writing style. Because he is focusing on decoding the text, the student accidentally stumbles over a backpack on the floor while reading. The rest of the students giggle, and the reader gets embarrassed. The reader quickly "tags" the student nearest to him by handing her the book. Since the students do not all have copies of the text, the new reader does not know where to begin reading. She gets guidance from the first reader and eventually starts walking and reading, but this text is even more difficult for her to read because she is not a strong reader. The student gets increasingly flustered as she stumbles through the text. The rest of students are getting restless and noisy. Sensing the reader's discomfort, Mrs. Gonzalez decides that a read-aloud was not a good idea and changes to a different activity.

Based on her experience with this read-aloud, Mrs. Gonzalez should:

- **a.** wait until the next day and continue with the read-aloud using the Tag Reading strategy.
- **b.** reevaluate if the Tag Reading strategy is appropriate for the chosen text and make the appropriate changes for the next read-aloud.
- **c.** conduct future read-alouds herself so students do not get embarrassed.
- **d.** only use read-alouds sparingly in her classroom because students do not seem to enjoy them.

Answer: b. reevaluate if the Tag Reading strategy is appropriate for the chosen text and make the appropriate changes for the next read-aloud.

Mrs. Gonzalez should reevaluate what went wrong in the read-aloud. Her lack of planning, spontaneous selection of a text, and random choice of read-aloud protocol all came together to result in an unsuccessful read-aloud experience. By incorporating read-alouds into her planning, carefully selecting texts, and paying attention to which read-aloud strategies work best under certain circumstances, Mrs. Gonzalez should be able to effectively utilize read-aloud protocols with her students.

Effective Read-Aloud Tools

This chapter has provided you with a collection of read-aloud tools. Now, let us place them in the appropriate toolboxes to help ensure that we use the right tool for the right job. Use the descriptions of the read-aloud activities presented previously to determine which should be used with proficient and non-proficient readers. Check the appropriate boxes and then record explanations for your choices in figure 9.2. Finally, check for possible responses in figure 9.3.

Figure 9.2 Effective Read-Aloud Tools

Activity	Proficient Readers	Non-Proficient Readers	Both
Teacher Read-Aloud			
Train Reading			
Jump-In Reading			
Fade In/Fade Out			
Echo Reading			
Buddy Reading (Paired Reading)			
Choral Reading			
Tag Reading			
Fill-in-the-Blank Reading			
Radio Reading			

Proficient Readers	Non-Proficient Readers
Reasons for my choices:	Reasons for my choices:

Figure 9.3 Possible Answers to Effective Read-Aloud Tools

Activity	Proficient Readers	Non-Proficient Readers	Both
Teacher Read-Aloud			X
Train Reading	X		
Jump-In Reading	X		
Fade In/Fade Out	X		
Echo Reading			X
Buddy Reading (Paired Reading)			X
Choral Reading		X	
Tag Reading			X
Fill-in-the-Blank Reading			X
Radio Reading	X		

Proficient Readers	Non-Proficient Readers
Reasons for my choices:	Reasons for my choices:
Teacher Read-Aloud—All types of readers benefit from listening to text read aloud with fluency and prosody.	Teacher Read-Aloud—All types of readers benefit from listening to text read aloud with fluency and prosody.
Train Reading—Proficient readers can model fluency and prosodic features for non-proficient readers.	Echo Reading—Non-proficient readers hear and then copy the fluency and prosody modeled by a proficient reader.
Jump-In Reading—Students follow along precisely with the reader so they can decide to jump in and keep reading without long delays.	Buddy Reading—Non-proficient readers benefit from listening to the text read aloud by proficient readers in a cooperative activity.
Fade In/Fade Out—Students modulate the level of their voices and listen to other students fading in and out while reading at the same time.	Choral Reading—Non-proficient readers follow along and practice reading aloud without being put on the spot.
Echo Reading (to model prosody)—The teacher selects several proficient readers to read the text aloud while the rest of the class echoes it back.	Fill-in-the-Blank Reading—All readers benefit from following along and listening to text read aloud with fluency and prosody and then responding chorally when prompted.
Buddy Reading—Proficient readers pair with less-proficient readers and act as mentors and models for reading fluency.	Tag Reading—Students are moving and engaged and only need to read a small amount of text if tagged.
Radio Reading—Students read fluently with emotion and expression.	
Fill-in-the-Blank Reading—All readers benefit from following along and listening to text read aloud with fluency and prosody and then responding chorally when prompted.	
Tag Reading—Students are moving and engaged and can choose to read for as long as they want.	

Incorporating Engaging Read-Alouds into Instruction

How do you incorporate engaging read-alouds into your instruction? Take a moment to describe your practice using figure 9.4. Check figure 9.5 for possible answers.

Figure 9.4 Incorporating Engaging Read-Alouds

Before a Read-Aloud
During a Read-Aloud
After a Read-Aloud

Figure 9.5 Possible Answers to Incorporating Engaging Read-Alouds

Before a Read-Aloud

- Choose a high-interest text that supports the content (considering different types of text to motivate and engage readers).
- Pre-read the text to identify places to stop and either ask questions or ask students to quickly reflect on the text orally or in writing.
- Identify students who will participate in the read-aloud activity.
- Identify response or discussion protocols to use during the read-aloud.
- Ensure the read-aloud supports specific standards, instructional purposes, and targeted literacy skills.

During a Read-Aloud

- Model targeted fluency or comprehension skills.
- Facilitate instructional conversations at appropriate times.
- Try to ensure that think-alouds, partner shares, vocabulary, or other activities enhance students' ability to comprehend the text.

After a Read-Aloud

- Reflect on it.
- Talk about it.
- Write about it.

Sample Lesson—Incorporating Engaging Read-Alouds

The following lesson provides one example of how to use an engaging read-aloud.

Procedure

1. Before beginning the read-aloud, select a text based on instructional objectives and cultural authenticity. This sample lesson uses *Tar Beach* by Faith Ringgold. This picture book tells the story of an eight-year-old girl, Cassie Louise Lightfoot, who dreams of being able to escape the constraints of her daily life and go wherever she wants to go. One night, as she lies on "Tar Beach," the rooftop of her apartment building in Brooklyn, Cassie discovers she can fly and follow her dreams.

2. Select the read-aloud strategy that best fits your instructional goals and the chosen text. For example, *Tar Beach* is an excellent text to use with the Buddy Reading protocol, especially when it is possible to pair older students with younger students. On the surface, the book contains a relatively simple storyline that young children will find engaging. However, the story has deeper meaning and historical significance that allows older students to explore themes of discrimination and organized labor.

3. Say, "Today you are going to be reading *Tar Beach* to your buddy in Mr. Larkin's second grade class. To prepare for the Buddy Reading, I am going to read the text aloud to you first so you can familiarize yourselves with the type of words and language the author uses. As I read, pay close attention to the way my voice changes to add expression to the text."

4. Read the text aloud. As you read, stop periodically to discuss the illustrations, point out challenging words in the text, and ask comprehension questions to ensure the class is following the storyline.

5. When you finish reading, ask, "What did I do to make sure that you could understand and enjoy listening to the text?" Discuss the pace at which you read, your use of pauses to give the listener time to absorb the text, and the way you pointed out details in the text and illustrations. Remind students to try to use these strategies when they read aloud to their younger buddies.

6. Later in the day, when the younger students arrive, have each pair of buddy readers find a place to sit comfortably together. Give each pair of students a copy of the text. Have the older students read the story to the younger students.

7. As students read, circulate and monitor. Do not interrupt the reading unless a student is truly struggling or reading in such a way that the younger listener cannot follow the story.

8. When all pairs have finished reading the book, use an attention signal, such as "Time to/ End." Say, "Now we are going to use the Think-Pair-Share strategy to discuss the story with our reading buddies. I am going to write a question on the board and read it aloud to the

class. Then I am going to set a timer for one minute. During that time, I would like everyone to think about the question silently. When the timer goes off, I will give you three minutes to discuss the question with your reading buddy. The younger buddies share their ideas first and then the older buddies will share. After three minutes, you will combine with another pair of reading buddies, making new groups of four students. After joining a group, you will have another three minutes to discuss the question in your groups."

9. Write a discussion question on the board and read it aloud to the class. Make sure that both the younger and the older students can discuss the question. For example, a question for *Tar Beach* might be "What does the title of the book mean? Why is this important?"

10. Set the timer and have students consider the question silently for one minute. When the timer goes off, have students discuss the question with their reading buddies. After the designated amount of time, assign each pair of students to another pair and give the groups time to share their thoughts about the question.

11. When the groups are finished discussing, ask volunteers, both younger and older students, to share their thoughts with the rest of the class.

12. After the younger students return to their classroom, have the older students continue their discussion using a protocol such as Put Your Two Cents In to take turns contributing to the discussion around a given topic or set of questions. In this example, the students could discuss a question such as "What role does discrimination play in Cassie's life? How do you know?"

13. As a final activity, encourage the class to discuss the illustrations that accompany the text in small groups. Explain that the illustrations are based on a story quilt that combines written text, painting, and quilt making into one piece of art. After examining and discussing the illustrations, invite students to write a journal entry responding to the question "How do the illustrations in *Tar Beach* contribute to your understanding of the characters' culture in the story?"

14. When students are finished with their journal entries, use the Merry-Go-Round discussion protocol to have students share their responses with the class.

Post-Reading Assessment

Now, it is your turn to start "swimming" by implementing engaging read-alouds. Start today. As you plan your next lesson, think about how you will incorporate the various read-aloud activities. Be intentional and strategic. As always, allow yourself the time and space to fail, to make mistakes, and to be uncomfortable. After two weeks of implementing CLR, come back to this chapter and complete figure 9.6 on how you use engaging read-alouds.

Figure 9.6 Engaging Uses of Read-Alouds: Survey After Infusing CLR Principles

0: *Never Emerging* 1: *Rarely Splashing* 2: *Sometimes Floating* 3: *Mostly Kicking* 4: *Always Freestyling*				
I read aloud to my students at least twice a week.	0	1 2 3 4		
I use a variety of materials for read-alouds.	0	1 2 3 4		
I encourage my students to engage in the activity of reading aloud as much as possible.	0	1 2 3 4		

STUDENT VOICE

Allowing Your Students to Be Engaged in Their Own Way, or "BeYou": Nonverbal Language Cues

BeYou is a call to action, reminding teachers to adjust instruction and classroom practices, ensuring that students can be themselves at school culturally and linguistically. In this section, we consider how students might express the importance of being validated and affirmed when using nonverbal language cues at school.

How can nonverbal language cues be culturally misunderstood in the classroom? Talking with words is only one way to communicate, and there are a lot of ways to say something, without really *saying* anything at all. You feel me? I can have a whole conversation with my friends, and we get it, even though no one actually *said* anything. Everything from the way we shake hands to how we style our hair communicates something about us and affects how we connect with others. The tricky part is sometimes this can get us in trouble in school, especially when nonverbal cues are assumed to mean something wrong or negative. Sometimes a certain look on my face or how I move my body might be misinterpreted as attitude or being disruptive when I'm actually trying to convey something else.

How does it feel to be misunderstood? A lot of what we do in school focuses on spoken or written language, but sometimes nonverbal cues can say something so much better. Honestly, this is one of the main ways I "talk"! These nonverbal cues and behaviors, like how I stand, my facial expressions, where I look, the gestures I make, and even the tone of my voice, are valid and important ways that I communicate. It's tough when these cues are misunderstood or seen as being rude or disrespectful, which can lead to getting in trouble, like being sent out of class or worse.

What do I need to be myself? Even when I'm not speaking, I am still saying a lot through my facial expressions, gestures, and body language. The key in the classroom is to try to work out what I am trying to say before assuming the worst or taking it personally. I am validated when my teachers recognize my nonverbal cues as a legitimate way to communicate. I feel affirmed when teachers try to read the situation and understand what I am trying to or need to say before assuming it means something negative or take it personally. It's also really cool when teachers look for ways to highlight nonverbal communication in the classroom, like making it part of our greetings or a way to check in with us throughout class.

What CLR activities validate and affirm nonverbal language cues? Activities like Silent Appointment and Tea Party Meet 'n' Greet encourage students to use nonverbal cues as a way to partner up, work together, and express themselves. And when teachers use nonverbal cues to check in with students or communicate with students, they validate and affirm students' use of these cues.

Build CLR Community and Collaboration

In CLR, we talk about how what is truly essential for cultural and linguistic responsiveness is love. This is beyond your ordinary love. It is *more* love. It is when you are loving in the best way that you can, and yet the situation, the students, the parents, your staff, a colleague, or the institution says to you, "But I need more." This "more" is defined as outrageous love, which is cultural and linguistic responsiveness.

Knowing that it happens to the best of us, even when we have the best intentions, identify a student who, for whatever reason, you have stopped responding to with "outrageous love." A student who has gotten on your "bad" side, your non-validating and non-affirming side. Reflect on how things got to this point with the student, and consider what you feel like you need to do to start giving outrageous love again. Create a plan to do so. Share your plan with a colleague.

Reflection

_____

_____

_____

_____

_____

_____

_____

Plan for Responding with Outrageous Love

_____

_____

_____

_____

_____

_____

_____

CHAPTER 10

Fill Your Toolbox: Common Literacy and Writing Activities Used Responsively

Now that you have learned specific responsive literacy techniques, it is time to fill your toolbox with general language and writing activities. These activities are used throughout literacy instruction to provide students with an even deeper culturally and linguistically responsive classroom experience. In this chapter, I present a collection of research-based reading and writing activities that CLR educators across the country use. All of these activities are intended to increase engagement and give you a variety of ways to support your students' literacy development.

These activities are appropriate for instruction across the curriculum. Content-area teachers looking for ways to incorporate reading and writing into their lesson plans will find models that enable them to enhance content learning through effective literacy strategies. Many of the activities can be considered validating and affirming or, at least, responsive. By using these activities, you are able to cover the content while incorporating a culturally responsive methodology.

Today's college and career readiness standards ask students to read stories and literature, as well as more complex texts that provide facts and background knowledge in areas such as science and social studies. Students will be challenged and asked questions that push them to refer back to what they have read. This stresses critical-thinking, problem-solving, and analytical skills that are required for success in college, career, and life.

Standards require that instruction include the following:

1. Regular practice with complex texts and their academic language
2. Reading, writing, and speaking grounded in evidence from texts, both literary and informational
3. Building knowledge through content-rich nonfiction

It is likely that many of the activities in this chapter are familiar to you; however, I hope that the descriptions and suggestions for use will provide new insights about how to use these activities with underserved students. This collection is not meant to be exhaustive by any measure. What CLR teachers must do is find the "right" fit for their students and strategize about how to effectively implement activities into their instruction.

The literacy resources in this chapter are organized into three parts:

◆ **Part One:** Reading Strategy Activities. Each strategy includes a list of related culturally and linguistically responsive (CLR) elements, an overview, when to use it, and implementation steps.

◆ **Part Two:** Writing Strategies. Each strategy includes a list of CLR elements, a description, and when to use it.

◆ **Part Three:** Writing Activities. Each activity includes a description and a list of CLR elements.

As you read through the activities, choose a few that will work with your teaching philosophy, your curriculum standards, and, most importantly, your students.

Part One: Reading Strategy Activities

The twenty reading strategy activities that follow address a range of literacy concepts and skills, including word recognition, vocabulary development, concept relationships, oral reading, prediction, using prior knowledge, understanding text structure, comprehension, literary interpretation, and questioning strategies.

ANTICIPATION/REACTION GUIDE

Validate and Affirm Cultural Behaviors: Sociocentrism, Linguistic or cultural appropriateness depending on the situation

Overview: An Anticipation/Reaction Guide utilizes two steps to increase reading comprehension—stimulating prior knowledge and experiences before reading and reinforcing key concepts after reading.

When to Use: Before and after reading

Process

1. Outline the main ideas (no more than five to six) in a reading selection. Write the ideas in a short list using clear declarative statements. Do not include generalizations or abstractions in this list. For example:

   ◆ Voting allows you to have a say in what the government does.

   ◆ You have to be 18 years old to vote.

   ◆ Women could not vote before 1920.

2. Rewrite the statements as questions to activate students' prior knowledge and elicit their reactions and responses.

   ◆ What is the purpose of voting?

   ◆ How old do you have to be to vote?

   ◆ Have women always been able to vote?

3. Have students write responses to each of the questions, including explanations and/or evidence to support the answers.

4. Allow students to openly discuss their responses prior to reading. Note any recurring themes in the discussion and any opposing or contradictory points of view.

5. Have students read the passage. Encourage them to write comments noting agreement and disagreement between their answers and the author's message or purpose.

DRAWING CONCLUSIONS

Validate and Affirm Cultural Behaviors: Sociocentrism, Linguistic or cultural appropriateness depending on the situation

Overview: The Drawing Conclusions strategy helps students review facts, details, and prior knowledge to form a conclusion about a text. This strategy is effective for all content areas.

When to Use: During and after reading

Process

1. Give each student a copy of the Drawing Conclusions activity sheet, found in appendix A (page 306).

2. Remind students that a conclusion is more than an inference. A conclusion is an explanation based on evidence.

3. Model for students the process of filling in the facts/details and inferences columns. Then, make a conclusion based on the text.

4. Put students in pairs and have them complete the activity sheet based on a shared reading or text.

5. Have students share their conclusions with the entire class.

HOT SEAT

Validate and Affirm Cultural Behaviors: Cooperation/Collaboration, Sociocentrism, Conversational Patterns, Orality and Verbal Expressiveness

Overview: Students take turns sitting in the Hot Seat and adopting the persona of a specific character from the text. The student in the Hot Seat answers questions posed by the rest of the class by taking into account the character's personality, perspective, and opinions.

When to Use: After reading

Process

1. Students read part or all of a selected piece of literature.

2. Divide the class into groups of three to five students. Assign each student a character from the book, or allow students to choose their own characters. Have each student adopt their character's persona by thinking about the character's attitudes, views, and personal characteristics. Encourage students to look back through the text and examine the information about the characters' actions, thoughts, and feelings.

3. Have all students, working independently or in small groups, prepare questions for each character. Questions may focus on the story's plot, a character's emotions, and so on.

4. Teachers may ask a panel of characters to assume the Hot Seat or limit it to one student. Using a response protocol, students take turns asking questions of the student(s) in the Hot Seat.

5. The student in the Hot Seat answers the questions from the perspective of their character.

Variation: Use puppets, character masks, or murals as a lead-in. This can also be used in content-area classes, such as social studies or science, with students taking on the personas of historical figures or scientists.

INTERACTIVE NOTES

Validate and Affirm Cultural Behaviors: Sociocentrism, Cooperation/Collaboration, Conversational Patterns

Overview: The Interactive Notes strategy helps students take an active role in the reading process and is effective for all content-area reading.

When to Use: Before, during, and after reading

Process

1. Provide students with the Interactive Notes three-column chart, found in appendix A (page 301).

2. Model how to answer a question such as "What do you think this text will be about? Why?" in the appropriate column.

3. Provide time for students to explore the text before reading it. Instruct students to look at the text's features and its visual elements. Then have students complete the first column of the activity sheet under the heading "Before Reading."

4. Read the text aloud together as a class. During the reading, periodically stop students and have them refer back to their interactive notes. Ask them to complete the "During Reading" column as they read the text.

5. When students have completed the reading, provide time for them to discuss the text in small groups of three to four. If appropriate, use a discussion protocol and provide questions to guide the students' discussion. Then have them complete the "After Reading" column independently.

6. Ask students to share their responses with the class.

7. Discuss how students' understanding of the text changed throughout the activity.

(Adapted from Burke 2002)

IT SAYS...I SAY...AND SO

Validate and Affirm Cultural Behaviors: Subjectivity, Field Dependence, Sociocentrism, Spontaneity

Overview: This strategy supports students in developing the skills to make inferences by combining information from the text with what they already know. This strategy is effective for all content areas.

When to Use: During and after reading

Process

1. Make a copy of the It Says…I Say…And So… activity sheet found in appendix A (page 302). Add two inferential questions to the activity sheet. Give each student a copy.

2. Model the strategy (or ask a student to model it) with a familiar text. Explain that inferential questions require readers to combine their prior knowledge with information in the text. For example, "What can we infer about the girl's father when she writes, 'I stayed up all night studying for the exam so I could prove my father wrong'?" To answer this question, the reader needs to infer that the girl's father did not believe she would do well on the test.

3. Ask students to read the first question.

4. Invite students to look at the text and write what the text says about the question. (It Says)

5. Encourage students to write what they already know about the question. (I Say)

6. Students write their conclusions or what they can infer about the question or answer. (And So)

7. Facilitate a classroom discussion about students' conclusions, using a discussion protocol such as Musical Shares or Silent Appointment.

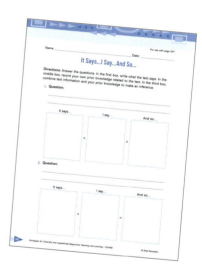

LANGUAGE EXPERIENCE APPROACH

Validate and Affirm Cultural Behaviors: Cooperation/Collaboration, Field Dependence, Linguistic or cultural appropriateness depending on the situation

Overview: The Language Experience Approach invites the students to work together with the teacher to create a collaborative narrative. During this activity, the teacher is the scribe as students dictate the narrative. The teacher uses the narrative as an authentic source for building reading fluency and increasing word knowledge. The only necessary material for this activity is a sheet of chart paper, a whiteboard, or another surface on which the teacher can write the students' story.

When to Use: Use for word recognition, vocabulary, and concept development

Process

1. Individually or in groups, students dictate a narrative as the teacher records it. The written passage is based on the students' oral language and personal expression. These features of language experience increase the likelihood that students, particularly readers who are below grade level, will be able to read and comprehend the dictated text.

2. When the dictation is complete, the teacher reads the narrative aloud and points to each word as students follow along. This process helps build a sight vocabulary for words that students already possess as part of a speaking vocabulary but have not yet mastered in written form. As the teacher reads the narrative, students are encouraged to make changes to clarify the text. These changes might be word substitutions, changes in sentence structure or sequence, or changes in punctuation.

3. When changes are complete, the teacher and students read the narrative together. The teacher once again points to each word as it is read aloud.

4. Students now try reading the narrative alone. If there are any words they cannot recognize or pronounce, the teacher notes these for later practice and review. These words might go into personal word banks or word walls that can serve as individual dictionaries for future reference during reading and writing activities.

5. When the teacher is confident that students can sight-read the words from the dictated composition, a final activity is to have students rewrite the narrative and illustrate it with a picture.

(Adapted from Ashton-Warner 1963)

LOGOGRAPHIC CUES

Validate and Affirm Cultural Behaviors: Subjectivity, Linguistic or cultural appropriateness depending on the situation

Overview: The Logographic Cues strategy has students use simple pictures or symbols to annotate the text while reading. This strategy helps struggling readers visualize, engage, and connect with the text and can be used in all content areas, for texts, notes, and vocabulary.

When to Use: During reading

Process

1. Introduce the concept of logographic cues. Display a chart showing sample logographic cues and what they represent, such as a heart to show how a character feels, a light bulb to indicate the main idea, and a house to allude to the setting. Model how to draw the pictures or symbols on sticky notes.

2. Think aloud as you read a section of text and demonstrate how to add the sticky notes to the text. For example, read a sentence, then pause and say, "I really don't understand what the author means in that sentence. I am going to add a sticky note with a question mark by that sentence so that I can come back later and clarify the meaning."

3. Depending on the needs of your students, you may want to use generic pictures or symbols initially. Encourage students to create their own pictures or symbols once the class is comfortable with the strategy.

4. Identify key ideas or concepts that your students need to be aware of as they read and have them place logographic cues on the appropriate pages when they encounter these.

5. Have students share their logographs or explain their thinking in writing when they are finished.

Sample Logographic Cue Chart

Logographic Cue	Meaning
?	I have a question./This doesn't make sense.
+	I agree./I like this point.
–	I disagree./I don't agree with this point.
!	This is unexpected/surprising.
	This gives me an idea.
	This gives information about a character.

MIND STREAMING

Validate and Affirm Cultural Behaviors: Sociocentrism, Cooperation/Collaboration, Subjectivity, Communalism

Overview: The Mind Streaming strategy is a structured way for students to tap into prior knowledge and comprehension of texts. It also helps students differentiate between main idea and details. This strategy is effective with content-area texts.

When to Use: Before reading

Process

1. Pair students and tell them what topic or text you will be discussing, providing a question if appropriate.

2. One student in the pair takes one minute to tell the other student everything they know about the topic or text. You can have students record their responses on a two-column chart with one column for each student.

3. The other student tells everything they know about the topic.

4. Give pairs about three minutes to discuss their answers. At the end of three minutes, each pair should have two examples to share with the class.

5. Discuss the answers as a class.

(Adapted from Santa, Havens, and Valdes 2014)

PHONOGRAMS—HINK-PINKS, HINKY-PINKIES, HINKETY-PINKETIES

Validate and Affirm Cultural Behaviors: Sociocentrism, Cooperation/Collaboration

Overview: Pairs of words that are one-syllable answers to riddles are called hink-pinks (frog-log), while answers of two syllables are called hinky-pinkies (gory-story), and three-syllable answers are called hinkety-pinketies (robbery-snobbery).

When to Use: Use for word recognition and building vocabulary after reading a text

Process

1. Before reading a book with multiple rhyming words, take students on a picture walk of the illustrations.

2. Encourage students to listen to the text for words that have endings that rhyme, such as *frog* and *log*. Read the story aloud.

3. Pause several times and have students name a word that rhymes with a word from the story.

4. Explain that you are going to give some clues and the class will think of rhyming words to guess the answer. At least one of the words should come from the story. For example, if the book included a fish, one clue and answer could be "a dream or request made by a water animal from our story." (fish/wish)

5. If students are having difficulty, provide one of the words in the hink-pink (the rhyming words that answer the clue) and have the students guess the second rhyming word.

6. To scaffold, begin as described in Step 5. Eventually, give the clues without providing hints and let the class guess both rhyming words.

7. When ready, allow students to create their own riddles with rhyming words as answers.

PICTURE THE FEELING

Validate and Affirm Cultural Behaviors: Sociocentrism, Field Dependence, Linguistic or cultural appropriateness depending on the situation

Overview: This strategy allows students to express their personal reactions to texts in a nonjudgmental setting. It also encourages students to develop mental images based on the text while reflecting on the importance of these mental pictures.

When to Use: After reading

Process

1. Have students read the selected text silently and independently. Tell students to highlight words, phrases, or sentences that they find meaningful or significant. Ask them to create vivid mental pictures that include the emotions that drew them to the piece of text.

2. Model sharing your own mental images. When sharing, read the selected words, phrases, or sentences from the text aloud and then explain the mental image to the class.

3. Invite students to share their own selected images from the literature.

Optional extensions: Students may record their selections in a double-entry journal, illustrate their mental pictures, and/or write about and share the importance of their selections.

QUESTION-ANSWER RELATIONSHIP (QAR)

Validate and Affirm Cultural Behaviors: Cooperation/Collaboration, Field Dependence, Linguistic or cultural appropriateness depending on the situation

Overview: The QAR strategy helps students develop various types of questions about a text to support comprehension. The four levels of questions are as follows:

- ◆ **Right There**—These questions are about facts or information that can be found directly in the text. For example, what was the name of the city where the characters lived?

- ◆ **Think and Search**—These questions pull information from the text. For example, what was the character struggling with in chapter 1 that he had resolved by chapter 4?

- ◆ **Author and You**—These are inference questions that consist of some information from the book and some from the reader's own thinking. For example, how did the character feel after the fight with his friend?

- ◆ **On My Own**—These questions ask the reader for an opinion based on their own knowledge and experiences. For example, how would the reader have handled the situation?

When to Use: During and after reading

Process

1. Explain the four levels of questions to students.

2. After reading a text, put students in pairs. Have each student write four questions. Then, have students trade papers with their partners. Students should identify the type of questions on their partners' papers and answer them.

(Adapted from Raphael 1982)

READER'S THEATER

Validate and Affirm Cultural Behaviors: Orality and Verbal Expressiveness, Sociocentrism, Communalism

Overview: Reader's Theater involves students in oral reading through reading parts in scripts. It helps build fluency through oral reading.

When to Use: During and after reading

Process

1. Select a text that can easily be made into a script based on the story. Identify the different characters, or student roles, in the text and create a script based on these roles. Or select a premade script or drama.

2. Assign each student a role or use a response protocol to decide which students will read specific parts.

3. Give students copies of the script and have them highlight their parts.

4. Provide time for students to practice reading through their parts independently.

5. Read through the script as a class with each student reading their designated part. Encourage students to use different voices and dramatic inflections to represent their characters or roles.

6. Discuss the text as a class. Use the text as a basis for learning about text structure, theme, and literary elements. Talk about how the Reader's Theater activity helps students comprehend specific aspects of the written text.

Optional: Have students produce a skit or play based on the script. Invite them to make costumes, props, and scenery. Perform the play for other classes or grade levels.

READING TEA PARTY

Validate and Affirm Cultural Behaviors: Kinesthetic, Sociocentrism, Cooperation/Collaboration, Subjectivity, Communalism, Dynamic Attention Span, Spontaneity

Overview: A Reading Tea Party serves as a valuable introductory activity by giving students a taste of the selection before they see the full text, novel, or play.

When to Use: Before and during reading instruction in all content areas

Process

1. Before beginning the lesson, write a selection of quotes from the text on small pieces of paper.

2. Divide the class into small discussion groups of four to five students. Distribute one quote to each group.

3. Invite students to read their assigned quotes. Ask them to discuss the quotes in their groups using the following questions:

   ◆ What do you think your quote means?

   ◆ Why do you think your quote might be important to the storyline?

   ◆ Who do you think says your quote?

   ◆ What predictions can you make based on your quote?

4. Have each group share its quote with the rest of the class. Ask one student to read the quote aloud and then have the other group members explain their thoughts and predictions about its significance.

5. Have students read the text either independently or as a class. During the reading, have them stop when they identify a quote. Instruct students to think about the actual context of the quote and the validity of their predictions.

6. When they have finished reading, encourage students to share their thoughts about the quotes with the rest of the class.

RECIPROCAL TEACHING

Validate and Affirm Cultural Behaviors: Cooperation/Collaboration, Sociocentrism, Communalism, Linguistic or cultural appropriateness depending on the situation

Overview: Reciprocal teaching involves teachers and students analyzing and discussing a segment of text to bring meaning to it. Four strategies structure the discussion: summarizing, generating questions, clarifying, and predicting. The teacher and students alternate assuming the instructor role to lead the discussion.

When to Use: Before, during, and after reading

Process

I. Summarizing helps the reader identify and integrate the most important information from the text.

1. Distribute the chosen text to students.

2. Invite students to summarize at the sentence, paragraph, and full-text levels.

Note: When students first begin employing reciprocal teaching, they typically remain at the sentence level. As students gain confidence and proficiency, they move to the paragraph and full-text levels.

II. Generating questions builds on summarizing and guides the learner one step further in the quest for comprehension.

1. Have students highlight the significant information in the text on which to base their questions.

2. Have students create questions and a self-assessment to validate their own questions.

Note: Question generating is an inclusive activity, encouraging students at all instructional levels to participate.

III. Clarifying is crucial for students who have a history of comprehension difficulty.

1. Explain that the purpose of reading is to comprehend the meaning of the text, not to read each word correctly. Clarifying eliminates barriers to understanding and enables the reader to fully comprehend a text.

2. Students are encouraged to be cognizant of the fact that many things can make a text difficult to understand, such as new vocabulary, unclear reference words, or challenging concepts.

Note: Clarifying provides a pathway to guide students to restore meaning.

IV. Predicting means generating a hypothesis about what will happen next in a text.

1. Review the relevant background knowledge students have on the topic.

2. Explain that the purpose of their reading is to confirm or disprove their hypothesis. As a result, they will link their new knowledge with their existing knowledge.

Note: This strategy builds on the knowledge of text structure, as students learn the role headings, subheadings, and embedded questions play in anticipating what might happen next.

(Adapted from Palincsar 1986)

Types of Text Structures

Text Structure	Description	Example
Cause and Effect	The cause-and-effect text structure describes the relationship between events, ideas, or concepts. Also, it describes the reasons something happened or the effects of a specific event or occurrence.	Description of how the assassination of Archduke Franz Ferdinand of Austria led to the beginning of World War I
Problem and Solution	This structure explains a particular problem or conflict and either proposes a solution or describes how the problem was resolved or overcome.	Discussion of how an increase in the use of bicycles as a form of transportation could decrease environmental pollution
Compare and Contrast	The compare-and-contrast text structure discusses the similarities and differences between two or more topics or ideas.	Essay about the similarities and differences between reptiles and amphibians
Chronological Order/ Sequence	This text structure explains a series of events in the order that they occurred. It may also be used to list the steps in a process.	An account of the major events, presented in chronological order, of the Battle of Gettysburg
Description	The description text structure provides an explanation of a concept, item, event, or location through the use of details and examples.	A description of what daily life was like for the early American colonists

SAVE THE LAST WORD FOR ME

Validate and Affirm Cultural Behaviors: Cooperation/Collaboration, Subjectivity, Communalism, Field Dependence

Overview: This strategy is used after reading to help students build confidence in their opinions and thoughts about a text.

When to Use: After reading

Process

1. Provide each student with an index card. Explain that after they read the text, they will record an interesting or important quotation from it on one side of the card. On the other side, they will explain why they think that quotation is interesting or important.

2. Put students into groups of three to four and have them read the text independently. When they finish, provide time for them to complete their index cards with a quotation on one side and an explanation on the other.

3. Select one student in each group to go first. This student reads the quotation on the front of their index card but does not comment on it. The rest of the students in the group take turns responding to the quotation and commenting on its significance. After everyone comments, the person who shared the quote concludes the discussion with the explanation on the back of the index card.

4. Repeat this process until all of the quotes have been shared and discussed.

(Adapted from Averette, n.d.)

SAY SOMETHING

Validate and Affirm Cultural Behaviors: Spontaneity, Subjectivity, Cooperation/Collaboration

Overview: This activity encourages students to work collaboratively to build meaning as they read a text together. Students stop periodically to make comments about the text to their partners.

When to Use: During reading

Process

1. Pair students together and give them a short text to read (or reread).

2. As students read, they should occasionally pause and say something to their partners about what they just read.

3. They should verbalize a prediction, connection, question, or comment.

4. Students continue until they reach the designated stopping point for their reading.

(Adapted from Short, Harste, and Burke 1996)

SKETCH TO STRETCH

Validate and Affirm Cultural Behaviors: Spontaneity, Subjectivity, Sociocentrism

Overview: The Sketch to Stretch strategy is a post-reading strategy where students think about what a passage or entire selection means to them and then draw symbolic representations of the text. This strategy is effective for all content areas.

When to Use: After reading

Process

1. Model for students how to create symbolic pictures for a text. As you share and discuss them, make sure students understand that the pictures are symbolic representations of the meaning of the text.

2. After students finish reading, have them work together or independently to create a sketch that symbolizes the meaning of the text.

3. When students finish their sketch, have them write an explanation of it. Instruct students to use evidence from the text to support their explanations.

4. Place students in groups to share their sketches. Encourage students to respond to one another's sketches to engage in a meaningful discussion.

(Adapted from Short, Harste, and Burke 1988)

SQ3R

Validate and Affirm Cultural Behaviors: Sociocentrism, Linguistic or cultural appropriateness depending on the situation

Overview: SQ3R stands for:

- ◆ **Survey:** The reader previews the material to develop a general outline for organizing information.
- ◆ **Question:** The reader raises questions with the expectation of finding answers in the material to be studied.
- ◆ **Read:** The reader attempts to answer the questions by reading silently.
- ◆ **Recite:** The reader deliberately attempts to answer aloud, or in writing, the questions.
- ◆ **Review:** The reader reviews the material by rereading portions of the assignment to verify the answers given during the Recite step.

When to Use: Before, during, and after reading informational text

Process

1. Lead students in a survey of a reading selection, paying special attention to headings, subheadings, topic sentences, and highlighted words.

2. Build a question for each heading and subheading in the text selection. These questions will be answered during the reading of the text.

3. Have students read the text carefully, keeping the questions in mind as they read.

4. Students recite the answers to the questions by verbalizing them in a group discussion or writing them down. The act of restating an answer reinforces learning.

5. This process is repeated for all questions.

6. Finally, students review all of their spoken or written answers. After modeling SQ3R several times, provide students with the SQ3R Guide found in appendix A (page 304). The guide contains cues for each step.

(Adapted from Robinson 1941)

THREE THINGS

Validate and Affirm Cultural Behaviors: Field Dependence, Subjectivity

Overview: The teacher provides students with three prompts before reading a text. As students read, they search for information related to the prompts. After reading the text, the class discusses the three elements using a discussion protocol.

When to Use: During reading

Process

1. Provide students with three prompts before having them read a text. The prompts can vary depending on the lesson objectives. For example, students might look for a connection, something surprising, something they knew already, something they agree or disagree with, a question, or a confusion.

2. Students work independently to read or reread the text.

3. As students read, they highlight or make notes based on the three prompts.

4. When students have their three things from the reading, they share them using a discussion protocol, such as Silent Appointment or Think-Pair-Share.

VISUAL ORGANIZERS

Validate and Affirm Cultural Behaviors: Field Dependence

Overview: Visual organizers are graphic representations of ways to think about and organize information. For example, some visual organizers show the whole-to-part relationships within a concept. Other organizers illustrate different ways to categorize, classify, define, or describe information. Visual organizers can be applied to many different concepts and activities, and students are encouraged to create the organizers themselves as they identify the type of thinking required for a particular activity or concept. Visual organizers can be used for many things:

- depicting order, sequence, or chronology
- comparing and contrasting
- categorizing and classifying
- illustrating cause-and-effect relationships
- understanding whole-to-part relationships
- describing
- showing problem-and-solution relationships

When to Use: Before, during, and after reading

Process

1. After selecting a text, consider the type of thinking necessary to understand the concepts presented in it. What types of relationships are explained? What is the purpose?

2. Decide if you want students to use a visual organizer before, during, or after reading.

   - If before reading, start the lesson by introducing the text through a picture walk or open-ended discussion about a topic related to the text. Then have students complete the visual organizer to activate their prior knowledge before reading the text.

   - If during reading, introduce the text and explain the purpose of the visual organizer. Think aloud as you model how to add a piece of information to the organizer. Have students complete the visual organizer as they read through the text.

   - If after reading, have students read the text independently, in small groups, or as a class. Then provide time for them to discuss the text with their peers before completing the visual organizer.

3. Incorporate information from the students' organizers as the class examines the text more closely through follow-up activities.

Part Two: Writing Strategies

The seven writing strategies in this section show the wide range of literacy skills that can be developed through writing. These strategies offer ways for students to work both independently and collaboratively to hone their skills through prewriting, writing, editing, and revising activities.

BRAINSTORMING

Validate and Affirm Cultural Behaviors: Subjectivity, Dynamic Attention Span, Immediacy, Spontaneity

When to Use: During prewriting

Description: Students are given a topic to discuss as a whole class or in a small group. Students use the language that is most comfortable for them. As ideas arise, students record the ideas. The teacher facilitates a whole-class discussion of the topic, using standard language.

COLOR-CODING REVISION

Validate and Affirm Cultural Behaviors: Cooperation/Collaboration, Subjectivity, Immediacy

When to Use: During revising

Description: Students work collaboratively to identify essential elements in each other's writing. Students are provided with highlighters and use different colored highlighters to indicate focus elements in a composition, such as yellow = thesis statement; blue = supporting evidence; green = topic sentences; and pink = transition words. After identifying the elements in the writing by color, students return the writing samples to the original authors. The authors then use the color-coding to identify any missing areas of information. For example, a lack of blue would indicate missing evidence to support a particular point. Students revise their compositions to include all the necessary elements.

JOURNAL WRITING

Validate and Affirm Cultural Behaviors: Spontaneity, Subjectivity

When to Use: During prewriting and writing

Description: Students engage in a free write about a specific topic or a meaningful experience in either nonstandard or standard language.

PEER RESPONSE GUIDES

Validate and Affirm Cultural Behaviors: Sociocentrism, Cooperation/Collaboration, Immediacy

When to Use: During revising

Description: Students work collaboratively to read and give structured feedback to one another about their writing, such as "Your introduction really grabs my attention because the anecdote is so realistic" or "The text example you use to support the topic sentence in paragraph three is not relevant to the topic." The teacher supplies a peer response feedback form to help students structure their feedback effectively. If appropriate, the teacher can structure the peer response feedback form to focus on particular skills or components of the text. For example, the following questions and prompts are designed to help students provide feedback about character development.

- List the characters in the text.
- Which characters do you find believable?
- If there are characters that you find unbelievable, what could be done to make them more believable?
- Does the author provide physical descriptions of the characters?
- Does the author describe the characters' thoughts, feelings, and opinions?
- Do the characters interact in a believable way?
- Are the characters' actions and dialogue consistent throughout the story?

PREWRITING TOOLS

Validate and Affirm Cultural Behaviors: Subjectivity, Field Dependence

When to Use: During prewriting

Description: Students use the following prewriting tools to help consolidate and visualize the information about their writing topic. **Note:** These tools are often used after brainstorming as the next step of organization in the writing process.

- *Free Writing*—Students engage in free writing as a way to start getting their initial ideas down on paper. During free writing, students write down whatever comes to mind without explaining the relationships between different ideas or types of information. They do not need to pay attention to spelling, punctuation, format, style, or grammar during this activity.
- *Diagramming*—Diagramming consists of visually organizing information and ideas around a certain topic. When using diagramming as a prewriting tool, students can draw lines and arrows to show connections between concepts, use various symbols or shapes to represent different topics, and illustrate relationships between main ideas and supporting details or evidence visually.
- *Outlining*—Outlining is a more structured prewriting tool that enables the student to create headings and subheadings to show the flow of information and the connections between topics.

READ-AROUND GROUPS

Validate and Affirm Cultural Behaviors: Sociocentrism, Cooperation/Collaboration, Immediacy

When to Use: During revising

Description: Students work in small groups and read one another's papers with specific criteria in mind. For example, students may be asked to respond to the development of a theme or moral in the writing, the correct use of grammar and punctuation, or the presence of topic sentences and supporting details. Each student reads their neighbor's paper and responds in writing using a peer feedback form designed to assess the identified criteria. After a specified amount of time, each student passes the paper clockwise to the next student. The process is repeated until group members have read the papers of everyone in the group.

After the rotation is complete, the writing sample and the peer feedback forms are returned to the student who wrote the text. Students then read the feedback and revise their writing accordingly.

WRITING TEMPLATES AND FRAMES

Validate and Affirm Cultural Behaviors: Supports inductive learning

When to Use: During prewriting and writing

Description: Students use writing templates or frames to plan their writing. Writing templates support students' ability to organize their ideas in a more linear format or one that is appropriate for the type of writing. For example, a story strip is a useful template for writing narratives. When using a story strip, students draw and write a series of events they plan to include in their narratives. When writing an opinion piece, templates that allow students to state their opinions and then record the reasons, evidence, and details to support these opinions can be very beneficial.

Since informative writing often follows specific text structures based on the purpose of the writing, writing templates based on these text structures can help students organize their ideas before they start writing.

Part Three: Writing Activities

The fifteen universally applicable writing activities that follow offer a range of writing experiences for students at all levels. Some of the activities build on collaborative actions, some serve to extend students' understanding of the writing process, and others support cultural understanding and responsiveness.

ACROSTICS

Validate and Affirm Cultural Behaviors: Subjectivity, Cooperation/Collaboration, Sociocentrism, Dynamic Attention Span, Kinesthetic

Description: Acrostics are poems created by writing a name or concept down the left side of a page. For each letter, write a word that describes the name or concept to you. The following example is an acrostic poem for the word *validate*, an especially important concept in culturally responsive teaching and learning.

Example:

V—value

A—affirm

L—love

I—individuality

D—distinguish

A—acceptance

T—trust

E—engage

ALTERNATIVE ENDINGS

Validate and Affirm Cultural Behaviors: Spontaneity, Subjectivity

Description: Students develop a new ending for a written or oral story.

CAROUSEL WRITING

Validate and Affirm Cultural Behaviors: Kinesthetic, Sociocentrism, Cooperation/ Collaboration, Conversational Patterns, Dynamic Attention Span

Description: The teacher posts four to five sheets of chart paper around the room, each with a prompt. Students are placed into small groups and each group starts at one of the posters. When the teacher gives the signal, students begin collaborating to write a paragraph on the topic, with one person writing. The length of time spent at each chart paper will vary according to the age of the students, but five to ten minutes is usually sufficient.

When the teacher turns on the music (or gives another attention signal), students rotate clockwise to the next chart paper. Groups review where the last group left off and add to the paragraph, or make revisions and then add. This process continues until all groups are back at their original chart paper.

Then the groups read and revise their paragraphs for effectiveness (based on predetermined criteria, such as content, spelling, grammar, or structure). After revising, groups share their paragraphs with the whole class and students give feedback and ask questions based on criteria for an effective paragraph.

CHARACTER PORTRAITS

Validate and Affirm Cultural Behaviors: Supports inductive learning

Description: Concentrating on the roles of specific characters, students create pictures of the characters and describe how they fit into the story.

CHARACTER PROFILES

Validate and Affirm Cultural Behaviors: Supports inductive learning

Description: Students develop a short description of a character, using nonstandard language, standard language, or both.

CULTURE BITS

Validate and Affirm Cultural Behaviors: Sociocentrism, Field Dependence, Orality and Verbal Expressiveness

Description: Short bits of cultural information are provided to students at the beginning, the middle, or the end of class. Students must take notes and discuss the cultural topic.

DISCOVERY WORDS

Validate and Affirm Cultural Behaviors: Field Dependence, Subjectivity

Description: Students write a word representing a main concept or idea in the center oval. In the surrounding ovals, they add related words and concepts.

Example:

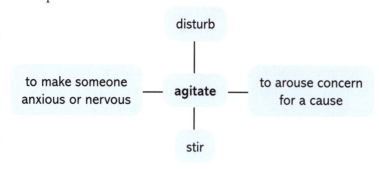

DRAW IT

Validate and Affirm Cultural Behaviors: Subjectivity

Description: Teachers give students a prompt or question, and students draw or paint a visual representation of their response. Then, students write a description of their picture.

INTERVIEWS

Validate and Affirm Cultural Behaviors: Sociocentrism, Cooperation/Collaboration, Subjectivity

Description: Students prepare a set of open-ended questions revolving around a cultural topic. Students use the questions to interview people within their family and community. Students share the information they gathered from their interviews through classroom presentations, written biographical reports, or using Silent Appointments. They can also integrate this information into larger research projects or units of study.

PASS IT ON

Validate and Affirm Cultural Behaviors: Sociocentrism, Cooperation/Collaboration, Subjectivity

Description: Students are put in small groups of four to five and given a prompt or sentence starter. One student writes the first sentence and then passes the paper to the next student to write the next sentence and so on until all students have written something and they have a paragraph. Students then share their paragraphs with the entire class.

PREDICTING

Validate and Affirm Cultural Behaviors: Subjectivity

Description: Students consider what will occur next in a reading selection and write their predictions in their own words or translate their predictions into standard language form.

QUESTION CIRCLE

Validate and Affirm Cultural Behaviors: Sociocentrism, Cooperation/Collaboration

Description: Students are seated in a circle. Each student writes a question at the top of a sheet of paper about a designated topic. For example, the teacher may instruct the students to write a question about the illustrations in a particular text. Students then pass their papers to the left. Students read the question and answer it. If time permits, students continue passing the papers and answering the questions several times.

Each paper is returned to the student who wrote the question at the top. Use a response protocol, such as Train/Pass It On, to have students call on one another to share their questions and answers with the rest of the class.

SCRAMBLED SENTENCES

Validate and Affirm Cultural Behaviors: Sociocentrism, Cooperation/Collaboration

Description: Students rearrange a list of scrambled words that the teacher provides to form a sentence that makes sense. They can work independently, in pairs, or in small groups.

SNAPSHOTS

Validate and Affirm Cultural Behaviors: Sociocentrism, Cooperation/Collaboration, Subjectivity

Description: Give each student a picture or photograph that shows a particular moment in time. Have students imagine that they are in the picture. Ask them to use their imaginations and write about what they see, hear, smell, taste, and feel.

Variation: This can also be used as a revision activity to help make students' writing more focused. Select a specific passage from a student's writing sample that needs more detail and have the student create a mental image of the scene. Then the student adds details to the writing by drawing upon all five senses.

STORY RETELLING

Validate and Affirm Cultural Behaviors: Sociocentrism, Cooperation/Collaboration, Subjectivity

Directions: Students retell a story in oral or written form using nonstandard language or standard language. They share their retelling with a partner.

STUDENT VOICE

Allowing Your Students to Be Engaged in Their Own Way, or "BeYou": Verbal Overlap and Nonlinear Conversational Patterns

BeYou is a call to action, reminding teachers to adjust practices, ensuring that students can be themselves at school culturally and linguistically. Here we consider how students might express the importance of being validated and affirmed when using verbal overlap and nonlinear conversational patterns.

How can verbal overlap, and nonlinear conversational patterns, be culturally misunderstood in the classroom? Conversations in my house are the best! When we talk, we get into it all and everyone is jumping in, adding on, shouting out… it's like this ball of energy that everyone is feeding. We jump around when it fits the topic, like we don't go straight from the beginning to the end of something that happened. Instead, we jump around to different parts, like starting in the middle, then going back to the beginning, and then skipping to the end. At school, it's so different. I've been told that when I jump in, or bounce around, it can feel like I am interrupting or can't keep track of what someone else is saying. I get told to focus or to wait my turn because it's rude to jump in when someone else is talking.

How does it feel to be misunderstood? My conversational style is what works best for me, because I get to hear different perspectives and ideas all at once, and no one really decides for anyone else when it's okay to jump in or how the conversation is going to flow. In school, though, we are usually asked to raise hands or wait our turn. I get the need for that sometimes. When it's the only way we get to talk in class, though, it can get frustrating. I have always talked this way, and I mean no disrespect. It's how we do it at home, and when I'm with my friends, and it actually takes verbal agility, you know? It means I AM paying attention, I'm interested, and I'm with you! That's a fact!

What do I need to be myself? Give me the chance to get into a conversation that welcomes verbal overlap and my nonlinear way of jumping in, and you will see how focused and connected I am. It makes talking in class more fun and that means we are more engaged! I am validated when the activities we do in class invite nonlinear conversations because it means my way of talking is accepted and valued by teachers. It's reassuring to talk freely without waiting for a turn or a cue.

What CLR activities validate and affirm verbal overlap and nonlinear conversational patterns?

Shout Out and Carousel Brainstorm validate and affirm verbal overlap and nonlinear conversational patterns, because they provide the opportunity to jump in, hear many responses at the same time, and talk in nonlinear ways. Having whole-class conversations that center verbal overlap and nonlinear discussion shows that you appreciate and respect different ways of talking. It's like saying, "Hey, I see how we all like to chat, and that's cool!"

Building CLR Community and Collaboration

Each teacher brings a student artifact (student work) to "show and not tell." See if the group members can reconstruct a description of the activity, the learning standard taught, and whether the outcome was achieved as shown by evidence (or not), by simply examining the student work.

Activity

Standards

Outcome

Culturally and Linguistically Responsive Language and Learning Environment

Culturally and Linguistically Responsive Language and Learning Environment Overview

This section, the final one for this book, continues our exploration of the overriding idea of the CLR approach: situational appropriateness. Situational appropriateness is the crux of CLR. Students are allowed to make choices around cultural and linguistic behaviors dependent on the situation without giving up or sacrificing what they consider to be their base culture or language. The action of being linguistically or culturally appropriate depending on the situation is what I sometimes call *culture switching* or *language switching*. In the context of CLR, being situationally appropriate is an intentional choice to skillfully make a cultural or linguistic adaptation or shift, without giving up, disavowing, or abandoning the home culture or language.

Chapter 11, which opens this section, focuses on language and the linguistic behaviors of students who are Standard English learners. Most Standard English learners speak what linguists call *nonstandard languages*. Institutions and schools do not typically accept them as legitimate languages. The most well-known and researched languages are African American Vernacular English (African American Language), Chicano English (Mexican American Language), Native American Languages, and Hawaiian Pidgin English (Hawaiian American Language). These languages are not the only unaccepted languages. There are a host of unaccepted languages depending on the region, such as the Appalachian English spoken in the Carolinas, Tennessee, and West Virginia. CLR educators are linguistically responsive when they see nonstandard languages as legitimate, rather than wrong, bad, or incorrect.

> In the context of CLR, being situationally appropriate is an intentional choice to skillfully make a cultural or linguistic adaptation or shift, without giving up, disavowing, or abandoning the home culture or language.

> Standard English learners are students for whom Standard English is not spoken as their home language.

Chapter 12 defines a responsive learning environment. This chapter takes you through a process for transforming your environment according to set criteria, moving your environment toward a more culturally responsive setting. During the process, you will closely examine your classroom for racial images and consider the possibility that it is overcommercialized.

Terms Central to Understanding Culturally and Linguistically Responsive Teaching

Term	Definition
Language	A legitimate linguistic entity defined around the parameters of phonics, markers, grammar, vocabulary, nonverbal uses, and discourse styles.
Home Language	The language utilized by family members in the home and others in the community that is different enough from the parameters defined by Standard English.

Terms Central to Understanding Culturally and Linguistically Responsive Teaching *(cont.)*

School Language	The language utilized in the context of school; commonly associated with Standard English.
Nonstandard Languages	Not the opposite of *standard language*; only used in the generic context of the term *language*; speaks to the non-acceptance of these languages, not to their lack of legitimacy. These languages are linguistically legitimate, following grammatical structures and rules just as "standard" language does.
Standard English	The English language that is uniform with respect to spelling, grammar, pronunciation, and vocabulary; the well-established language used in formal and informal speech and writing; widely recognized as acceptable wherever English is spoken and understood.
Academic Language	The language used in textbooks, in classrooms, and on tests; different in structure (e.g., heavier on compound, complex, and compound-complex sentences) and vocabulary (e.g., technical terms and common words with specialized meanings) from Standard English.
African American Language, African American Vernacular, or Black English	The systematic, rule-governed language that represents an infusion of the grammatical substratum of West African languages and the vocabulary of English.
American Indian Language	The language of American Indians used at home, on the job, in the classroom, and in other areas of daily experience. It shows extensive influence from the speaker's Native language tradition and differs accordingly from nonnative notions of standard grammar and appropriate speech (Leap 1993).
Chicano or Mexican American Language	The systematic, rule-governed language spoken by the Chicano and/or Mexican American community united by common ancestry in the Southwestern United States and/or Mexico.
Hawaiian American Language or Hawaiian Pidgin English	A native speech that evolved as a result of Hawaii's diverse background. It is also called *Da Kine* or, more commonly, *Pidgin*, though it really is not a pidgin anymore but actually a creole, or Hawaii Creole English, as termed by the Ethnologue database (ethnologue.com). Unlike other English-based pidgin, Hawaiian Pidgin is founded within several different languages, with the Hawaiian language contributing the most words. Still, the term *Pidgin* remains.

CHAPTER 11

Looking for Language in All the Right Places: Methods for Validating and Affirming Home Language

Understanding the Context

As you are becoming a CLR educator, you are embracing the three linguistic absolutes, or underlying assumptions. Even though there are strong disagreements and debates about the origins of nonstandard languages, there is much more agreement about these three assumptions. For that reason, I prefer to use the term *absolute*. The first absolute is that all language is good. There is no such thing as a bad language, incorrect English, or improper English. The second absolute is that the rules of nonstandard languages are not fabricated or random. They have grammatical structure, and some have their own dictionaries and grammar books. The third absolute is that we acquire our home language from our primary caregivers by the time we are four years old. These three absolutes establish the basis for the linguistic lens the responsive teacher must use.

This chapter walks a fine line between focusing too heavily on linguistics and relaying the three most critical factors applicable to CLR. Those factors are:

1. Recognizing linguistic behaviors
2. Providing opportunities for Standard English/Academic Language development
3. Using teachable moments to support students in being linguistically or culturally appropriate depending on the situation

Note that factors 1 and 3 are applicable to all educators, while factor 2 will mainly apply to those practitioners directly involved in providing English language arts or reading and writing instruction.

> The three linguistic absolutes:
>
> All language is good.
>
> Rules of nonstandard language are not fabricated or random.
>
> We acquire our home language from our primary caregivers by the time we enter school.

> When educators recognize students' linguistic behaviors or the use of the rules of home languages as positives and not deficits, they can then begin to validate and to affirm students' language. Consequently, teachers can begin the process of building and bridging that will enable students to succeed within the context of school culture and language (Hollie 2018, 45).

Teachable moments can be fun, especially when students ask you to move back and forth between home languages and school English. Make those moments a regular part of your classroom culture and use them to reinforce being culturally or linguistically appropriate in the situation.

Considering the Research

Research supports the use of strategies that validate and affirm students' home languages in conjunction with lessons about situational appropriateness. The following studies represent a sample of relevant research supporting the use of strategies regarding situational appropriateness in a culturally responsive classroom.

- The school literacy learning and achievement of students of diverse backgrounds is improved when educators acknowledge, value, and consider the role of home languages, interaction with students, and their relationships with the community (Au 1998).

- Already possessed competencies in nonstandard versions of English, such as African American Vernacular English (AAVE), can be leveraged by culturally responsive educators to improve literacy and content area learning of historically underachieving students (Lee 2007).

- By legitimizing students' experience with their nonstandard language through CLR techniques, educators can diminish achievement gaps (Hollie 2018).

- Teachers who had contact with the households of their students were able to leverage their understanding of the "funds of knowledge" available to the students at home in order to better design classroom instruction that would meet their students' needs (Moll et al. 2004).

- Utilizing the standard dialect in the context of writing and role play can serve as a bridge, supporting students in their nonstandard English dialects while instructing them in the standard dialect (Wyse et al. 2013).

Pre-Reading Assessment

Before reading this chapter, reflect on how you currently validate and affirm your students' home languages by completing the survey in figure 11.1. As you rate yourself, think about how frequently and effectively you give your students opportunities to practice situational appropriateness. If you are not doing any validating and affirming or practicing of situational appropriateness, think about ways that you can start implementing culturally responsive strategies.

Figure 11.1 Validating and Affirming Home Language Survey: Before Infusing the CLR Principles

0: *Never Emerging* 1: *Rarely Splashing* 2: *Sometimes Floating* 3: *Mostly Kicking* 4: *Always Freestyling*					
I validate and affirm my students' home languages whenever possible.	0	1	2	3	4
I proactively plan opportunities for my students to practice situational appropriateness.	0	1	2	3	4
I reactively use teachable moments to have my students use situationally appropriate language.	0	1	2	3	4

(Used with permission from Daniel Russell)

Beginning the Reflective Process

Learning happens when we reflect upon what we have experienced. Critical reflection generates, deepens, and documents learning (Ash and Clayton 2009). So, are you ready to validate and affirm students' home languages?

Use the following checklist to gauge your readiness and ability to effectively integrate activities about situational appropriateness into your teaching. Each item represents an important aspect of understanding and using situational appropriateness in a culturally responsive classroom. After completing the checklist, read the detailed descriptions of each item and reflect on how you plan to implement or increase your use of activities involving situational appropriateness in the classroom.

☑ The Use of Home Language Reflection Checklist

Item 11.1	Do I recognize the linguistic behaviors of my students?	○ Yes ○ No
Item 11.2	Do I explicitly plan for my students to practice situational appropriateness?	○ Yes ○ No
Item 11.3	Do I use teachable moments to have my students use situationally appropriate language?	○ Yes ○ No

Item 11.1 Do I recognize the linguistic behaviors of my students?

You must ask yourself this question. Some school districts have developed screeners to help identify Standard English learners. For instance, the Los Angeles Unified School District utilizes a Diagnostic Screener that can identify the use of features of AAVE, Mexican American English, and Hawaiian American Language (LAUSD 2012). Figure 11.2 shows a home language survey created by a group of CLR teachers. This survey was created for a particular population of African American students in Los Angeles. Thus, it is offered only as a possibility, depending on your population and context.

The best way to truly recognize the linguistic behaviors of your students is to be familiar with the rules of the more common unaccepted languages—namely African American Vernacular English (AAVE) and Mexican American (Chicano) English. Lists of the most common rules for each language are described in figures 11.3 and 11.4, respectively.

Figure 11.2 Home Language Frequency Writing Checklist Sample

Linguistic Feature	Example	Tally
Present Tense Copula Verb	She pretty.	
Third Person Singular Present Tense	He <u>run</u> fast.	
Past Tense Auxiliary Verb	We <u>was</u> here.	
Past Tense Marker *–ed*	He <u>visit</u> us yesterday.	
Plural Marker	I have 25 <u>cent</u>.	
Possessive Marker	That is my <u>sister</u> bike.	
Indefinite Article	I have <u>a</u> egg.	
Multiple Negation	He <u>don't</u> have <u>none</u>.	
Reflexive Pronoun	He hurt <u>hisself</u>.	
Same Voiced Consonant Clusters	I put my <u>tes'</u> on your <u>des'</u>.	
/th/ Sound	<u>Dis</u> is my <u>mouf</u>.	
/r/ Sound or /er/ Sound	<u>Yo</u> <u>sista</u> is <u>Ca'ol</u>.	
/l/ Sound	Did you <u>caw</u> me?	
It's a/There	<u>It's a</u> bird in here.	
Habitual *Be*	She <u>be</u> mean.	
African American Language Homonyms	Did you <u>fine</u> my book?	
Topicalization	That <u>boy he</u> funny.	
Ask/Ax	Can I <u>ax</u> you something?	
Present Tense Auxiliary Verb	<u>He coming</u> with us.	
Copula Verb Contraction	<u>Red</u> a pretty color.	
Short /ĕ//Short /ĭ/	I am <u>tin</u> years old.	

REFLECTIVE THOUGHT

The main point is that it is not so much about remembering the rules of different languages as it is about believing that your students come with linguistic differences, regardless of the language they use. While some of your students may appear proficient in Standard English, in actuality, they are not. You must recognize this fact through a linguistic lens. What is the linguistic lens you use to view your students' language? What actions do you take to help your native English speakers be respectful of linguistic differences?

Figure 11.3 African American Vernacular English (AAVE) Common Rules List

Categories	Examples
Sounds	**Sounds**
/th/ Sound (digraphs)	<u>Dis</u> is my <u>mouf</u>.
Consonant Clusters	I put my <u>tes'</u> on your <u>des'</u>.
Vowels Short /ĕ/ and Short /ĭ/	I am <u>tin</u> years old.
Reflexive /r/ Sound or /er/ Sound	<u>Yo</u> <u>sista</u> is <u>Ca'ol</u>.
Markers (Morphemes)	**Markers (Morphemes)**
Past Tense Marker –*ed*	He <u>visit</u> us yesterday.
Possessive Marker	That is my <u>sister</u> bike.
Plural Marker	I have 25 <u>cent</u>.
Syntax	**Syntax**
Multiple Negation	He <u>don't</u> have <u>none</u>.
Habitual *Be*	She <u>be</u> mean.
Topicalization	That <u>boy he</u> funny.
Present Tense Copula Verb	She pretty.
Regularized Patterns	**Regularized Patterns**
Reflexive Pronoun	He hurt <u>hisself</u>.
Present Tense Singular Verb	He <u>run</u> fast.
Past Tense Singular Verb	We <u>was</u> here.

Figure 11.4 Mexican American (Chicano) English Common Rules List

Categories	Examples
Sounds	**Sounds**
/th/ Sound (digraphs)	<u>Dis</u> teecher is mean.
Final Consonant Clusters and Medial Consonant Clusters	I <u>lef</u> my game over there. My dad went to da <u>harware</u> store.
Vowels Short /ĕ/ and Short /ĭ/	I don't got a <u>pin</u>.
/z/ and /v/ Sounds	The firemen <u>safed</u> many lifes. He won da <u>price</u> at the fair.
Circumflex Intonation (Nahuatl influenced from Native American Language)	<u>Doon't</u> bee <u>baaad</u>!
Breath H (Nahuatl influenced)	My hair was all <u>hwite</u>, so I dyed it.
Stress Patterns	I get paid <u>tooday</u>.
Markers (Morphemes) Phonologically Influenced	**Markers (Morphemes) Phonologically Influenced**
Past Tense Marker –*ed*	She <u>move</u> to San Diego.
Morphological Sensitive Rule (*thuh* before consonant/*thee* before a vowel)	We saw <u>thee</u> ocean over there.
Plural Marker (dropped when forming a separate syllable)	He always <u>ditch</u> school.
Syntax	**Syntax**
Multiple Negation	She <u>don't</u> like <u>nobody</u>.
Intensifiers	Mom was <u>all</u> lost on the way to my tia's. This movie <u>barely</u> came out.
Topicalization	My <u>brother he's</u> going to the movies.
Present Tense Copula Verb	This...a school.
Prepositional Variation	He was sitting <u>in</u> the couch.
Regularized Patterns	**Regularized Patterns**
Indefinite Article	Do you want <u>a</u> ice cream?
Present Tense Singular Verb	He <u>jump</u> rope to get in shape.
Pronoun	Now they can do it by <u>theirselves</u>.

Thought-Provokers: A Mindset for Moving Forward

1. How many languages do I speak? How did I acquire them?

   This reflection will help you create empathy for your students' experience.

2. The purpose of recognizing nonstandard languages is to validate and affirm students' languages. I acknowledge this and am remembering to build and bridge.

Thought-Blockers: A Mindset for Staying Stagnant

1. I find it difficult to resist the temptation to correct.

   Know that validating and affirming students' home languages does not mean you are not teaching academic language.

2. I need more knowledge building. I am, however, not willing to acquire this knowledge.

To learn more, read up on low-status languages or traditional languages in general. There are many books and articles of interest. Books like Peter Trudgill and Jean Hannah's (2008) *International English: A Guide to Varieties of Standard English* can help you understand the wide variety of even Standard English forms. Likewise, Wyse et al. (2013) describe many stories of students and teachers with low-status dialects functioning in the United Kingdom. *Language Endangerment and Language Maintenance: An Active Approach* by David and Maya Bradley (2013) gives a nice overview of the many traditional and low-status languages that have been rapidly disappearing and the efforts being made to record and maintain them. Finally, the article "Language Endangerment and Language Maintenance" by Wang Lie-qin (2012) describes similar processes and ongoing efforts specifically in China.

Item 11.2 Do I explicitly plan for my students to practice situational appropriateness?

This item may sound more daunting than it is. For many Standard English learners and English language learners, school is probably the only place where they will be exposed to proficient Standard English or academic language. As a CLR educator, providing students with opportunities to practice using Standard English and academic language in a linguistically affirming environment is a must. You have four options for explicitly creating situational appropriateness.

1. **Sentence Lifting.** Students take sentences directly from literature, poetry, songs, plays, student-elicited sentences, or scripts that incorporate specific contrasts of home and Standard English rule forms. Students perform contrastive analysis translations to determine the underlying rules that distinguish the two language forms. For example, teachers commonly take lines of rap music and ask students to change those lines into Standard English and then analyze the sound difference, effect on audience, or the grammar structure.

2. **Retellings.** Students first read or listen to a text presented in Standard English. Then, they use their home languages to retell the story or piece of text. The students' retellings are taped so that they can be compared and contrasted with the language of the text.

3. **Role-Playing.** Role-playing gives students opportunities to practice situations through acting and writing in Standard English. The emphasis is on situational appropriateness, which calls on students to weigh the language most suited to the environment, audience, purpose, and function.

4. **Teachable Moments.** The teacher elicits spontaneous responses from students about material read or presented, creating on-the-spot opportunities for situational appropriateness in the classroom.

REFLECTIVE THOUGHT

Students need practice with situational appropriateness. Your grade level or subject area will determine how deep you can go when planning explicit lessons for situational appropriateness. How can you incorporate practice with situational appropriateness into your daily instruction? What subject areas or specific parts of your instruction will be best suited for activities involving situational appropriateness?

To help students develop Standard English, English Language Development (ELD) instruction focuses on word recognition, academic language or vocabulary development, reading comprehension, and oral language. ELD techniques are strategies designed to help students who speak languages other than Standard English. If students have Basic Interpersonal Communication Skills (BICS) but need to develop Cognitive Academic Language Proficiency (CALP), employ the instructional method known as Specially Designed Academic Instruction in English (SDAIE). These are the five steps for creating an SDAIE lesson:

1. Consider the linguistic needs and cultural behaviors of the students in your class.

2. Know the rationale and rules for the instructional focus areas you plan to teach. Select an instructional focus area that aligns with state and grade-level standards.

3. Gather tools, relevant realia, resources, materials, music, posters, books, personal thesauruses, and supplies that will assist you in creating the SDAIE activity.

4. Designate the most beneficial place for the SDAIE activity within the lesson plan.

5. Teach a small group or the whole class and include an SDAIE learning center or instructional area for additional learning practice.

The following is an example of an SDAIE activity used with upper elementary students in Los Angeles for the linguistic rule of multiple negation.

Sample Mini-Lesson on Multiple Negation

Note: The main points can be displayed on the board or put on a handout for students. The mini-lesson can also be used for note-taking practice. The sentence "I don't never have no money" should be clearly visible for every student. The lesson centers on this sentence.

Teacher: Remember the other day when I gave you the journal starter "Tell me about a time when you wanted to buy something"? Well, this response came from that assignment. Who can tell me what they notice about the language used in this sentence?

Student: It's written in African American Language.

Teacher: That's right. It is written in AAL. Tell me again, class. What does AAL stand for?

Students: AAL means African American Language.

Teacher: Yes, African American Language. What is African American Language? Who can tell me?

Student: African American Language combines English words with West African language rules and structure.

Teacher: Correct again. African American Language is when English words and vocabulary are laid over West African language rules and structure. Does anyone remember what I mean when I say *linguistic feature*?

No students respond so the teacher continues.

Teacher: No? Okay, a linguistic feature is the "grammar rule" of a language. Today, we are going to talk about one of the linguistic features of African American Language.

Teacher underlines the displayed sentence as an example of multiple negation.

Teacher: Can someone read this sentence for me? Does anyone think they know what the linguistic feature or grammar rule for this sentence is?

No students respond so the teacher continues.

Teacher: This linguistic feature is called multiple negation. Why do you think that is what it is called?

Student: It has more than one negative in the sentence.

Teacher: Right. It has more than one negative in the sentence. Can someone come up and circle the negatives in this sentence?

A selected student walks up and circles the negatives don't, never, *and* no.

Teacher: Thank you. Okay, in West African languages, the rule is the more negatives that are in a sentence, the more negative the statement is. The multiple negatives are used for emphasis. "I don't never have no money." What is this sentence trying to emphasize?

Student: It means I don't have any money.

Teacher: Right, it is emphasizing the *never*. It's not that the person doesn't have money right now, but that they *never* have money. Now, in MAE—what is MAE again, class?

Students: It's Mainstream American English.

Teacher: Correct, Mainstream American English. In MAE, double or multiple negatives cancel each other out, like in math. So, when writing the sentence in MAE, we need to get rid of how many negatives, everyone?

Students: Two.

Teacher: That's right, two. So, the sentence could be written, "I never have money." So, let's review. Class, what is the linguistic feature in the underlined sentence?

Students: Multiple negation.

Teacher: That's correct, multiple negation. What is the rule for multiple negation in African American Language?

Student: More negatives make the statement more negative.

Teacher: Correct. The more negatives in a sentence, the more negative the statement is. Multiple negation is used for emphasis. What about MAE? What is the rule about negatives in MAE?

Student: One negative is used in Mainstream American English.

Teacher: Good. More than one negative in a sentence cancels out the negative and makes the statement positive. Good job. We will practice some more with multiple negatives tomorrow.

Thought-Provokers: A Mindset for Moving Forward

1. Once I recognize a behavior as linguistic, I validate and affirm *and* build and bridge.
2. I explicitly plan for situational appropriateness, which keeps me focused on building and bridging.

Thought-Blockers: A Mindset for Staying Stagnant

1. For me as a content-area teacher (or a physical education, art, music, or foreign language teacher), taking a little bit of time to focus on language seems like a distraction.
2. I am not willing to step outside of my comfort zone and focus on language.

Item 11.3 Do I use teachable moments to have my students use situationally appropriate language?

When you use SDAIE or create opportunities for your students to use situational appropriateness, you are taking a proactive approach. There will be times when teachable moments arise and you must take a more reactive approach. A teachable moment is when a student (or adult) uses their home language in a natural, authentic way, and then adjusts their language in that moment for situational appropriateness. No actual planning for these moments or teaching is immediately necessary. (See figure 11.5 for an example of how an interviewee adjusts their language to communicate appropriately in the situation.) These moments occur haphazardly and without warning. What you have to do is validate and affirm, and then build and bridge by asking the student to be linguistically or culturally appropriate depending on the situation. For instance, let us say a student uses their home language while explaining an answer in class. What are the steps you need to take?

1. Acknowledge and recognize the use of the home language by validating and affirming the statement with positive comments that recognize the use of the language, such as "I like how you expressed that," "I am impressed by your use of home language in your explanation," or "That sounded great, very authentic."

2. Use a build-and-bridge statement, signaling that being linguistically or culturally appropriate is necessary, such as "Now, tell me the exact same thing in school language," "Put that in academic language," or "Rephrase that information in a way that fits with our situation."

3. Praise the student for being linguistically or culturally appropriate and move on.

Within these three steps, I also want to give you three cautions:

♦ Home language does not always need to be adjusted. Sometimes, home language is appropriate at school, such as when on the yard or when writing dialogue.

♦ Students do not always have to switch from home language to school language. Sometimes students can switch from school language to home language, which is validating and affirming.

♦ You can switch from Standard English to academic language and vice versa when reading textbooks as a way of exposing students to the language of math, science, art, physical education, music, and other content areas. For example, take a scientific explanation of a term and ask students to explain it using Standard English.

Figure 11.5 Situational Appropriateness Example

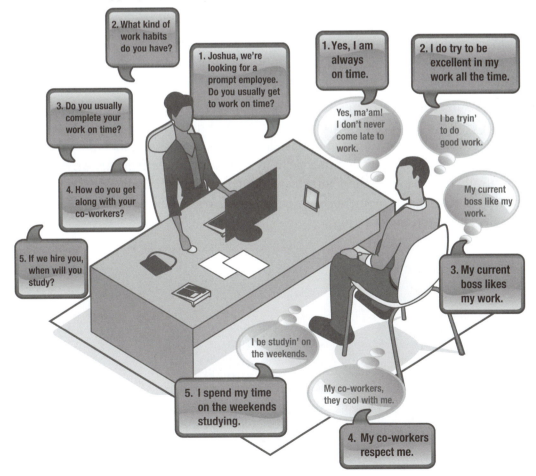

REFLECTIVE THOUGHT

Reflect on a recent lesson or unit you taught to your students. Can you recall any opportunities for teachable moments related to being linguistically or culturally appropriate for the situation? What could you do differently if a similar opportunity arises in a future lesson? Telling stories about personal experiences is a great way to connect with your students and motivate them to think about situational appropriateness. Think of two different personal experiences to share with your students where you had to take situational appropriateness into consideration before making a decision.

Thought-Provokers: A Mindset for Moving Forward

1. Regardless of the focus on situational appropriateness, I know the target language is always Standard English and academic language.

2. I acknowledge that teachable moments are not correctable moments.

Thought-Blockers: A Mindset for Staying Stagnant

1. I do not feel that teaching students to be linguistically or culturally appropriate is an essential part of teaching Standard English and academic language.

2. I feel that taking advantage of teachable moments detracts from instructional time.

Concluding Thoughts

Since a person's language is a crucial aspect of their culture, validating and affirming home languages carries deeper meaning. These opportunities are special, especially for our traditional English language learners. For Standard English learners, it comes as a relief more than anything else when teachers show that they get it by validating and affirming. As you have learned, culturally responsive teachers start by recognizing linguistic behaviors and end by taking advantage of teachable moments to help students learn to be linguistically or culturally appropriate depending on the situation.

Use these scenarios and exercises to assist you in processing, practicing, and applying the concepts from the chapter.

True/False

This exercise provides several true/false statements regarding the situational appropriateness of using nonstandard language in the school environment. As you answer each question, consider the implications of the statement for both the teacher and the student. Additionally, think about how a teacher with little or no training in cultural responsiveness might respond to these statements. What effect would these viewpoints have on the teacher's instructional practices? How could these beliefs affect students' ability to learn and achieve academically? Read each statement in figure 11.6, and indicate whether you believe it to be true or false.

Figure 11.6 True or False?

Situation	True or False
1. There are never times when it is appropriate for students to use nonstandard or unaccepted languages in school.	
2. Students should only speak to one another using nonstandard languages in the schoolyard, in the cafeteria, or when they are outside of the classroom.	
3. It is acceptable for students to speak to one another using nonstandard language variations while working together in small groups to complete a task.	
4. It is acceptable for students to use nonstandard language variations while participating in whole-class instructional conversations.	
5. It is acceptable for students to use their nonstandard home languages during formal presentations of their group assignments.	

Answers: 1. False, 2. False, 3. True, 4. False, 5. False

Classroom Applications

Think about your own classroom and teaching practices. Use the following prompts to reflect on your past experiences and consider how you can effectively help students use situationally appropriate language in your classroom.

1. Consider the daily schedule in your classroom. When is it appropriate for students to use nonstandard home languages? When is it not appropriate?

   _____

   _____

2. The concept of using situationally appropriate language can be applied to a variety of subject areas, activities, and instructional practices. What are some creative and engaging ways

you can integrate activities that focus on using situationally appropriate language into your classroom?

_____

_____

Recognizing Linguistic Behaviors

Look at the following sample of a student's writing. Use the checklist in figure 11.7 to record the frequency of each linguistic feature present in the writing sample. Check your answers in figure 11.8.

> LeBron James is my favorite athlete. He play for the Lakers. He is a champion because he won 4 NBA championship. He work hard because he believe in hisself.

Figure 11.7 Linguistic Feature Checklist

Linguistic Feature	Example	Tally
Third-Person Singular Present Tense	He _run_ fast.	
Plural Marker	I have 25 _cent_.	
Reflexive Pronoun	He hurt _hisself_.	

Figure 11.8 Answers to Linguistic Feature Checklist

Linguistic Feature	Example	Tally
Third-Person Singular Present Tense	He play; He work; He believe.	|||
Plural Marker	4 NBA championship		
Reflexive Pronoun	He believe in hisself.		

Analyzing Linguistic Behavior

Now that you have had a chance to practice analyzing a writing sample, it is time to think about applying this type of analysis to the students in your classroom. You will need a writing sample from a student to proceed. When selecting a writing sample, consider the different cultural backgrounds and languages represented by the students in your classroom. Be sure to pick a writing sample that is reflective of a prominent culture or language in your classroom.

1. Make a copy of the writing sample so that you can return the original to the student.

2. Read the text aloud. While you are reading, underline all the examples of nonstandard English in the text.

3. Using the appropriate "Common Rules" chart, such as the Mexican-American (Chicano English) Common Rules List (page 268), assign a different color to each category using colored markers.

4. Read through the writing sample and use the colored markers to highlight examples of different types of rules in the writing.

5. Review the types of rules present in the writing sample. Brainstorm several ways to use the information you learned through this exercise with your students.

Sentence Lifting

The following student's writing reflects the regularized use of the present tense singular verb. While you want to validate and affirm the student's rule-governed language difference, you also want to teach a mini-lesson about the Standard English grammar rules that apply to third-person singular subject-verb agreement.

> LeBron James is my favorite athlete. He play for the Lakers. He is a champion because he won 4 NBA championship. He work hard because he believe in hisself.

One way to teach this mini-lesson is to follow these three steps. See figure 11.9 for additional clarification.

1. Highlight the sentences that you would lift from the student's writing sample.

2. Rewrite the sentences using Standard English grammar rules.

3. Suggest a grammar rule.

Figure 11.9 Example of Sentence Lifting

Lifted Sentence	Rewrite the Sentence	Suggest a Grammar Rule
He play for the Lakers.	He plays for the Lakers.	When you identify a singular subject, add an *s* to the end of the verb.
He work hard because he believe in hisself.	He works hard because he believes in himself.	When you identify a singular subject, add an *s* to the end of the verb.

Note: These are the only two sentences chosen for this sentence-lifting activity because the mini-lesson focuses on third-person singular subject-verb agreement rules.

Classroom Applications

Think about your own classroom and teaching practices. Use the following questions to reflect on your past experiences and consider how you can effectively use sentence-lifting activities in your classroom.

1. Reflect on the writing activities you use to teach your students. Do your students use different types of language in different types of writing assignments? What types of writing activities would provide good samples for sentence-lifting exercises?

_____

_____

2. Think about specific students in your class. Do they share the same home languages? If not, how can you use sentence-lifting activities to benefit all of the students in your class?

_____

_____

Sample Lesson—Using Sentence-Lifting Exercises in the Classroom

The following lesson provides an example of how to use sentence lifting to help teach students Standard English.

Procedure

1. Before beginning the lesson, review students' writing samples and analyze the linguistic behavior in their writing using the appropriate "Common Rules" charts from this chapter (pages 267–268).

2. Choose a rule that is frequently used in the students' writing as a focus for the lesson. For example, one sentence-lifting activity might focus on the use of the past tense marker *–ed*.

3. Select several examples of the rule from the students' writing and "lift," or copy, the examples onto the "Home Language" column of the Types of Language activity sheet (page 305). Do not include students' names or identifying information in the examples. Make a copy of the activity sheet for every student.

4. As an optional but fun way to engage the students in the activity, bring in two different hats to use with the activity. Ideally, one hat should be a casual hat that would normally be worn in a relaxed setting, such as a baseball hat. The other hat will represent situations that require the use of Standard English, so a more formal hat, such as a graduation cap or top hat, will help the students remember this distinction. However, any two hats will work.

5. Explain, "Different situations require that we use different types of English. For example, if I walked in the front door of my house and said, 'Good evening. May I please use the restroom before we commence our evening meal?' my family would think that I was completely ridiculous. However, if I walked into a meeting with the superintendent of the school district and used similar language, such as, 'Good morning. May I please use the restroom before we commence the meeting?' that language would be appropriate for the situation. In order to practice using different types of language, we are going to use this hat (hold up the casual hat) to show when we should use our home languages and this hat (hold up the other hat) to show when we should use Standard English. So in the example I just shared, I would wear this hat (put on the formal hat) when I want to use Standard English in my meeting with the superintendent of the school district."

6. Say, "Today, we are going to practice this concept using examples from your writing. I have read through your writing and selected several examples for the activity. We are going to practice switching from home language (put on casual hat) to Standard English (switch to the other hat), because school writing assignments generally require you to use Standard English."

7. While wearing the casual hat, display the first example on the board and read it aloud. Ask students why this sentence is an example of home language. Say, "Now I am going to switch hats so that I can change this sentence into Standard English." Literally switch hats and say the same sentence in Standard English. Write the Standard English version of the sentence on the displayed activity sheet in the "Standard English" column. Discuss the rule, past tense marker –*ed*, which was used in the example.

8. Ask a student volunteer to translate the next example from home language to Standard English. Have the student put on the casual hat and read the sentence from the writing sample aloud. Then have the student change hats and write the Standard English version of the sentence on the chart and read it aloud to the class.

9. Choose two to three other students to come to the front of the class and demonstrate translating examples using the same procedure. After each example, review the rule used.

10. Distribute copies of the activity sheet to students and assign each student a partner. Have the partners work together to translate the remaining home language sentences into Standard English.

11. Once students have completed their activity sheets, select several pairs of students to share their answers with the class. After discussing and agreeing upon the answers, record them on the projected version of the activity sheet.

12. Review the linguistic rules addressed in the activity and summarize the importance of using different types of language depending on the situation.

Figure 11.10 Types of Language Chart

Reversing Language Use

As we validate and affirm to build and bridge, we are asking students who are familiar with and proficient users of nonstandard languages to translate their use of this language into Standard English. Test your knowledge by translating these sentences from Standard English to a home language using figure 11.11. You can use the African American Vernacular English and Chicano English Common Rules to help you. Check your answers in figure 11.12.

Figure 11.11 Language Practice

Standard English	Home Language
He jumps rope to get into shape.	
She runs fast.	
We were here.	
He hurt himself.	

Figure 11.12 Answers to Language Practice

Standard English	Home Language
He jumps rope to get in shape.	He jump rope to get in shape. (Present Tense Singular Verb)
She runs fast.	She run fast. (Present Tense Singular Verb)
We were here.	We was here. (Past Tense Singular Verb)
He hurt himself.	He hurt hisself. (Reflexive Pronoun)

As you become increasingly aware or familiar with the rules of the more common nonstandard languages, you will begin to recognize patterns. This is important when helping students recognize the patterns of both languages. At this point, you should be noticing that the language rules are the same, but they are expressed differently in Standard English and home languages.

Sample Lesson—Language Switching Games

Alternating between languages is a necessary and practical skill for students to learn. Not only will the ability help students succeed in school, but it will also aid them in a variety of different situations throughout their lives, such as college interviews and job applications. This can be taught formally using structured lesson plans and assessments and also informally using teachable moments and spontaneous examples. The following lesson uses a game format to teach students to translate their language use.

Procedure

1. Before beginning the lesson, remind students how they can apply different linguistic rules in order to consciously move back and forth between two or more languages. After providing several examples of how to change home language to Standard English and vice versa, give students several sentences and ask them to practice switching back and forth from one language to another.

2. Say, "Now we are going to play a game called Beat the Teacher. In this game, you will develop sentences, and I will have to translate them in a certain amount of time. I get a point for every sentence that I complete in the specified amount of time, and you get a point for every sentence that stumps me. At the end of the game, we will count our points and determine the winner."

3. Give each student four index cards. On each index card, have students use a colored marker to write a sentence. Explain that two of the sentences should be in a home language and two should be in Standard English.

4. Place students into small groups of three to five students. Have students take turns reading their sentences aloud to the group. After reading each sentence, the group should discuss how

to change the sentence into the other language (Standard English into home language and vice versa). Once the group agrees on the correct way to switch the sentences, the students write the new sentences on the backs of the cards using a different colored marker.

5. Ask students to return to their seats. Select one student to be the scorekeeper and one student to be the timekeeper. Give the timekeeper a stopwatch and explain that they are going to be responsible for timing the rounds, roughly ten seconds.

6. Use the Pick-a-Stick response protocol to select a student to go first. Have the student read one of their sentences from the front of the card. As soon as the student finishes reading the card, the timekeeper starts the stopwatch. You have ten seconds to respond with the changed version of the sentence. If you are correct, the scorekeeper records a point for you. If you run out of time or give an incorrect response, the scorekeeper records a point for the students.

7. Stop periodically throughout the game to discuss the different linguistic rules students are using in their sentences. If there is disagreement about the correct way to change a particular sentence, write the sentence on the board and discuss the applicable linguistic rules with the class.

8. Play the game for the designated amount of time or until every student has had a chance to read one sentence. At the end of the game, add up your points and the students' points to determine a winner.

9. Use a similar game format to continue practicing in the future, but instead of playing against students yourself, put students into two teams and have them play against each other.

Post-Reading Assessment

Now, it is your turn to start "swimming" by validating and affirming home languages. Start today. As you plan your next lesson, think about how you will validate and affirm, build and bridge. Be intentional and strategic. As always, allow yourself the time and space to fail, to make mistakes, and to be uncomfortable. After a couple of weeks of implementing CLR, come back to this chapter and complete the survey in figure 11.13 on validating and affirming home languages.

Figure 11.13 Validating and Affirming Home Languages Survey: After Infusing the CLR Principles

0: *Never Emerging* 1: *Rarely Splashing* 2: *Sometimes Floating* 3: *Mostly Kicking* 4: *Always Freestyling*					
I validate and affirm my students' home languages whenever possible.	0	1	2	3	4
I proactively plan opportunities for my students to practice situational appropriateness.	0	1	2	3	4
I reactively use teachable moments to have my students use situationally appropriate language.	0	1	2	3	4

STUDENT VOICE

Allowing Your Students to Be Engaged in Their Own Way, or "BeYou": Realness

BeYou is a call to action, reminding teachers to adjust instruction and classroom practices, ensuring that students can be themselves at school culturally and linguistically. Here we consider how students might express the importance of being validated and affirmed when using realness at school.

How can realness be culturally misunderstood in the classroom? At home and with my friends, we're all about honesty and being straightforward. We don't beat around the bush or sugarcoat things because we value being real and authentic. We believe it's important to speak our minds and tell the truth, even if it's not always what others want to hear.

In school, though, sometimes that directness can be misunderstood or unwelcome. People might think I'm being rude or critical when I'm just trying to be honest. For me, being upfront and avoiding confusion is actually my way of showing respect and staying true to myself at the same time.

How does it feel to be misunderstood? Being direct or telling it like it is at school can cause trouble because that honesty isn't always understood or welcomed, so I have to be more careful of how I say things than I do at home. Communication tends to be more indirect and saying things at the right time or in a way that protects people's feelings is preferred. It can be really confusing! Indirect communication can be sus to me because it feels like someone is avoiding the truth or trying to make it something it's not. When I say things directly, I am never trying to be rude or disrespectful. I am just keeping it real, and for me that is what matters most.

What do I need to be myself? Being authentic is important to me. I know there will be times I have to say things a certain way, more indirectly or at the situationally appropriate time, and I am working on it. I need times, though, where I can be direct in the moment, as it helps me to communicate clearly by getting straight to the point. It is affirming when people at school recognize directness as a valid way to communicate, and recognize that it is not meant to be critical, rude, or disrespectful. It is validating when directness becomes part of our learning, like in debates and group conversations, and is accepted in class when I am talking with my friends. It matters in my relationships with teachers too.

What CLR activities validate and affirm realness? Three-Step Interview and Carousel Brainstorm are great activities to use in class because they give students the opportunity to share what they think honestly. The more students get to talk to and with each other in ways that encourage them to authentically say what they think, the better.

Build CLR Community and Collaboration

In the name of self-care, do your own group's version of "What Are You Reading, Watching, Listening To?" Each person shares with the group their top three for one, two, or all three categories.

CHAPTER 12

Creating a Responsive Learning Environment

Understanding the Context

This chapter offers insights into the qualities of an effective culturally responsive learning environment and provides opportunities for you to reflect on the learning environment in your classroom. You cannot be 100 percent responsive in your teaching without a culturally responsive learning environment. What Barbara Shade, Cynthia Kelly, and Mary Oberg wrote in 1997 remains true today. A culturally responsive learning environment means that your room meets these characteristics:

◆ is inviting to students and welcoming to guests

◆ has a sense of belonging that is student centered, with an "our room" feel

◆ has a positive energy, vibe, and rhythm that can be felt—not heard

◆ uses a variety of colors and designs

◆ is arranged with space for movement and collaborative learning

◆ has opportunities for learning centers or places to work

◆ includes multimedia

◆ is clean, aromatic, and non-institutional

These eight elements can be summed up in three categories: physical attraction, arrangement, and atmosphere. When I walk into any classroom, these three areas influence my first impression. I ask myself, "Is this room physically attractive? Does it draw me in?" I put on my interior design hat and look at how the room is arranged. Is the room conducive to movement, collaboration, and facilitation? I take a deep breath and feel the atmosphere of the room, wanting to observe a sense of calmness conducive to learning.

Considering the Research

While not specifically focused on cultural responsiveness, Kathleen Roskos and Susan Neuman (2011) offer their research-based suggestions for an environment conducive to learning. As you can see, these fit nicely into the three categories previously listed. Their suggestions include the following:

◆ **Physical space is aligned to instructional goals.** A design fundamental is to link environment to purpose. For example, if your classroom uses learning centers, there must be adequate space for students to move back and forth between the centers comfortably. Peter Barrett, Lucinda Barrett, and Fay Davies found that up to 73 percent of student performance variations driven at the class level are linked to work environment (2013). Their study indicates that placing an average student in the least effective rather than the most effective learning environment decreases the student's learning progress by as much as one whole year.

◆ **Sufficient materials are well organized.** From a design perspective, the materials principle is made evident in two basic ways: the availability of materials and the accessibility of materials. The classroom environment should contain a variety of literacy materials— sufficient amounts for both the teacher (manuals, books, and charts) and students to use (a variety of literary and informational texts, word cards/letter tiles, class- or student-created charts, dictionaries, and relevant realia).

◆ **The walls teach.** Wall color, white space, interface, and functional organization influence learning. Walls, in fact, matter and have an impact on the learning environment. A wall design that is too busy can create distraction, particularly for small children (Amirault 2024; Fisher, Godwin, and Seltman 2014). However, student work and meaningful bulletin boards involving culturally diverse images enhances a student's sense of cultural membership in the class (Krasnoff 2016; Montgomery 2001).

◆ **The environment is participatory.** The social environment brings the physical environment of the classroom to life. Research shows the powerful role of the social environment in shaping individual literacy experience—a sense of belonging, identity, ownership, and choice (Rogoff 1990). For example, as students begin to feel a stronger sense of membership in their classroom environment, they respond by assuming greater responsibility in their own educational experience. Barbara Rogoff gives an example of Girl Scouts during a cookie sale. Initially the girls would rely on their mothers to do the cash handling. But, as the girls became more socially involved and invested in the sale process, they began to take on more and more of the activities on their own.

◆ **The environment is green.** Light, temperature, air quality, noise, and crowding—all of these elements affect the instructional process (Graetz and Goliber 2003; Moore 2001). Too much or not enough of each aspect can erode environmental quality in ways that lead to negative effects on learning. For instance, a classroom that is too warm may lead to sleepy students, while one that is too cold can make them too uncomfortable to focus.

Beginning the Reflective Process

Are you ready to make your classroom environment culturally responsive? Before diving headfirst into the topic of culturally responsive learning environments, it is important to stop and reflect on your current classroom environment. By systematically surveying your classroom environment, you can identify areas that need improvement to make your classroom more culturally responsive.

The Use of the CLR Learning Environment Survey

Complete the survey in figure 12.1. (Note: the survey can also be used for classroom walk-throughs so that teachers can gain feedback from their colleagues.) Following the survey, you will find some suggestions and key points to consider for your room makeover.

Figure 12.1 CLR Learning Environment Survey

CLR Environment Survey

Teacher _____

Grade/Class _____

Observer _____

Date of Observation _____

Rate your learning environment's cultural responsiveness on two levels:

- **Quantitative:** Are the environmental features (page 283) in place?
- **Qualitative:** What are the aspects of responsiveness, including creativity, presentation, and atmosphere?

For each category below, rate the quality of responsiveness on a five-point scale from very responsive (5) to least responsive (1).

Walls That Teach

Quantitative: Is there a 70:30 ratio of authentic to commercially produced print resources evident in the classroom? yes or no (circle one)

Qualitative: Rate the level of responsiveness (creativity, presentation, and atmosphere). Circle your selection.

Very Responsive				Least Responsive
5	4	3	2	1

Comments/Suggestions:

_____

_____

Physical Space Aligned to Instructional Goals

Quantitative: Are a variety of learning centers present? yes or no

Is space for them set up in an organized manner? yes or no

Qualitative: Rate the level of responsiveness (creativity, presentation, and atmosphere).

Very Responsive				Least Responsive
5	4	3	2	1

Comments/Suggestions:

_____

_____

Inviting and Welcoming

Quantitative: Does the room feature a variety of colors that are relevant to various cultures or to the cultures and activities of the school? yes or no

Qualitative: Rate the level of responsiveness (creativity, presentation, and atmosphere).

Very Responsive				Least Responsive
5	4	3	2	1

Comments/Suggestions:

_____

_____

Space for Movement and Collaboration

Quantitative: Does the room arrangement facilitate ease of movement, management, and presentations? yes or no

Qualitative: Rate the level of responsiveness (creativity, presentation, and atmosphere).

Very Responsive				Least Responsive
5	4	3	2	1

Comments/Suggestions:

_____

_____

Resource Rich

Quantitative: Do the classroom library and other resources support a focus on multiple literacies and cultures? yes or no

Qualitative: Rate the level of responsiveness (creativity, presentation, and atmosphere).

Very Responsive				Least Responsive
5	4	3	2	1

Comments/Suggestions:

_____

_____

Technology and Multimedia

Quantitative: Are technology resources present and ready for use? yes or no

Qualitative: Rate the level of responsiveness (creativity, presentation, and atmosphere).

Very Responsive				Least Responsive
5	4	3	2	1

Comments/Suggestions:

_____

_____

Relevant Bulletin Boards

Quantitative: Are the bulletin boards relevant to the content areas and the cultural diversity of the students? yes or no

Qualitative: Rate the level of responsiveness (creativity, presentation, and atmosphere).

Very Responsive				Least Responsive
5	4	3	2	1

Comments/Suggestions:

_____

_____

REFLECTIVE THOUGHT

Ask your students to help you make your classroom environment more culturally responsive. Invite them to give feedback about items and displays that they feel accurately represent their cultural backgrounds and those they do not relate to on a cultural level.

Thought-Provokers: A Mindset for Moving Forward

1. I know that when a classroom environment is culturally responsive, everyone benefits. Environments that reflect CLR principles create a sense of community within the classroom and help engage my students in learning.

2. It is easier to implement CLR activities in an environment that is set up to support the CLR framework. It is easier to use movement activities with my students if the classroom furniture is arranged to allow for movement.

Thought-Blockers: A Mindset for Staying Stagnant

1. The physical environment of my classroom has very little impact on my students' ability and willingness to learn.

2. It looks more professional to display commercial products in my classroom rather than student work.

Revising the Learning Environment

When it comes to the learning environment, there is no one right answer for all classrooms. The preceding survey is meant to encourage thinking about a variety of factors. In addition to the areas referenced in the survey, you need to consider what I call the three Ds: de-Blumenbaching, de-commercializing, and de-superficializing. Assessing the three Ds will help you uncover the ways your mindset affects your classroom learning environment.

De-Blumenbaching

As mentioned in the introduction, Blumenbach was an anthropologist who developed a system of racial classification that divided the human race into five classes based on physical features and perceived beauty. Blumenbach's work upheld the common belief that Caucasians were the superior race because they were directly descended from the biblical figures Adam and Eve.

While Blumenbach's theories about racial classification were discarded long ago, the underlying concept of the superiority of the Caucasian race persists in many subconscious and less-explicit ways. As discussed in chapter 8, texts focused on the mainstream (Caucasian) culture are far more common than ones that include authentic descriptions and representations of diverse cultures. The media overwhelmingly focuses on individuals of the Caucasian race, and consumer products are often dominated by images of Caucasians. Products published for classroom use have historically been dominated by Caucasians as well. Research has demonstrated how seeing or not seeing oneself, racially, in media and literature can negatively impact one's identity. Thus, as culturally responsive educators, it is necessary to "de-Blumenbach" ourselves, especially in the context of schooling and classroom learning environments. This means making deliberate decisions about the images you display in your classroom and seeking out materials that represent all your students' cultures, rather than only the mainstream Caucasian culture. It is important that you critically examine your learning environments, textbooks, and the images displayed at your school and make changes to move toward a more representative and culturally responsive environment. To learn more, conduct an internet search on "racial identity and the media," since extensive coverage is beyond the scope of this book. Here are a few good places to start:

> It is important that you critically examine your learning environments, textbooks, and the images displayed at your school and make changes to move toward a more representative and culturally responsive environment.

- Grace Kao's "Group Images and Possible Selves Among Adolescents: Linking Stereotypes to Expectations by Race and Ethnicity" (2000)

- Chalmer E. Thompson and Robert T. Carter's *Racial Identity Theory: Applications to Individual, Group, and Organizational Interventions* (1997)

◆ Charmaine L. Wijeyesinghe and Bailey W. Jackson III's *New Perspectives on Racial Identity Development: Integrating Emerging Frameworks* (2012)

The bottom line is to critically examine your learning environments, textbooks, and the images around your school to see how they have been "Blumenbached" and then more importantly how to change them to more accurately reflect the students in your school.

De-Commercializing

Perhaps the best way to ensure that your classroom environment is representative of your student population is to display students' work, rather than commercial products. By developing your classroom environment around work created by students, you are automatically making it more culturally responsive. When students see their own work on classroom walls and bulletin boards, they immediately see themselves as an integral part of the classroom and school. By creating a classroom community that is based on students, rather than commercial materials, you are validating and affirming both students' talents and their own personal perceptions of cultural identity.

De-Superficializing

As seen in the Iceberg Concept of Culture (page 15), there are many different layers and levels of culture. When you are working to make your classroom environment more culturally responsive, it is important to go beyond superficial images of cultural diversity and strive for authentic and genuine representations of your students' culture. For example, simply displaying a woven African basket in the corner of your classroom does not make your classroom environment more culturally responsive. Most students, even if they are from an African American background, will probably not notice, let alone identify with, this type of cultural artifact without intentional instruction. However, the purposeful use of bright and culturally meaningful colors to make a classroom environment more inviting and conducive to learning is an authentic and effective way to make your classroom more responsive.

Concluding Thoughts

Creating a responsive learning environment takes into consideration both physical and social factors. The physical factors include elements that make the classroom intellectually attractive and stimulating to students: furnishings and their arrangement, learning resources and their organization, displays of student work, and displays of items that reflect who the students are. There is always room for teacher innovation in creating a learning environment that is responsive to students' cultural and linguistic needs and expectations.

Building CLR Community and Collaboration

CLR Community and Collaboration is about sustainability, continuing your CLR-ness going forward and making it part of all that you do. Discuss the following with your CLR colleagues.

◆ Are you ready for sustainability? In what ways? In what ways are you not ready?

◆ What are your next steps? What planning needs to occur to sustain and increase your cultural and linguistic responsiveness? What processes need to be established?

How to Begin Swimming in Your CLR Pool: The Last Chapter

CLR Commencement

While this chapter is the last one in this book, it is the beginning chapter of your development as a culturally responsive teacher. How do you begin CLR? The steps are outlined in this chapter. The previous chapters of this book provided the nuts and bolts on how to implement CLR teaching in the four instructional areas, category by category: classroom management, academic vocabulary, academic literacy, and academic language. There is, however, one question that remains: Where do you start?

CLR Infusion Levels

Let us start by going back to the introduction and my metaphor of diving into the CLR pool. I likened CLR infusion levels to swimming lessons. Now that the entire CLR framework has been described, let us discuss what exactly needs to be accomplished to be fully swimming in your CLR pool. Figure 13.1 shows the infusion levels again.

Figure 13.1 CLR Infusion Levels

Emerger	Splasher/High Splasher	Floater/High Floater	Kicker	Freestyler
1–2 CLR activities demonstrated in at least 1 instructional area	3–5 CLR activities demonstrated in at least 1 instructional area	6–7 CLR activities demonstrated in at least 2 instructional areas	8–9 CLR activities demonstrated in at least 3 instructional areas	10–12 CLR activities demonstrated in at least 4 instructional areas

Characteristics of the CLR infusion levels are as follows:

Emerger: An Emerger is the teacher who sits on the side of the pool, dangling their toes in the water. Myriad reasons could be the basis for this stagnation, including fear, skill level, or school or district constraints. In terms of CLR, this teacher does not incorporate culturally specific activities during instruction. For example, a teacher who refuses to try using discussion protocols in the classroom because they fear the students will get out of control would be considered an Emerger.

Splasher: A Splasher is someone who has jumped into the CLR pool and is splashing away. Often, the Splasher's attitude is *what do I have to lose?* This teacher will be doing at least three to five CLR activities in at least one instructional area. For instance, a teacher who consistently reads aloud to the class and frequently uses a response protocol, such as Whip Around, to have students respond to a question or prompt would be considered a Splasher.

Floater: A Floater is a teacher who is clearly intent on becoming culturally responsive and has spent some time in reflection about their instructional practices. With such reflection, the Floater will be doing six to seven CLR activities across at least two instructional areas. For example, a teacher who is considered a Floater might have students use a discussion protocol to collaboratively discuss a culturally authentic social studies text. As part of these collaborative small-group discussions, the teacher has students identify and add new words to their personal thesauruses and personal dictionaries. After they discuss the text, the teacher has students use the Give One, Get One movement activity to choose students from different groups to share their ideas from the discussion. After this activity, the teacher uses the Pick-a-Stick response protocol to call on several students to share their newly acquired knowledge about the text with the rest of the class. In this example, the students learn social studies content while also engaging in vocabulary-building activities through a variety of different culturally responsive activities.

Kicker: Being a Kicker is our goal for cultural responsiveness and moves the CLR implementation into automation. Becoming a Kicker takes time. Rarely does someone start off kicking. The Kicker will be doing eight or nine CLR activities in at least two instructional areas. An important aspect of being a Kicker is the support they can offer to other teachers, especially Floaters. Teachers who are considered Kickers have a collection of CLR activities and protocols that they employ frequently and automatically. A teacher might regularly use three different attention signals to get students' attention and communicate certain expectations. For example, the "Get up, stand up/Stand up for your rights" attention signal might be used to indicate it is time to move, the "Time to/End" attention signal might be used to signify the end of an activity, and the "Do your best/Forget the rest" attention signal could be used to notify the students that it is time to start an activity.

> Kickers strive to create responsive language and learning environments in their classrooms. They use teachable moments and planned instruction to teach situational appropriateness for both cultural language and behavior.

In addition to using attention signals consistently, a Kicker incorporates responsive vocabulary and literacy activities throughout their teaching. This means reading aloud a variety of texts in different instructional areas. It means consistently leveling words and incorporating word-building activities with Tier Two words across different domains. It also means continually adding culturally authentic texts and materials to the classroom library.

Kickers strive to create responsive language and learning environments in their classrooms. They use teachable moments and planned instruction to teach situational appropriateness for both cultural language and behavior. They evaluate the physical environment in their classrooms and ensure that it authentically represents students' cultural backgrounds. Lastly, teachers at this stage frequently reflect on their teaching practices in order to improve their own pedagogy and identify effective strategies that can be used by other teachers as well.

Freestyler: Anything beyond a Kicker is considered exemplary. Freestylers provide models to their colleagues. They are doing at least ten activities consistently across four or more instructional areas. Freestylers are at the deepest end of the pool. They have immersed their pedagogy into cultural responsiveness. The beauty of the CLR framework is that there are myriad ways to expand and apply it to almost any situation. Teachers in this category are adept at designing their instruction around the CLR framework and can spontaneously respond to their students' needs in a culturally responsive manner. These teachers use CLR strategies both inside and outside the classroom. They integrate the CLR principles in study trips, assessments, individual activities, and group projects. They serve as mentors for teachers who are new to the framework and strive to promote the use of culturally responsive teaching practices across the school. Although teachers in this category have reached the highest level of CLR implementation, they never stop searching for new and better ways to improve their instruction in culturally responsive ways.

> REFLECTIVE THOUGHT
>
> Looking at the infusion levels, where are you starting and where do you intend to be in six weeks? How will you get there?

 ## Thought-Provokers: A Mindset for Moving Forward

1. I acknowledge that implementing CLR can be a challenging task, and I do not expect to be able to do everything overnight. I set reasonable goals for myself and will not give up if it takes me longer to reach the next level than I initially expected.

2. I know I am not alone in this process. I have identified people and resources both inside and outside the school environment that can help me modify my teaching practices and reflect on my progress.

 ## Thought-Blockers: A Mindset for Staying Stagnant

1. I do not share the same cultural background as my students, and I sometimes fear that I will never fully understand their cultures.

2. I feel that I will never be able to master all of the numerous components of the CLR framework, so I resist even trying.

Three Steps to Start

The three steps to your official CLR start are QQS—quantity, quality, and strategy. *Quantity* speaks to filling your instructional toolbox with the necessary CLR activities to start swimming. The number one inhibitor to cultural responsiveness is not a mindset orientation but actually a skill-set issue. The first step is to fill your toolbox. *Quality* refers to implementing each strategy accurately and with fidelity. Many times, teachers new to CLR try something and find that it does not work the first time. They may give up. Given that teaching is, to some extent, trial and error, it is to be expected that when initially trying new activities, you may not have 100 percent success. The quality step grabs your attention so that you can focus on the effectiveness of your implementation. *Strategy* is an ongoing step that asks two questions: "Why am I doing this particular activity at this particular time?" and "What do I intend to accomplish?" Using the CLR activities must accompany a strategy. Think of strategy here as a plan of action or a method for accomplishing a goal. Plan your CLR use with intention and purpose each and every time. Remember the formula:

$$\text{Quantity} + \text{Quality} + \text{Strategy} = \textbf{CLR}$$

Step 1: Quantity

To fill your toolbox with CLR activities, use a collaborative activity based on the graphic organizer shown in figure 13.2. Use this process to support your CLR infusion and to achieve the goal of having four or more activities in each category. The graphic organizer has five categories. The process involves two steps for each category.

1. In the first box, write a CLR activity you already do or know.
2. For the second box, talk to a colleague and find out what they do. Borrow their idea and write it in the second box.

To be a Splasher, you need at least two activities in each category. Once you begin, you will find it easier to discover other activities until you reach the goal of four or more. Figure 13.2 provides a sample of CLR activities representing a teacher at the Splasher level. The activities listed there are a small sample of the many activities you can include in your CLR toolbox.

Figure 13.2 Building a Quantity of CLR Activities

	Attention Signals	Response Protocols	Discussion Protocols	Movement Activities	Extended Collaboration
A CLR activity I know	When I say _____, you say _____.	Shout Out	Jigsaw	Give One, Get One	Book clubs for small-group discussion about a text
A CLR activity from a colleague	Se puede/Sí, se puede!	Put Your Two Cents In	Merry-Go-Round	Musical Shares	Collaborative research project that culminates with a group presentation

Figure 13.3 models how CLR strategies and activities can be infused into common literacy activities and components of instruction.

Figure 13.3 Sample CLR and Literacy Activities

Leveling Vocabulary Words	Vocabulary Strategies	Practice and Assessment
Select words that are important to understanding the text or concept.	Context Clues	Multiple-choice tests to assess students' ability to use context clues and word parts to determine word meaning
Identify Tier Two words and focus on these words in your instruction.	Personal Thesaurus	Rubrics or other open-ended assessments to assess the usage of the new words in students' speech and writing.

Use of CR text	Use of Engaging Read-Alouds	Revising Writing
For teaching content material	Jump-In Reading	Students revise their writing assignments by changing examples of home language to academic language.
For read-alouds	Buddy Reading	Students develop characters in their writing by including dialogue in their home languages.

Sentence Lifting	Role-Playing	Retellings
Examples from students' speech	Interview related to content being studied	Retell "Cinderella" using home language.
Examples from literary sources	Family conversation at home	Retell "Mother to Son" by Langston Hughes using academic language.

Step 2: Quality

After acquiring a repertoire of CLR activities for your toolbox, it is time to evaluate the quality of your CLR instruction. Going through the motions of including culturally responsive activities in your instruction does not necessarily mean that they are effective for your students. In general, assessment of the quality of a particular lesson or activity occurs for two reasons. One reason is that sometimes in early implementation of CLR, teachers are not concerned about the fidelity and accuracy of the activity. There can be a tendency to be random or even inconsistent about the use. A second reason is that early implementers may do the activities incorrectly and need to be corrected. Therefore, keep in mind that the following questions are typically asked in reflection, depending on the level of success of the activity. As you become more experienced, many of these questions can easily be asked at the beginning of a CLR activity to help you prepare.

1. Where did I learn about this activity? What is my source? In what ways has that source of information been helpful?

2. Do I have clarity about all of the steps? If not, what am I missing? How will I get clarity?

3. What adjustments will I need to make for my grade level, content area, or student population? How will I go about making these adjustments?

4. Do I have all the necessary resources and structures in place for complete success? If not, what resources and structures do I need, and how will I go about getting them?

5. How did my students respond to this activity? Why did they respond this way?

6. What steps did I take to prepare for this activity? What additional steps could I take in the future to improve it?

7. Did this activity help my students achieve the academic objective of the lesson? How?

8. Did this activity engage my students in a culturally responsive way? How so?

Addressing the quality of CLR instruction helps you gauge the effectiveness of your teaching practices with regards to academic and cultural objectives. Just as good teachers always assess their students, culturally responsive teachers need to evaluate their own performance and assess the results of their instruction. By engaging in a thorough evaluation of the quality of your CLR activities, you will not only improve your instructional practices but also challenge yourself to become a more flexible and open-minded teacher.

Step 3: Strategy

This last step is ongoing. For this step, begin with your lesson plan. A sample template is available in appendix B and in the digital resources. After your lesson plan is written, go back and look for places where you can make it culturally and linguistically responsive. These opportunities for CLR moments will occur throughout your lesson. Look for opportunities for response, discussion, times to move, and collaboration. These opportunities appear all the time in any quality lesson. As you find them, infuse a CLR activity. If you are intentional and purposeful, then your strategy for CLR activities will be successful.

Figure 13.4 shows a sample lesson outline from San Lorenzo High School near Oakland, California. You will see how Nicole Lusiani, an Advanced Placement history teacher, infused CLR into her lesson. The template incorporates professional teaching standards, CLR areas of engagement (responsive classroom management, responsive academic literacy, responsive academic vocabulary, and responsive academic language), and college and career readiness standards.

> This history lesson is just one example. I do not prescribe any particular model, since many districts and schools have different lesson planning templates. There is only one scenario where this infusion cannot happen and that is if there is no lesson planning in the first place.

Figure 13.4 Sample Judiciary Liberties Lesson Outline

Unit: Judiciary Liberties

Lesson: Judicial Philosophy and the Power of the Courts

Content Standards

- Students formulate questions about and defend their analyses of tensions within our constitutional democracy.
- Students analyze judicial activism and judicial restraint and the effects of each.
- Students discuss Article III as it relates to judicial power.

English Language Arts Standards

- Cite specific textual evidence to support analysis of primary and secondary sources, connecting insights gained from specific details to an understanding of the text as a whole.
- Determine the central ideas or information of a primary or secondary source; provide an accurate summary that makes clear the relationships among the key details and ideas.
- Draw evidence from informational texts to support analysis, reflection, and research.

Continued ➜

Figure 13.4 Sample Judiciary Liberties Lesson Outline *(cont.)*

Learning Goals

- Define, compare, and contrast judicial activism (JA) with judicial restraint (JR).
- Apply JA and JR accurately in analysis of how judges would decide a hypothetical case.
- Identify appropriate checks and balances and constitutional provisions for support.

Materials

- Copies of current event article (one per student)
- Copies of questions (one per student)

Introduction

Warm-Up: Personal dictionary with table partner

Procedure Outline

1. Group Circle: Share personal dictionaries and Venn diagram the two.
2. Fist-to-Five Check for Understanding, plus questions
3. Teacher Read-Aloud: "President Obama's Executive Order on Gun Control"
4. Give One, Get One: What was familiar in this article?
5. Attention Signal: Grizzly Pride
6. Raise a Hand: What did President Obama do? Why was it controversial?
7. Group Circle: Visual Organizer—Three Branches, Clarify Activism and Restraint for Judiciary
8. Attention Signal: Thinking's on Fire
9. Number Draw: What does your partner's paper say about each?

Close

Judiciary Scenario

The NRA mounts a case against President Obama, suing him for infringing on the rights of gun owners. Students prepare a decision in table partners; two in a group are activist and two are restraint.

Evaluation

Each student submits written responses to the questions.

REFLECTIVE THOUGHT

The primary goal of any lesson plan should be to help students reach educational objectives. Remember, the CLR framework is not curriculum; it is a tool to help your students succeed academically by making your instructional practices and classroom environment culturally and linguistically responsive.

Thought-Provokers: A Mindset for Moving Forward

1. Any teacher is capable of creating a culturally and linguistically responsive classroom. If I am dedicated to the CLR principles and devote the necessary time and effort to implement them in my classroom, I can become a Kicker.

2. By incorporating the CLR framework in my classroom, I will not only help my students reach academic goals and standards but will also improve my teaching practices through critical reflection and collaboration with other teachers.

 ### Thought-Blockers: A Mindset for Staying Stagnant

1. My daily classroom schedule is already too full with other tasks and activities to implement CLR activities.

2. I do not believe that CLR activities will actually improve my instruction or help my students learn.

Concluding Thoughts

I want to leave you with these lasting phrases. If you teach by them, then you will be a successful, culturally responsive educator. All the success to you and your students!

Dive into the pool of cultural responsiveness.

It is not my first thought but my last thought that counts.

Cultural responsiveness is liberating for my students and me.

Is it cultural or not? If it is cultural, then I must validate and affirm.

Validate, affirm, build, and bridge.

When I teach this way, I am empowered and inspired, empowering and inspiring.

ACKNOWLEDGMENTS

A book that has had great influence on me is Seth Godin's *Tribes: We Need You to Lead Us*. With the utmost simplicity, mainly through anecdotes, Godin lays out the concept that a group of like-minded people, no matter the size, committed around a single focus, idea, and goal can make a change through a movement. He says that those engaged in a movement are all leaders in some way or another and what they do is not work in the traditional sense but as a valued contributor, motivated and inspired by passion and service, to the movement.

Tribes perfectly describes how I see CLR. Cultural responsiveness is a movement, led by people who are singularly focused on a high-quality, equitable, and liberating education for all students. There is no single leader in CLR per se. There are a host of leaders, depending on where you are in your CLR. Whether you're a student, a parent, a member of the support staff, an office manager, a bus driver, a cafeteria worker, a teacher, an instructional coach, a building administrator, a director of equity, a professional development coordinator, a deputy superintendent of instruction, a superintendent, a board member, or a CLR coach, if you are committed to validating, affirming, building, and bridging, then you can be a leader in CLR.

I count myself as a leader, reluctantly. What convinces me most is that I have never looked at doing CLR as work, a job, or something that I do for a living. This is my calling and my passion. It is what I live, breathe, eat, and drink. Therefore, anyone who knows me knows that CLR is my first thought and my last thought. That said, I'm deeply grateful to my family (all of you) for your understanding, patience, and support as my passion keeps me away from you on most days, whether I am home or away. I want to acknowledge the entire Academic English Mastery Program (AEMP) Nation and the Culturally and Linguistically Academy of Success School (CLAS) Community. I also want to acknowledge two inspirations for this book in particular. Each forced me to conceptualize CLR for a wider audience and a more universal application, showing me that cultural responsiveness is truly for everyone. Both are directly responsible for the first edition of this book. First, I honor the bold ambition of the San Ramon Valley Unified School District in northern California to become CLR. Second, I appreciate the open-mindedness of the teachers and staff at Hopkins High School in Minnesota during the early stages of our work. You have made a difference for central Minnesota. New districts to the work have been the Ithaca Schools, University City Schools and Parkway Schools in St. Louis, and the Etiwanda Schools in southern California. Additionally, I want to commend Jamila Gillenwaters, Ed.D., for her contribution on the exercises and scenarios in this book; Lydia McClanahan for updating and adding to the protocols Amy Coventry initially created; Kiechelle Russell for the Call and Response attention signals; Nicole Lusiani for her lesson on judiciary liberties; and Carrie Eicher for the BeYou sections found throughout this new edition.

Lastly, I want to thank Rachelle Cracchiolo, founder and CEO of Teacher Created Materials, and her staff for beckoning me to Huntington Beach in November 2013 and gently nudging me to take the time and get this done.

* Please note that I have intentionally not mentioned everyone by name as to not forget anyone and cause *offensitiveness*. Those in the CLR movement will understand what I am saying.

Name _____ Date: _____

Personal Thesaurus Template

Strategies for Culturally and Linguistically Responsive Teaching and Learning—152468

Name _____ Date: _____

Personal Dictionary Template

1. Academic Term	2. My Personal Illustration
3. My Personal Connection/ Analogy/Example	4. My Personal Definition

1. Academic Term	2. My Personal Illustration
3. My Personal Connection/ Analogy/Example	4. My Personal Definition

Strategies for Culturally and Linguistically Responsive Teaching and Learning—152468   © Shell Education

For use with page 236.

Name _____ Date: _____

Interactive Notes

Directions: Record notes before, during, and after reading the text using the questions below.

Before Reading	During Reading	After Reading
What do you think this text will be about? Why?	What are the main ideas presented in the text?	What is the purpose of the text? How do you know?
What do you notice when you look at the text?	What is the format and style of the text?	What is the overall theme or message of the text?
What prior knowledge do you have about the subject of the text?	What do you notice while reading the text?	How does this text relate to other academic concepts?

Name _____ Date: _____

It Says...I Say...And So...

Directions: Answer the questions. In the first box, write what the text says. In the middle box, record your own prior knowledge related to the text. In the third box, combine text information and your prior knowledge to make an inference.

1. **Question:**

   _____

   _____

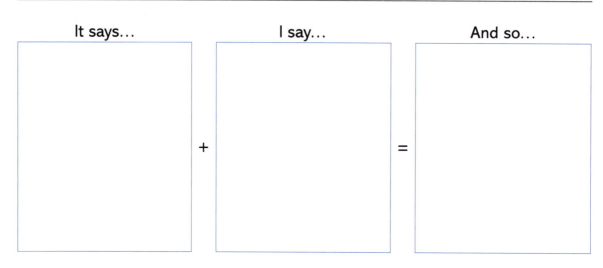

It says...		I say...		And so...

2. **Question:**

   _____

   _____

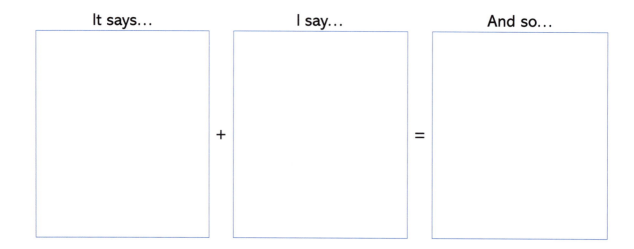

It says...		I say...		And so...

Name _____ Date: _____

Logographic Cue Chart

Directions: Use the symbols to mark your text as you read.

Logographic Cue	Meaning
?	I have a question./This doesn't make sense.
+	I agree./I like this point.
—	I disagree./I don't agree with this point.
!	This is unexpected/surprising.
	This gives me an idea.
	This gives information about a character.

For use with page 248.

Name _____ Date: _____

SQ3R Guide

Directions: Use the prompts and questions below to analyze the text.

Survey

Look over the text. Take notes on the following features in the text.

- Title
- List the headings in the text
- List the subheadings in the text
- Describe any charts/pictures/graphs in the text
- Note any vocabulary words or words in bold or italics
- Record any other interesting or notable text features

Question

Use the information from your survey to write a question for each heading and subheading. Consider using who, what, where, when, why, and how in your questions.

Read

Read through the text. While you read, keep thinking about the questions you wrote.

Recite

Reread your questions and then recite the answers based on the text. If you do not know an answer, go back and reread that section of text. After reciting your answers verbally, write down the answer to each question.

Review

Review the answers to your questions.

Name _____ Date: _____

Types of Language Chart

Directions: Write a sentence in a home language. Then write how it would be said in Standard English.

Home Language	Standard English

Name _____ Date: _____

Drawing Conclusions

Directions: Record notes about important facts and details from the text. Next, record inferences that you make. Then, write conclusions you can draw using the facts and your inferences.

Facts/Details from the Text	Inferences

Conclusions

Strategies for Culturally and Linguistically Responsive Teaching and Learning—152468

Validate, Affirm, Build, and Bridge: VABB

The protocols described in this book include the specific behaviors they validate and affirm and/ or build and bridge. If a protocol includes both validate and affirm behaviors *and* build and bridge behaviors, then it can be used for both purposes.

Cultural Behaviors Validate and Affirm	Mainstream Behaviors Build and Bridge
Non-maintenance of Eye Contact	Maintenance of Eye Contact
Proximity (Physical Closeness)	Distance
Kinesthetic (High Movement)	Stationary (Low Movement)
Collaboration/Cooperation	Competition
Spontaneity (Improvising)	Prompted/Standardized
Pragmatic Language Use (Nonverbal Expression)	Written or Spoken Communication
Realness	Indirectness
Contextual Conversation Pattern (Verbal Overlap)	Turn-taking
Orality and Verbal Expressiveness (Verve or expressiveness with verbal and non-verbal cues)	Less Emotional Communication
Sociocentrism (Social Interaction)	Autonomous
Communalism (Collective Success)	Individual Success
Subjectivity	Objectivity
Relative Time	Precise Time
Dynamic Attention Span	One Way to Show Focus
Field Dependence	Decontextualized
Sense of Immediacy (Connectedness)	Unconnected

For use with chapter 4.

Planning Extended Collaborative Learning Template

Unit:

Standards, Objectives, and Learning Goals—List the standard, objective, and ultimate learning goal that students will achieve by the end of the unit.

Culminating Collaborative Project—Explain the final project that students will complete collaboratively at the end of the unit. The project should allow students to demonstrate mastery of the objectives.

Assessment for Culminating Collaborative Project—Describe an assessment for evaluating the culminating collaborative project. This assessment should be tied to the goal previously listed.

Planning Extended Collaborative Learning Template *(cont.)*

Lessons—Consider the skills and knowledge the students need to demonstrate mastery of the objectives through the culminating project. Briefly outline how you will teach these skills through a set of lessons. Describe how you will integrate opportunities for collaboration.

- Lesson 1: _____

  Collaboration: _____

  _____

- Lesson 2: _____

  Collaboration: _____

  _____

- Lesson 3: _____

  Collaboration: _____

  _____

- Lesson 4: _____

  Collaboration: _____

  _____

- Lesson 5: _____

  Collaboration: _____

  _____

- Additional Lesson: _____

  Collaboration: _____

  _____

Planning Extended Collaborative Learning Template *(cont.)*

Collaboration Summary—Explain how the collaborative opportunities previously described help students meet academic objectives while also affirming and validating them culturally.

_____

_____

_____

_____

_____

_____

_____

_____

_____

Notes:

_____

_____

_____

_____

_____

_____

_____

_____

_____

For use with chapter 8.

Responsive Literacy Guide

Questions to Determine If a Text Is Culturally Authentic or Generic

1. Do the majority, if not all, of the characters in the story represent various underserved racial identities?

   ◆ If the answer is yes, the text could be either culturally authentic or generic.

   ◆ If the answer is no, this text is probably culturally generic.

2. Does the text include specific details about the characters' culture, such as culturally specific traditions, lifestyles, challenges, and language throughout the book?

   ◆ If the answer is yes, the text is probably culturally authentic.

   ◆ If the answer is no, the text is probably culturally neutral.

3. Could you replace the characters of color in this book with mainstream characters with little or no effect?

   ◆ If the answer is yes, the text is probably culturally generic.

   ◆ If the answer is no, the text is culturally authentic.

Questions to Determine If a Text Is Culturally Neutral or Culturally Generic

1. Does the text include main characters who represent underserved groups?

   ◆ If the answer is yes, the text could be either culturally neutral or culturally generic.

   ◆ If the answer is no, this text is probably culturally neutral.

2. Does the text include some information about the characters' culture, such as generic references to superficial cultural preferences like food or clothing?

   ◆ If the answer is yes, the text is probably culturally generic.

   ◆ If the answer is no, the text is probably culturally neutral.

3. Imagine substituting the characters of color in the text with dominant culture characters. Would that change affect the story? Would you have to rewrite any of the text?

   ◆ If the answer is yes, the text is probably culturally generic.

   ◆ If the answer is no, the text is culturally neutral.

Responsive Literacy Guide *(cont.)*

Tips for Avoiding the Pitfalls of Selecting Culturally Neutral Texts

- Choose well-known authors, illustrators, publishers, and sellers who have already developed solid reputations for producing culturally appropriate materials.
- Critically analyze how the characters are portrayed in the story, how the facts are presented, and in what context they are presented.
- Evaluate factual information for accuracy.
- When applicable, analyze the author's use of nonstandard language for authenticity and thoroughness.
- Carefully examine the illustrations for appeal, ethnic sensitivity, and authenticity.

Decision Tree for Deciding If a Text Is Culturally Neutral, Generic, or Authentic

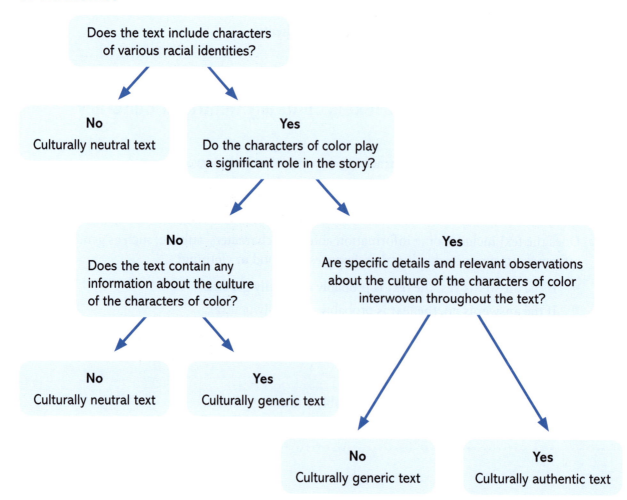

Text Evaluation Guide

Culturally Authentic Text Selected: _____

Evidence to Support My Conclusion

Superficial Cultural Details:

Food:

_____

Traditions:

_____

Rings of Culture:

Age:

_____

Orientation:

_____

Gender:

_____

Ethnicity:

_____

Nationality:

_____

Religion:

_____

Socioeconomic Status:

_____

For use with page 295.

Sample CLR Lesson Outline Template

Unit
Lesson
Content Standard(s)
Learning Goal(s)
Materials
Introduction
Procedure Outline
Close
Evaluation

LIST OF PROTOCOLS AND STRATEGIES

Strategies for Culturally and Linguistically Responsive Teaching and Learning—152468

© Shell Education

REFERENCES

Adams, Brittany, and Annemarie Bazzo Kaczmarczyk. 2021. "Initiating Courageous Conversations about Race and Racism with Read-Alouds." *Language and Literacy Spectrum* 31 (1): Article 3.

Adjapong, Edmund S., and Christopher Emdin. 2015. "Rethinking Pedagogy in Urban Spaces: Implementing Hip-Hop Pedagogy in the Urban Science Classroom." *Journal of Urban Learning, Teaching, and Research* 11: 66–77.

Alamirew, Fikre Diress. 2022. "The Acquisition of Inflectional Morphology: The Representation of Nominal Inflections in Amharic Speaking Children's Speeches." *Journal of Child Language Acquisition and Development-JCLAD* 10 (2): 534–556. science-res.com/index.php/jclad/article/view/87.

Alghamdy, Rashed Zannan. 2019. "EFL Learners' Reflections on Cooperative Learning: Issues of Implementation." *Theory and Practice in Language Studies* 9 (3): 271–277. doi.org/10.17507/tpls.0903.03.

Allen, David, and Tina Blythe. 2004. *The Facilitator's Book of Questions: Tools for Looking Together at Student and Teacher Work*. Teachers College Press.

Allen, Rich. 2008. *Green Light Classrooms: Teaching Techniques That Accelerate Learning*. Corwin.

Alvermann, Donna E., and Shelley Hong Xu. 2003. "Children's Everyday Literacies: Intersections of Popular Culture and Language Arts Instruction." *Language Arts* 81 (2): 145–155.

Amirault, Chris. 2025. *Sparking Learning in Young Children: Classroom Best Practices*. Shell Education.

Amorsen, Adele, and Melinda G. Miller. 2017. "Children's Oral Language Development and Early Literacy Practices." *Educating Young Children: Learning and Teaching in the Early Childhood Years* 23 (1): 24–27.

Armstrong, Amanda LaTasha. 2022. "The Representation of Social Groups in US Educational Materials and Why It Matters: A Research Overview." *New America*, February 16. newamerica.org/education-policy/briefs/the-representation-of-social-groups-in-us-education-materials-and-why-it-matters/.

ASCD Scientific Advisory Committee. 2023. "Looking to Research for Literacy Success." Knowledge Matters Campaign. February 28, 2023. ASCD blog. ascd.org/blogs/looking-to-research-for-literacy-success/.

Ash, Sarah L., and Patti H. Clayton. 2009. "Generating, Deepening, and Documenting Learning: The Power of Critical Reflection in Applied Learning." *Journal of Applied Learning in Higher Education* 1 (Fall 2009): 25–48.

Ashton-Warner, Sylvia. 1963. *Teacher*. Bantam Books.

Aslan Berzener, Ümmü, and Selma Deneme. 2021. "The Effect of Cooperative Learning on EFL Learners' Success of Reading Comprehension: An Experimental Study Implementing Slavin's STAD Method." *Turkish Online Journal of Educational Technology-TOJET* 20 (4): 90–100.

Au, Kathryn H. 1998. "Social Constructivism and the School Literacy Learning of Students of Diverse Backgrounds." *Journal of Literacy Research* 30 (2): 297–319.

August, Diane, Maria Carlo, Cheryl Dressler, and Catherine Snow. 2005. "The Critical Role of Vocabulary Development for English Language Learners." *Learning Disabilities Research and Practice* 20 (1): 50–57.

Averette, Patricia. n.d. "Save the Last Word for Me." National School Reform Faculty. Accessed July 26, 2024. nsrfharmony.org/wp-content/uploads/2017/10/save_last_word_0.pdf.

Bacon, Mary Montle. 2015. *A Strategies, Reference, and Resource Manual for Eliminating the Achievement Gap Implementing Culturally Relevant and Responsive Instruction.* Accessed February 4, 2015. notebook.lausd.net/pls/ptl/docs/page/ca_lausd/fldr_organizations/committee_main/committee_curr_instruct/committee_curr_instruct_ agenda/item%20225301.pdf.

Baker, Doris Luft, Lana Santoro, Gina Biancarosa, Scott K. Baker, Hank Fien, and Janet Otterstedt. 2020. "Effects of a Read Aloud Intervention on First Grade Student Vocabulary, Listening Comprehension, and Language Proficiency." *Reading and Writing* 33 (2020): 2697–2724.

Barrett, Peter, Lucinda Barrett, and Fay Davies. 2013 "Achieving a Step Change in the Optimal Sensory Design of Buildings for Users at All Life-stages." *Building and Environment* 67 (2013): 97–104.

Battistich, Victor, Daniel Solomon, and Kevin Delucchi. 1993. "Interaction Processes and Student Outcomes in Cooperative Learning Groups." *The Elementary School Journal* 94 (1): 19–32.

Beck, Isabel, Margaret McKeown, and Linda Kucan. 2013. *Bringing Words to Life, Robust Vocabulary Instruction.* 2nd ed. Guilford.

Beltrano, Natalie. 2023. "Call and Response: Inquiry-Based Learning as a Critical Pedagogy in the Scholarship of Teaching and Learning to Promote Transformation and Transformational Leadership." *Imagining SoTL* 3 (1): 46–61. doi.org/10.29173/isotl678.

Betances, Samuel. 1990. "Growing Beyond the Isms." Paper presented at the Black Aspirations Conference. Cleveland, Ohio.

Biancarosa, Gina, and Catherine E. Snow. 2006. *Reading Next—A Vision for Action and Research in Middle and High School Literacy: A Report to Carnegie Corporation of New York.* Alliance for Excellent Education.

Biemiller, Andrew, and Naomi Slonim. 2001. "Estimating Root Word Vocabulary Growth in Normative and Advantaged Populations: Evidence for a Common Sequence of Vocabulary Acquisition." *Journal of Educational Psychology* 93 (3): 498–520.

Blachowicz, Camille, and Peter Fisher. 2015. *Teaching Vocabulary in All Classrooms.* 5th ed. Pearson.

Bradley, David, and Maya Bradley. 2013. *Language Endangerment and Language Maintenance: An Active Approach.* Routledge.

Bucholtz, Mary. 2000. "Language and Youth Culture." *American Speech* 75 (3): 280–283.

Burke, Jim. 2002. *Tools for Thought: Graphic Organizers for Your Classroom.* Heinemann.

Caine, Renate, Geoffrey Caine, Carol Lynn McClintic, and Karl Klimek. 2004. *12 Brain/Mind Learning Principles in Action: The Fieldbook for Making Connections, Teaching, and the Human Brain.* Corwin.

Carlo, Maria S., Diane August, Barry McLaughlin, Catherine E. Snow, Cheryl Dressler, David N. Lippman, Teresa J. Lively, and Claire E. White. 2004. "Closing the Gap: Addressing the Vocabulary Needs of English Language Learners in Bilingual and Mainstream Classrooms." *Reading Research Quarterly* 39 (2): 188–206.

Chall, Jeanne S., and Vicki A. Jacobs. 2003. "Poor Children's Fourth-Grade Slump." *American Educator* 27 (1): 14–15.

Clark, Eve. 1993. *The Lexicon in Acquisition*. Cambridge University Press.

Cohen, Elizabeth G., Celeste M. Brody, and Mara Sapon-Shevin, eds. 2004. *Teaching Cooperative Learning: The Challenge for Teacher Education*. State University of New York Press.

Colliot, Tiphaine, and Éric Jamet. 2018. "Does Self-Generating a Graphic Organizer While Reading Improve Students' Learning?" *Computers and Education* 126: 13–22. doi.org/10.1016/j.compedu.2018.06.028.

Colliot, Tiphaine, and Éric Jamet. 2021. "Improving Students' Learning by Providing a Graphic Organizer After a Multimedia Document." *British Journal of Educational Technology* 52 (1): 252–265. doi.org/10.1111/bjet.12980.

Conklin, Wendy, and Andi Stix. 2014. *Active Learning Across the Content Areas*. Shell Education.

Conradi Smith, Kristin, Craig A. Young, and Jane Core Yatzeck. 2022. "What Are Teachers Reading and Why?: An Analysis of Elementary Read Aloud Titles and the Rationales Underlying Teachers' Selections." *Literacy Research and Instruction* 61 (4): 383–401. doi.org/10.1080/19388071.2021.2008558.

Cooper, J. David. 2000. *Literacy: Helping Children Construct Meaning*. Houghton Mifflin.

Cunningham, Anne, and Keith Stanovich. 1998. "What Reading Does for the Mind." *American Educator* 22: 8–15.

Darling-Hammond, Linda. 2010. *The Flat World and Education: How America's Commitment to Equity Will Determine Our Future*. Teachers College Press.

Dembo, Myron. 1988. *Teaching for Learning: Applying Educational Psychology in the Classroom*. Longman.

Dickinson, Kari. 2024. "CCBC's Diversity Statistics Show Small Changes in Number of Diverse Books for Children and Teens Published Last Year." University of Wisconsin–Madison School of Education, April 3. education.wisc.edu/news/ccbcs-diversity-statistics-show-small-changes-in-number-of-diverse-books-for-children-and-teens-published-last-year/.

Dolan, Lawrence J., Sheppard G. Kellam, C. Hendricks Brown, Lisa Werthamer-Larsson, George W. Rebok, Lawrence S. Mayer, Jolene Laudolff, Jaylan S. Turkkan, Carla Ford, and Leonard Wheeler. 1993. "The Short-Term Impact of Two Classroom-Based Preventive Interventions on Aggressive and Shy Behaviors and Poor Achievement." *Journal of Applied Developmental Psychology* 14 (3): 317–345.

Duman, Bilal. 2010. "The Effects of Brain-Based Learning on the Academic Achievement of Students with Different Learning Styles." *Educational Sciences: Theory and Practice* 10 (4): 2077–2103.

Fatiu, Indrei, and Irene Rodgers. 1984. "The Iceberg Concept of Nature." *American Field Scholarship Orientation Handbook 4*.

Fisher, Anna V., Karrie E. Godwin, and Howard Seltman. 2014. "Visual Environment, Attention Allocation, and Learning in Young Children When Too Much of a Good Thing May Be Bad." *Psychological Science* 25 (7): 1362–1370. doi.org/10.1177/0956797614533801.

Fisher, Douglas, and Nancy Frey. 2023. *The Vocabulary Playbook: Learning Words That Matter, K–12*. Corwin.

Fisher, Douglas, James Flood, Diane Lapp, and Nancy Frey. 2004. "Interactive Read-Alouds: Is There a Common Set of Implementation Practices?" *The Reading Teacher* 58 (1): 8–17.

Fitzsimons, Aidan, and Eabhnat Ní Fhloinn. 2023. "The CoPS Model for Collaborative Problem-Solving in Mathematics." *Irish Educational Studies* 1–18. doi.org/10.1080/03323315.2023.2189137.

Ford-Connors, Evelyn, and Jeanne R. Paratore. 2014. "Vocabulary Instruction in Fifth Grade and Beyond: Sources of Word Learning and Productive Contexts for Development." *Review of Educational Research* 85 (1): 50–91. doi.org/10.3102/0034654314540943.

Foster, Michele. 2001. "Pay Leon, Pay Leon, Pay Leon Paleontologist: Using Call-and-Response to Facilitate Language." *Sociocultural and Historical Contexts of African American English* 27: 281.

Frayer, Dorothy Ann, Wayne C. Frederick, and Herbert John Klausmeier. 1969. *A Schema for Testing the Level of Cognitive Mastery.* Wisconsin Center for Education Research.

Garan, Elaine M., and Glenn DeVoogd. 2008. "The Benefits of Sustained Silent Reading: Scientific Research and Common Sense Converge." *The Reading Teacher* 62 (4): 336–344.

Gay, Geneva. 2018. *Culturally Responsive Teaching: Theory, Research, and Practice.* 3rd ed. Teachers College Press.

Giovanni, Nikki. 1968. "Knoxville, Tennessee." In *The Collected Poetry of Nikki Giovanni*, 59. HarperCollins.

Giroir, Shannon, Leticia Romero Grimaldo, Sharon Vaughn, and Greg Roberts. 2015. "Interactive Read-Alouds for English Learners in the Elementary Grades." *The Reading Teacher* 68 (8): 639–648. doi.org/10.1002/trtr.1354.

Goodwin, Bryan. 2011. *Simply Better: Doing What Matters Most to Change the Odds for Student Success.* ASCD.

Graetz, Ken A., and Michael J. Goliber. 2003. "Designing Collaborative Learning Places: Psychological Foundations and New Frontiers." In *The Importance of Physical Space in Creating Supportive Learning Environments: New Directions in Teaching and Learning*, edited by Nancy Van Note Chism and Deborah J. Bickford. Jossey-Bass.

Graves, Michael F. 2000. "A Vocabulary Program to Complement and Bolster a Middle-Grade Comprehension Program." In *Reading for Meaning: Fostering Comprehension in the Middle Grades*, edited by Barbara M. Taylor, Michael F. Graves, and Paulus Willem van den Broek. Teachers College Press.

Graves, Michael F. 2006. *The Vocabulary Book: Learning and Instruction.* Teachers College Press.

Green, Clarence. 2021. "The Oral Language Productive Vocabulary Profile of Children Starting School: A Resource for Teachers." *Australian Journal of Education* 65 (1): 41–54. doi.org/10.1177/0004944120982771.

Gregory, Anne, Russell J. Skiba, and Pedro A. Noguera. 2010. "The Achievement Gap and the Discipline Gap: Two Sides of the Same Coin?" *Educational Researcher* 39 (1): 59–68. doi.org/10.3102/0013189X09357621.

Gregory, Gayle, and Terence Parry. 2006. *Designing Brain-Compatible Learning.* Corwin Press.

Haataja, Eetu, Muhterem Dindar, Jonna Malmberg, and Sanna Järvelä. 2022. "Individuals in a Group: Metacognitive and Regulatory Predictors of Learning Achievement in Collaborative Learning." *Learning and Individual Differences* 96: 102146. doi.org/10.1016/j.lindif.2022.102146.

Hammond, Zaretta. 2013. "The Neuroscience of Call and Response." Culturally Responsive Teaching & the Brain, April 1. crtandthebrain.com/the-neuroscience-of-call-and-response/.

Han, Weifeng, and Chris Brebner, eds. 2024. *Typical and Atypical Language Development in Cultural and Linguistic Diversity.* Routledge.

Heller, Mia C., Arne Lervåg, and Vibeke Grøver, V. 2019. "Oral Language Intervention in Norwegian Schools Serving Young Language-Minority Learners: A Randomized Trial." *Reading Research Quarterly* 54 (4): 531–552. doi.org/10.1002/rrq.248.

Hiebert, Elfrieda. 2005. *Quickreads: A Research-Based Fluency Program.* Modern Curriculum Press.

Hiebert, Elfrieda. 2023. *Teaching Words and How They Work: Small Changes for Big Vocabulary Results.* Teachers College Press.

Hollie, Sharroky. 2012. *Culturally and Linguistically Responsive Teaching and Learning: Classroom Practices for Student Success.* Shell Education.

Hollie, Sharroky. 2018. *Culturally and Linguistically Responsive Teaching and Learning: Classroom Practices for Student Success.* 2nd ed. Shell Education.

Hollins, Etta R. 2015. *Culture in School Learning: Revealing the Deep Meaning.* 3rd ed. Routledge.

Howard, Lotus Linton. 2017. "Yellow Ribbons: Interactions Stress Collectivity as well as Individuality." In *Bright Ribbons: Weaving Culturally Responsive Teaching into the Elementary Classroom.* Corwin. doi.org/10.4135/9781071800423.n9.

İlter, İlhan. 2017. "Teaching Word Meanings to Students at Different Reading Ability: A Controlled Assessment of the Contextual-Based Vocabulary Instruction on Reading Comprehension." *Education and Science* 42 (190): 437–463.

İlter, İlhan. 2018. "Effects of the Instruction in Inferring Meanings from Context on the Comprehension of Middle School Students at Frustration Reading Level." *Journal of Education* 198 (3): 225–239. doi.org/10.1177/0022057418818818.

İlter, İlhan. 2019. "The Efficacy of Context Clue Strategy Instruction on Middle Grades Students' Vocabulary Development." *Research in Middle Education: RMLE Online* 42 (1): 1–15. doi.org/10.1080/19404476.2018.1554522.

Ivey, Gay. 2003. "The Intermediate Grades: 'The Teacher Makes It More Explainable' and Other Reasons to Read Aloud in the Intermediate Grades." *The Reading Teacher* 56 (8): 812–814.

Jaffe, Brooke. 2013. "Dearth of Racial Diversity in Children's Books Is Terrible: Depressingly Unsurprising." *The Mary Sue*, July 1. themarysue.com/racial-diversity-childrens-books/.

Jensen, Eric P. 2008. *Brain-Based Learning: The New Paradigm of Teaching.* 2nd ed. Corwin.

Jensen, Jamie Lee, and Anton Lawson. 2011. "Effects of Collaborative Group Composition and Inquiry Instruction on Reasoning Gains and Achievement in Undergraduate Biology." *CBE Life Sciences Education* 10 (1): 64–73. doi.org/10.1187/cbe.10-07-0089.

Johnson, David W., and Roger T. Johnson. 1987. *Learning Together and Alone: Cooperative, Competitive, and Individualistic Learning.* Prentice-Hall.

Johnson, David W., Roger T. Johnson, and Mary Beth Stanne. 2000. "Exhibit B—Cooperative Learning Methods: A Meta-analysis." University of Minnesota.

Jolliffe, Wendy. 2007. *Cooperative Learning in the Classroom: Putting It into Practice.* SAGE Publications.

Kagan, Spencer. 2009. *Kagan Cooperative Learning*. Kagan Publishing.

Kame'enui, Edward J., Robert C. Dixon, and Douglas Carnine. 1987. "Issues in the Design of Vocabulary Instruction." In *The Nature of Vocabulary Acquisition*, edited by Margaret G. McKeown and Mary E. Curtis. Lawrence Erlbaum Associates.

Kane, Britnie Delinger, and Evthokia Stephanie Saclarides. 2023. "Doing the Math Together: Coaches' Professional Learning Through Engagement in Mathematics." *Journal of Mathematics Teacher Education* 26 (2): 241–270. doi.org/10.1007/s10857-021-09527-y.

Kao, Grace. 2000. "Group Images and Possible Selves Among Adolescents: Linking Stereotypes to Expectations by Race and Ethnicity." *Sociological Forum* 15 (3): 407–430.

Karten, Toby. 2009. *Inclusion Strategies That Work for Adolescent Learners*. Corwin.

Kieffer, Michael J., and Nonie K. Lesaux. 2007. "Breaking Down Words to Build Meaning: Morphology, Vocabulary, and Reading Comprehension in the Urban Classroom." *The Reading Teacher* 61 (2): 134–144.

Kindle, Karen. 2012. "Vocabulary Development During Read-Alouds: Primary Practices." In *Issues and Trends in Literacy Education*, 5th Edition, edited by Richard D. Robinson, Michael C. McKenna, and Kristin Conradi. Pearson.

Koçak, Zeynep Fidan, Radiye Bozan, and Özlem Işık. 2009. "The Importance of Group Work in Mathematics." *Procedia- Social and Behavioral Sciences* 1 (1): 2363–2365. doi.org/10.1016/j.sbspro.2009.01.414.

Konza, D. 2016. "Vocabulary." *Best Advice Series: Department for Education and Child Development* 1 (4): 1–6.

Krasnoff, Basha. 2016. *A Guide to Evidence-Based Practices for Teaching All Students Equitably*. Region X Equity Assistance Center at Education Northwest.

Ladson-Billings, Gloria. 2021. "I'm Here for the Hard Re-Set: Post Pandemic Pedagogy to Preserve Our Culture." *Equity and Excellence in Education* 54 (1): 68–78. doi.org/10.1080/10665684.2020.1863883.

Lariviere, Danielle O., Vishakha Agrawal, and Jiaxin Jessie Wang. 2022. "Intensive Intervention Practice Guide: Mathematics-Language Instruction for Emergent Bilingual Students with Mathematics Difficulty." National Center for Leadership in Intensive Intervention. Office of Special Education Programs, US Department of Education.

Leap, William L. 1993. "American Indian English and Its Implications for Bilingual Education." *Linguistics for Teachers* 207–208.

Lee, Carol D. 2007. *Culture, Literacy, and Learning: Taking Bloom in the Midst of the Whirlwind*. Teachers College Press.

LeMoine, Noma. 1999. *English for Your Success: A Language Development Program for African American Children Grades Pre-K–8: A Handbook of Successful Strategies for Educators*. Peoples Publishing Group.

Long, Michael H. 1977. "Group Work in the Teaching and Learning of English as a Foreign Language—Problems and Potential." *English Language Teaching Journal* 31 (4): 285–292.

Los Angeles Unified School District Board of Education (LAUSD). 2012. Title III Master Plan Institute 2012-13; Chapter 4: Instructional Services for Standard English Learners "Ensuring Access to Core Academic Content." LAUSD Board of Education.

Lovell, Elyse D'nn, and Denise Elakovich. 2018. Developmental Math Pilot: Massive Open Online Course (MOOC), Psychology Concepts, and Group Work." *Community College Journal of Research and Practice* 42 (2): 146–149. doi.org/10.1080/10668926.2016.1251353.

Lujan, Heidi L., and Stephen E. DiCarlo. 2006. "Too Much Teaching, Not Enough Learning: What Is the Solution?" *Advances in Physiology Education* 30 (1): 17–22.

Marzano, Robert J. 2007. *The Art and Science of Teaching: A Comprehensive Framework for Effective Instruction*. Heinle ELT.

Marzano, Robert J., and Lindsay Carleton. 2010. *Vocabulary Games for the Classroom*. Marzano Research Laboratory.

Marzano, Robert J., and Debra J. Pickering. 2010. *The Highly Engaged Classroom*. Marzano Research Laboratory.

May, Laura A., Gary E. Bingham, and Meghan L. Pendergast. 2014. "Culturally and Linguistically Relevant Read Alouds." *Multicultural Perspectives* 16 (4): 210–218.

McCauley, Joyce K., and Daniel S. McCauley. 1992. "Using Choral Reading to Promote Language Learning for ESL Students." *The Reading Teacher* 45: 526–535.

McDonald, Joseph. 2007. *The Power of Protocols: An Educator's Guide to Better Practice*. Teachers College Press.

Mohr, Nancy. 2007. *The Power of Protocols: An Educator's Guide to Better Practice*. New York: Teachers College Press.

Molinsky, Andy. 2013. *Global Dexterity: How to Adapt Your Behavior Across Cultures without Losing Yourself in the Process*. Harvard Business Review Press.

Moll, Luis, Cathy Amanti, Deborah Neff, and Norma Gonzalez. 2004. "Funds of Knowledge for Teaching: Using a Qualitative Approach to Connect Homes and Classrooms." In *Funds of Knowledge: Theorizing Practices in Households, Communities and Classrooms*, edited by Norma Gonzalez, Luis Moll, and Cathy Amanti. Lawrence Erlbaum Associates.

Montag, Jessica L. 2019. "Differences in Sentence Complexity in the Text of Children's Picture Books and Child-Directed Speech." *First Language* 39 (5): 527–546. doi.org/10.1177/0142723719849996.

Montgomery, Winifred. 2001. "Creating Culturally Responsive, Inclusive Classrooms." *Teaching Exceptional Children* 33 (4): 4–9.

Moody, Stephanie Michelle, and Sharon D. Matthews. 2020. "Pathways to Becoming a Culturally Responsive Teacher: Narrative Inquiries into a Translanguaging Read Aloud." *Journal of Curriculum Studies Research* 2 (2): 170–188. doi.org/10.46303/jcsr.2020.15.

Moore, Gary. 2001. "Children, Young People and Their Environments." Keynote Address at the 4th Child and Family Policy Conference, Dunedin, NZ.

Nagy, William, Richard Anderson, and Patricia Herman. 1987. "Learning Word Meanings from Context During Normal Reading." *American Educational Research Journal* 24: 237–270.

Nagy, William, Irene-Anna Diakidoy, and Richard Anderson. 1993. "The Acquisition of Morphology: Learning the Contribution of Suffixes to the Meanings of Derivatives." *Journal of Reading Behavior* 25 (2): 155–170.

Nagy, William E., and Judith A. Scott. 2000. "Vocabulary Processes." In *Handbook of Reading Research*, edited by Michael L. Kamil, Peter B. Mosenthal, P. David Pearson, and Rebecca Barr. Vol. 3. Lawrence Erlbaum Associates.

National Reading Panel. 2013. "National Reading Panel (Historical/For Reference Only)." Accessed September 26, 2024. nichd.nih.gov/research/supported/Pages/nrp.aspx/.

National School Reform Faculty. 2015. "It Takes a Village." Harmony Education Center. www.nsrfharmony.org/wp-content/uploads/2017/10/it_takes_a_village.pdf.

Navarro Martell, M. A. 2021. "Learning and Teaching en dos idiomas: Critical Autoethnography, translenguaje, y rechazando English Learner." *Association of Mexican American Educators Journal* 15 (3): 11–29.

New America Foundation. 2008. "Changing the Odds for Children at Risk." Accessed September 26, 2024. newamerica.org/education-policy/events/changing-the-odds-for-children-at-risk/.

Nobles, Wade W. 1987. "Psychometrics and African American Reality: A Question of Cultural Antimony." *Negro Educational Review* 38 (2–3): 45–55.

O'Kane, Caitlin. 2022. "Over 1,600 Books Were Banned in U.S. School Districts in One Year—And the Number Is Increasing." CBS News, September 20. cbsnews.com/news/banned-books-list-increased-schools-ban-critical-race-theory-sexuality-pen-america-report/.

Orange, Tonikiaa, and Sharroky Hollie. 2014. "A Model for Educating African American Students." In *Proud to be Different: Ethnocentric Niche Charter Schools in America*, edited by Robert A. Fox and Nina K. Buchanan. Rowman and Littlefield Education.

Palincsar, A. S. 1986. "Reciprocal Teaching." In *Teaching Reading as Thinking*. Oak Brook, IL: North Central Regional Educational Laboratory as discussed on North Central Regional Educational Laboratory. 2014. "Reciprocal Teaching." Accessed November 21, 2014. ncrel.org/sdrs/areas/issues/students/atrisk/at6lk38.htm.

Park, Clara C. 1997. "Learning Style Preferences of Korean-, Mexican-, Armenian-American, and Anglo Students in Secondary Schools. Research Brief." *NASSP Bulletin* 81 (585): 103–11.

Quin, Daniel. 2016. "Longitudinal and Contextual Associations Between Teacher–Student Relationships and Student Engagement: A Systematic Review." *Review of Educational Research* 87 (2): 345–387. doi.org/10.3102/0034654316669434.

Rafique, Adnan, Muhammad Salman Khan, Muhammad Hasan Jamal, Mamoona Tasadduq, Furqan Rustam, Ernesto Lee, Patrick Bernard Washington, and Imran Ashraf. 2021. "Integrating Learning Analytics and Collaborative Learning for Improving Student's Academic Performance." *IEEE Access* 9. doi.org/10.1109/ACCESS.2021.3135309.

Rahmat, Yurike Nadiya, Andri Saputra, M. Arif Rahman Hakim, Eko Saputra, and Reko Serasi. 2021. "Learning L2 by Utilizing Dictionary Strategies: Learner Autonomy and Learning Strategies." *Lingua Cultura* 15 (2): 175–181. doi.org/10.21512/lc.v15i2.7339.

Raphael, Taffy. 1982. "Improving Question-Answering Performance Through Instruction." *Reading Education Reports* 32: 64.

Rasinski, Timothy, Nancy Padak, Rick M. Newton, and Evangeline Newton. 2020. *Building Vocabulary with Greek and Latin Roots: A Professional Guide to Word Knowledge and Vocabulary Development*. Shell Education.

Rasinski, Timothy, and Chase Young. 2024. *Build Reading Fluency: Practice and Performance with Reader's Theater and More*. Shell Education.

ReadWriteThink. 2006. "Literature Circle Roles." readwritethink.org/sites/default/files/resources/lesson_images/lesson19/lit-circle-roles.pdf.

ReadWriteThink. 2014. "No Teachers Allowed: Student-Led Book Clubs Using QAR." Accessed November 26, 2014. readwritethink.org/classroom-resources/lesson-plans/teachers-allowed-student-book.

Reutzel, D. Ray, Parker C. Fawson, and John A. Smith. 2008. "Reconsidering Silent Sustained Reading: An Exploratory Study of Scaffolded Silent Reading." *The Journal of Educational Research* 102 (1): 37–50.

Reutzel, D. Ray, Paul M. Hollingsworth, and J. Lloyd Eldredge. 1994. "Oral Reading Instruction: The Impact on Student Reading Development." *Reading Research Quarterly* 29: 40–65.

Reyes, Angela. 2005. "Appropriation of African American Slang by Asian American Youth." *Journal of Sociolinguistics* 9 (4): 509–532.

Robinson, Francis Pleasant. 1941. "The SQ3R Method." In *Effective Study*. Harper and Row Publishers.

Rogoff, Barbara. 1990. *Apprenticeships in Thinking: Cognitive Development in Social Context*. Oxford University Press.

Roskos, Kathleen, and Susan B. Neuman. 2011. "The Classroom Environment: First, Last, and Always." *The Reading Teacher* 65 (2): 110–114.

Ryan, Allison M., and Helen Patrick. 2001. "The Classroom Social Environment and Changes in Adolescents' Motivation and Engagement During Middle School." *American Educational Research Journal* 38 (2): 437–460. doi.org/10.3102/00028312038002437.

Sadieda, Lisanul Uswa, Afik Wildan Muzakie, Risqi Putri Rahmawati, Renaldi Bimantoro, and T. A. Bagus. 2019. "The Effect of Using Dictionary to Develop Students' Vocabulary in MTs. Al-Musthofa." International Conference on English Language Teaching. *Advances in Social Science, Education and Humanities Research* 434.

Safir, Shane, and Jamila Dugan. 2021. *Street Data: A Next-Generation Model for Equity, Pedagogy, and School Transformation*. Corwin.

Santa, Carol M., Lynn T. Havens, and Bonnie J. Valdes. 2014. *Project CRISS: Creating Independence Through Student-Owned Strategies, 4th ed.* Kendall/Hunt.

Schiller, Pam, and Clarissa A. Willis. 2008. "Using Brain-Based Teaching Strategies to Create Supportive Early Childhood Environments That Address Learning Standards." *Young Children* 63 (4): 52–55.

Scholes, Laura. 2021. "Year 3 Boys' and Girls' Enjoyment for Reading Across Demographics in Australia. Implications for Boys and Students from Lower SES Communities." *International Journal of Inclusive Education* 28 (5): 509–524. doi.org/10.1080/13603116.2021.1941319.

Shade, Barbara J., Cynthia Kelly, and Mary Oberg. 1997. *Creating Culturally Responsive Classrooms: Psychology in the Classroom*. American Psychological Association.

Sharan, Shlomo. 1976. *Small-Group Teaching*. Educational Technology Publications.

Shea, Mary, and Maria Ceprano. 2017. "Reading with Understanding: A Global Expectation." *Journal of Inquiry and Action in Education* 9 (1): 48–68.

Short, Kathy, Jerome Harste, and Carolyn Burke. 1988. *Creating Classrooms for Authors*. Heinemann Publishing.

Short, Kathy, Jerome Harste, and Carolyn Burke. 1996. *Creating Classrooms for Authors and Inquirers*, 2nd ed. Heinemann Publishing.

Slade, Malcolm, and Faith Trent. 2000. "What the Boys Are Saying: An Examination of the Views of Boys about Declining Rates of Achievement and Retention." *International Education Journal* 1 (3): 201–229.

Slavin, Robert E. 2010. "Co-operative Learning: What Makes Group-Work Work?" In *The Nature of Learning: Using Research to Inspire Practice*, 161–178. OECD Publishing. doi. org/10.1787/9789264086487-9-en.

Sosa, Teresa. 2017. "Recently I Was in a Fatal Incident: Personal Narratives and Social Identities." *Linguistics and Education* 42: 34–42. doi.org/10.1016/j.linged.2017.08.002.

Sparks, Sarah D. 2019. "Why Teacher-Student Relationships Matter." *EdWeek*, March 12. edweek. org/teaching-learning/why-teacher-student-relationships-matter/2019/03.

Stahl, Steven A., and William E. Nagy. 2006. *Teaching Word Meanings*. Lawrence Erlbaum Associates.

Stix, Andi, and Frank Hrbek. 2013. *Exploring History Through Primary Sources: Ancient Mesopotomia*. Reprint. Teacher Created Materials.

Swanborn, Machteld, and Kees de Glopper. 1999. "Incidental Word Learning While Reading: A Meta-Analysis." *Review of Educational Research* 69: 261–285.

Tate, Marcia L. 2025. *Engaging the Brain: 20 Unforgettable Strategies for Growing Dendrites and Accelerating Learning*. 4th ed. Corwin.

Thompson, Chalmer E., and Robert T. Carter, eds. 2013. *Racial Identity Theory: Applications to Individual, Group, and Organizational Interventions*. Routledge.

Toney, Jermaine, and Hillary Rodgers. 2011. "16 Solutions That Deliver Equity and Excellence in Education." *Organizing Apprenticeship Project* (OAP) 2: 1–20.

Torgesen, Joseph, and Roxanne Hudson. 2006. "Reading Fluency: Critical Issues for Struggling Readers." In *Reading Fluency: The Forgotten Dimension of Reading Success*, edited by S. Jay Samuels and Alan A. Farstrup. International Reading Association.

Trelease, Jim. 1982. *The Read-Aloud Handbook*. 1st ed. Penguin Books.

Trelease, Jim, and Cyndi Giorgis. 2019. *Jim Trelease's Read-Aloud Handbook*. 8th ed. Penguin Books.

Troyer, M. 2023. "Teacher Knowledge and Questioning in Classroom Talk About Text." *Literacy Research and Instruction* 62 (2): 101–126. doi.org/10.1080/19388071.2022.2074328.

Trudgill, Peter, and Jean Hannah. 2008. *International English: A Guide to Varieties of Standard English*. Routledge.

Tudge, Jonathan. 1990. "Collaborative Problem-Solving in the Zone of Proximal Development." Presented at the American Educational Research Association Meeting. Boston, MA.

Umbel, Vivian M., Barbara Z. Pearson, Maria C. Fernandez, and D. K. Oller. 1992. "Measuring Bilingual Children's Receptive Vocabularies." *Child Development* 63: 1012–1020.

U.S. Department of Education, Institute of Education Sciences, National Center for Education Statistics, National Assessment of Educational Progress (NAEP). 2022. Reading Assessment. www.nationsreportcard.gov/highlights/reading/2022/.

Villegas, Ana, and Tamara Lucas. 2004. "Diversifying the Teacher Workforce: A Retrospective and Prospective Analysis." *Yearbook of the National Society for the Study of Education* 103 (1): 70–104.

Villicana, Adrian J., Luis M. Rivera, and Nilanjana Dasgupta. 2011. "The Effect of a Group-Affirmation on Prejudice." *Psychology Student Research Journal* 1: 31–37.

Vlach, Saba K., Tova S. Lentz, and Gholnecsar E. Muhammad. 2023. "Activating Joy Through Culturally and Historically Responsive Read-Alouds." *The Reading Teacher* 77 (1): 121–130. doi.org/10.1002/trtr.2203.

Walpole, Sharon, Steve Amendum, Adrian Pasquarella, John Z. Strong, and Michael C. McKenna. 2017. "The Promise of a Literacy Reform Effort in the Upper Elementary Grades." *The Elementary School Journal* 118 (2): 257–280. doi.org/10.1086/694219.

Wang, Lie-qin. 2012. "Language Endangerment and Language Maintenance." *Journal of Hebei University (Philosophy and Social Science)* 5: 111–113.

Whorrall, Jennifer, and Sonia Q. Cabell. 2016. "Supporting Children's Oral Language Development in the Preschool Classroom." *Early Childhood Education Journal* 44 (4): 335–341. doi.org/10.1007/s10643-015-0719-0.

Wickersham, Kelly, and Brett Ranon Nachman. 2023. "'I Never Learned More in My Life in Such a Short Period of Time': Math Contextualization as Momentum Toward Community College Student Success." *Community College Journal of Research and Practice* 47 (4): 273–289. doi.org/10.1080/10668926.2021.1999341.

Wijeyesinghe, Charmaine L., and Bailey W. Jackson III. 2012. *New Perspectives on Racial Identity Development: Integrating Emerging Frameworks*. NYU Press.

Winkleman, Sabrina. 2025. *50 Strategies for Cooperative Learning*. Shell Education.

Wiseman, Angela. 2011. "Interactive Read Alouds: Teachers and Students Constructing Knowledge and Literacy Together." *Early Childhood Education Journal* 38: 431–438.

Woo, Ashley, Sabrina Lee, Andrea Prado Tuma, Julia H. Kaufman, R. A. Lawrence, and Nastassia Reed. 2023. "Walking on Eggshells—Teachers' Responses to Classroom Limitations on Race- or Gender-Related Topics." RAND. rand.org/content/dam/rand/pubs/research_reports/RRA100/RRA134-16/RAND_RRA134-16.pdf.

Wright, Tanya S. 2023. *A Teacher's Guide to Vocabulary Development Across the Day*. The Classroom Essentials Series, edited by Katie Wood Ray. Heinemann.

Wyse, Dominic, Russell Jones, Helen Bradford, and Mary Anne Wolpert. 2013. *Teaching English, Language and Literacy*, 3rd ed. Routledge.

Yang, Kou. 2003. "Hmong Americans: A Review of Felt Needs, Problems, and Community Development." *Hmong Studies Journal* 4 (1): 1–23.

Young, Terrell A., Paul H. Ricks, and Kathryn Lake MacKay. 2023. "Engaging Students with Expository Books Through Interactive Read-Alouds." *The Reading Teacher* 77 (1): 6–15. doi.org/10.1002/trtr.2210.

Yuan, Yuxin, Xiaofen Li, and Wanxu Liu. 2022. "Dance Activity Interventions Targeting Cognitive Functioning in Older Adults with Mild Cognitive Impairment: A Meta-Analysis." *Frontiers in Psychology* 13: 966675. doi.org/10.3389/fpsyg.2022.966675.

Zeichner, Kenneth. 2003. "The Adequacies and Inadequacies of Three Current Strategies to Recruit, Prepare, and Retain the Best Teachers for all Students." *The Teachers College Record* 105 (3): 490–519.

Strategies for Culturally and Linguistically Responsive Teaching and Learning—152468

Dr. Sharroky Hollie is an esteemed educator and author known for his passionate advocacy of culturally and linguistically responsive teaching practices. With over three decades of experience in education, Dr. Hollie has dedicated his life to promoting the validation and affirmation of underserved students.

As the founder and executive director of the non-profit organization The Center for Culturally Responsive Teaching and Learning (The Center), Dr. Hollie has been instrumental in empowering educators to effectively engage students from diverse backgrounds. Since 2004, The Center has brought the concept of cultural and linguistic responsiveness to hundreds of school districts in the United States and Canada and thousands of educators.

In addition to his work with The Center, Dr. Hollie is the author of several influential books and articles, including *Culturally and Linguistically Responsive Teaching and Learning: Classroom Practices for Student Success, Second Edition*, *The Will to Lead and the Skill to Teach*, and *Supporting Underserved Students: Aligning Cultural and Linguistic Responsiveness to PBIS*. He is a contributing author to several texts, namely *Proud to be Different: Ethnocentric Niche Charter Schools in America*, *Teaching African American Learners to Read: Perspectives and Practices*, and *The Oxford Handbook on African American Language*.

Dr. Hollie is a former tenured assistant professor in teacher education at California State University and has been a visiting professor at UCLA, Stanford, Hebrew Union College in Los Angeles, and Webster University in St. Louis, Missouri.

Hollie's teaching career began in Los Angeles Unified School District, where he taught middle and high school English Language Arts and served as a district administrator and professional development provider for the Academic English Mastery Program. His proudest work is the founding of the Culture and Language Academy of Success, a K–8 independent laboratory school that existed from 2003 to 2013.

Accessing the Digital Resources

The digital resources can be downloaded by following these steps:

1. Go to www.tcmpub.com/digital

2. Use the ISBN number to redeem the digital resources.

3. Respond to the question using the book.

4. Follow the prompts on the Content Cloud website to sign in or create a new account.

5. The content redeemed will now be on your My Content screen. Click on the product to look through the digital resources. All resources are available for download. Select files can be previewed, opened, and shared.

For questions and assistance with your ISBN redemption, please contact Teacher Created Materials.

email: customerservice@tcmpub.com

phone: 800-858-7339

Contents of the Digital Resources

The Digital Resources include a Year of Reflections Journal with more than 40 reflection prompts, essentially one for each week of the school year. You'll also find digital versions of the student pages and teacher forms in this book.